ESSAYS IN LITERARY HISTORY

J. MILTON FRENCH

Essays in Literary History

presented to

J. MILTON FRENCH

edited by RUDOLF KIRK *and* C. F. MAIN

PR14
.K59

NEW YORK / RUSSELL & RUSSELL

1965

Preface

The contributors to this book, members of the Department of English in the College of Arts and Sciences of Rutgers University, wish by their essays to honor Professor J. Milton French, who will retire from the Faculty on June 30, 1960, after having served as Chairman of the Department of English for the past twenty years. Had they greater gifts to bestow, they would gladly have presented them. Like the Juggler to Our Lady in the medieval tale, however, they give of the talents they possess and hope that their essays will be received as an expression of their deep appreciation of the privilege of working with Milton French.

The editors are indebted to Professor Don M. Wolfe of Brooklyn College, a distinguished seventeenth-century scholar, for writing the appreciation of Milton French which precedes the essays. David P. French, who took the photograph of his father, has kindly allowed it to be used as a frontispiece.

The editors also wish to thank the Rutgers Research Council for a substantial grant that made possible the publication of this volume. Mr. William Sloane, the Director of the Rutgers University Press, has aided the authors and editors in every way.

R. K.
C. F. M.

21 May 1960

Contents

ESSAYS IN LITERARY HISTORY

J. Milton French

BY DON M. WOLFE

In every generation of American scholars, a few individuals emerge who embody pre-eminently the ideals and accomplishments that the profession most cherishes but frequently fails to fulfill. The scholar, perhaps more than any other professional man, is conscious of the gap between dream and reality in his own life; he is, therefore, happy to know a few fellow seekers who have emerged whole and sweet, their creative powers unscathed, from the hazards he knows so well.

Among these select few Milton French takes his place, a man mellow in spirit and a scholar of astonishing resources. The stature of some scholars, whatever the poverty or riches of their accomplishments, is apparent even in the briefest conversation. But Milton French's true stature emerges only from years of knowing him and reading his books. In conversation with two or three he is always the best listener and the least assertive talker. He is a tall man, with graying sandy hair and modest blue eyes. When Emerson wrote that "every man carries in his glance the sense of his own worth in the immense range of men," he did not describe Milton French. French expects every man he sits down with to be more brilliant than himself; when he is disappointed, he is ready at the next meeting of minds to revise his estimate upward. He looks for more generous action and more creative ideas from his fellow scholars than even they expect from themselves. Self-assertion is foreign to French's outlook. His humility comes from the ripeness of his manhood rather than from a lack of confidence. His genius as a scholar is his talent for long patience in exploring one inexhaustible author. When the history of American scholarship is written, two or three centuries from now, the name of J. Milton French will surely occupy a conspicuous place in it. His achievements will appear in true perspective; meanwhile his friends and colleagues have strong reasons to assess the man as well as the scholar.

II

Milton French was born in Randolph, Massachusetts, on March 7, 1895. Eighteen miles from Boston, Randolph was at the time a small, peaceful village, full of tree-shaded streets. Across the street from the French home stood the Baptist Church, to which the family belonged. Four doors away lived the Plunkett family, with a bright-eyed child by the name of Elva. Milton's father, whose first American ancestor had landed in Salem in 1630, was sturdy, affectionate, and public-spirited. In early life he had been a shoemaker, following his father's trade. Then he turned to the business of insurance to support his family, meanwhile serving in various town offices, later in the Massachusetts Legislature. Before the first family automobile, he kept a carriage and horses in the barn back of the house, which his son Milton helped to care for; on the second floor of the barn there was still a shop containing the family's old shoemaking tools. When his son Milton had graduated from grammar school, he sent him to Thayer Academy, a few miles away, to which Milton commuted on horse-drawn trolleys. Thayer was a preparatory school of some distinction, and it did not occur to the elder French and his wife that their child should not attend the university of his choice.

In 1913 Milton French entered Harvard, where his leisure to work was made possible mainly by his father's farsighted thrift; for three years he held an honorary Harvard College Fellowship. He had courses in Bacon and Milton with William Allan Neilson and in Shakespeare with Kittredge. He took the M.A. in 1921, the doctorate in 1928; for encouragement and guidance during his graduate years he was most indebted to Hyder Rollins. His interest was now centered in the seventeenth century, though not yet in Milton. Out of his doctoral study of George Wither grew an edition from manuscript of Wither's *The History of the Pestilence* (Harvard University Press, 1932). This book is a valuable and exciting record of seventeenth-century life and thought. Among the first sentences of the introduction we find an anticipation of the range and emphasis of French's future interests as a scholar:

> The poem which is herewith printed for the first time was written by George Wither in 1625, while the terrible English pestilence of that year was at its height. It is the record of the horror and anguish of a poet to whom "art for art's sake" was as unthinkable and meaningless as "emotion recollected in tranquillity." Wither wrote while his emotion burned hot within him and with an all-absorbing purpose. He had been

living in London during the awful devastation of the plague, had helped to nurse some of the victims, and had seen in it the hand of an offended Deity eager to chasten and reclaim an erring people. Out of the fullness of his heart he wrote with the flaming zeal of an Old Testament prophet. . . .

One is . . . conscious of a certain fatuous priggishness and a deplorable lack of humor throughout. . . . Wither was no Milton; yet he possessed in rudimentary form most of the merits as well as the defects of his greater contemporary.

In these sentences we see French's rejection of aesthetics as the sole concern of the literary critic; his fascination with historical events; his interest in Puritan ideas, of which his own childhood upbringing had been a continuing, if gentler, confrontation; finally, his concern with Milton as an artist-prophet.

Meanwhile, upon graduation from Harvard in 1919, Milton French had enlisted for World War I and been trained as a radio officer. As a second lieutenant in the Army of Occupation, he arrived in France at the end of hostilities and was discharged after two years of service.

In 1921, a few months after receiving his M.A., Milton French married Elva Lenore Plunkett, a registered nurse and at that time night supervisor in a branch of Massachusetts Memorial Hospital. Almost immediately she helped nurse her husband through a mild siege of tuberculosis, from which he recovered in the spring of 1922. No more charming person or kindlier spirit than Elva French has graced academic life. Their son David (born in 1925), who followed in his father's graduate and undergraduate footsteps at Harvard, married Betty Woodhouse and now teaches English at Queens College. David's sister Jane (born in 1932) graduated from Radcliffe College and is married to John L. Lumley, a teacher of aeronautical engineering at Pennsylvania State University. The Lumleys have three children; the David Frenches, two.

Milton French's teaching experience began at Lafayette College in 1919–1920, where he served as instructor in English; then followed five years at New York University, 1922–1927, and eight years as assistant professor at Dartmouth, 1928–1936. In 1936–1938, he served as instructor and tutor at Harvard, after which he was assistant professor at the University of Akron (1938–1939) and at Queens College (1939–1940). In 1940 he was appointed professor and head of the Department of English at Rutgers University. If, as William James said, the function of an education is to be able to know a good man when you see one, the men at Rutgers who chose French were singularly perceptive. The flowering of this scholarly talent has reached full bloom at Rutgers, in the midst of warm appreciation from his colleagues, from brilliant younger men he has helped select, and from Milton scholars the world over.

III

Almost thirty years ago Milton French made a commitment to himself such as few scholars find possible or desirable. He decided to spend the remaining decades of his scholarly endeavors on Miltonic research. To accomplish this end, he selected as his first task the close examination of every source, in chronological order, to which David Masson refers in his *Life of Milton*. Such a task, if completed, meant that there would be no fact or idea in Milton's life and thought that he would not touch and examine anew. He

reasoned correctly that this method would also bring to
light many new facts about Milton unknown to Masson
and later scholars. No more exhaustive analysis of Milton's
many-sided life could have been projected. French began to
assemble, one by one, copies of documents, records, letters,
and books upon which Masson and his successors had relied. Such was the scholarly task that was to crystallize
twenty years later in his great series, *Life Records of John
Milton* (sponsored by the Rutgers Research Council and
published by the Rutgers University Press). It was a task
that required an almost daily expansion of a scholar's mind
and scope of resources. No man as a scholar is equal to the
task of assessing Milton with full insight in all departments
of his mind and art. But Milton French chose a humbler
task of durable usefulness: to lay before the critics and biographers of the future the indispensable documents upon
which they must depend.

In the middle 1930's the first yields of French's new approach to Milton began to appear in a series of articles
strikingly diverse in texture and aim. New facts about Milton, like those revealed in "A New Letter by John Milton"
(*PMLA*, 1934) and "An Action Against Milton" (*TLS*,
1935 and 1936), were to French the richest of all rewards
for his labor. Then came a valuable article, "Milton, Needham, and *Mercurius Politicus*" (*Studies in Philology*, 1936),
that gave for the first time the full picture of the Needham-
Milton relationship and uncovered Needham's use of his
own previous writings as articles for *Mercurius*. Still another
article, "Milton as Satirist"(*PMLA*, 1936), laid emphasis on
the quality and sources of Milton's satiric diction. In "Milton as a Historian" (*PMLA*, 1935) French brought into
full focus Milton's gift for scientific inquiry in contrast to
the psychology of the poet. To the student of Milton this

article is far more satisfying than an earlier excellent article on the same topic by Sir Charles Firth. For some years French had been gradually training himself to handle the historian's tools; but Firth had not known Milton well enough to place the rationalistic seeker and the frenzied poet side by side. The reading of these several articles shows, as nothing else can, the range of scholarly resources French was able to muster for the advancement of his great aim. The gaining of such resources brought a cumulative insight and made sudden illumination, such as the scholar most cherishes, an almost daily experience.

Steady application to the embracing plan he had chosen also made it possible for Milton French to make vital contributions to the Columbia *Milton*. He was called upon to edit the *State Papers* for Volume XIII. With Thomas O. Mabbott he edited Volume XVIII, which scholars generally find one of the most useful of the Columbia series, and certainly the richest in illuminating annotations and hints for future research. Legal documents written or dictated by Milton and others, which French analyzed in his *Milton in Chancery* (1939), were now published in full for the first time. *Proposalls of Certaine Expedients* was also published for the first time in Volume XVIII and identified by Mabbott and French as Milton's work. With the encouragement of the two editors, Volume XVIII included Maurice Kelley's excellent presentation of texts and notes of Milton marginalia and William R. Parker's discovery of new texts of the Hobson poems. In this collaborative effort Milton French's own contributions were rich and informative; moreover, he was now assuming a leadership in Miltonic studies that was to encourage new research projects among both younger men and contemporaries in the decades that followed.

In the 1940's while the *Life Records* were in preparation for the press, Milton French found time to help initiate and guide two other important Milton projects, the Variorum edition of *Milton's Poetry* for the Columbia University Press and the *Complete Prose* for the Yale University Press. Under his leadership of the seventeenth-century group of the Modern Language Association, Merritt Hughes was chosen to edit the poetry, and this project has moved forward with the aid of French, A. S. P. Woodhouse, and Douglas Bush as members of the editorial board. The other project was the *Complete Prose*, initiated in 1948. Milton French was the first scholar asked to join the *Prose* board; of all American Miltonists, he now possessed the most diverse resources needed to supervise a study of Milton in which biography, intellectual history, historical sources, documents, and editions, rather than aesthetics, would be dominant considerations. When the *Prose* board was complete, it included Hughes, Kelley, Bush, Woodhouse, Sir Herbert Grierson, and John Diekhoff; James Holly Hanford helped to see the project under way at the first meeting and attended many subsequent ones. Partly for geographical reasons, the burden of the project's labors has fallen upon French, Kelley, Alexander M. Witherspoon, and the general editor, Don M. Wolfe. In the twelve years that have passed, French has been a tower of strength to the *Prose* board. Except for times of illness, he has not missed a single meeting; his patience is indefatigable, his courtesy and imagination unfailing, his advice always informed by the immense range of his reading in the sources. In these twelve years of meetings, those who have come to know Milton French value the sweetness and mellowness of the man as much as the versatility and insight of the scholar.

IV

The first volume of the *Life Records* appeared in 1949; the fifth and last volume in 1958. One sentence thus summarizes the crystallization of three decades' devotion to a scholarly dream. But the complexities and variations of this great dream elude us. It was planned and carried out amid burdens and responsibilities, in the mounting of despair and the glimmering of hope. The *Life Records* is not a series for new critics of literature or new critics of intellectual history. Milton himself was a man devoted to facts: he knew that the history of his country, and the revolution in which he engaged, the fall of kingship, the ideas of *Areopagitica*, were an essential part of the history of man; nor could any action of his passionate life remain unlinked, in the recesses of his mind and heart, to the art of *Paradise Lost* or *Samson Agonistes*. But such a statement is not made by French himself; the *Life Records* imposes no predilections; it leaves each critic free to recreate his own Milton from the indispensable sources.

And now, on the verge of laying down his academic responsibilities, Milton French is free to give more time to his first love: the creative scholarship that has proved more fruitful than he or any of his contemporaries could have imagined thirty years ago. He is still youthful, exuberant, eager for the new day and the two-mile walk, for the letter about Milton, for the voices of his friends. He has been awarded a Huntington Library Fellowship for the year following his retirement. As never before, he is prepared to make new discoveries and substantial contributions to Milton scholarship. He is to edit, with Maurice Kelley, Volume VII of the

Milton *Prose;* and his resources are indispensable to both the board of the *Prose* and that of the Variorum. But his friends cherish the ripeness of the man even more than the lore of the scholar. "Walk with mean men," wrote Emerson, "and you think life is mean; but walk with Plutarch, and the world is filled with great spirits that will not let you sleep." Those who have walked with Milton French know that in this one man are embodied greatness of spirit and superlative scholarly stature.

March 1960

Beowulf's Fight with Grendel

BY ALLAN H. ORRICK

In *Beowulf*, the fight between the hero and Grendel is introduced by a prologue (710–745a) in which the monster arrives at Heorot, breaks down the door, and devours a Geatish warrior, Handscioh. He then turns his attention to Beowulf. This paper deals with the next four and one-half lines (745b–749), the passage in which the fight has its beginning. As usually printed, these lines contain a metrically anomalous half-line and are so punctuated that the meaning is obscured. Given their usual interpretation, they contribute very little to the narrative; yet, logically, the actions described here should determine, partially at least, the nature of the fight's later stages and should help with the meaning of other passages in the poem. It is, therefore, worthwhile to attempt a more accurate and less ambiguous text and a different interpretation. I begin with my suggested text and follow with a commentary:

Forð, near ætstop,
nam þa mid handa   higeþihtigne.
Rinc on ræste   (hine) ræhte ongean
feond mid folme;   he onfeng hraþe
inwitþancum   ond wið earm gesæt.

Forð, near ætstop: Although not usually so considered, *forð* and *near* very likely represent a type of asyndetic parataxis, "stepped forward, [stepped] nearer." I would put a comma between them for the sake of clarity (see Klaeber, edition, p. clxiv, on punctuation of variations; but also E. A. Kock, *Jubilee Jaunts and Jottings, Lunds Universitets Årsskrift*, N.F. Avd. I, Bd. 14, No. 25 [1918], p. 11).[1]

nam þa mid handa: Kemp Malone has suggested, though never in print so far as I know, a conative sense for *nam*, "tried to take, tried to seize," a meaning which is necessary here, for it is nowhere evident that Grendel got a grip on Beowulf, nor are we told that Beowulf was injured in the fight. Moreover, in the usual interpretation, the monster is said to have reached after he had seized, an unsatisfactory sequence of actions unless this is a case of histeron proteron. Earle translated, "he was then taking"; similarly Wrenn (p. 198), "he was in the act of seizing," explaining that *nam* is a "progressive or continuous" tense.

higeþihtigne: This adjectival compound has been assigned several meanings. Among them are "mighty-minded" (Kemble), "animo validus" (Grein, *Sprachschatz*; Holthausen-Köhler), "doughty-minded" (Thorpe), "stout-hearted" (Arnold; Wrenn), "doughty of heart" (B-T), "great-hearted" (Earle; Wyatt-Chambers), "strong-hearted, determined" (Klaeber). Any one of these meanings is generally applicable to Beowulf,. but none seems especially appropriate in this specific context. Without implying an allegorical interpretation, it is safe to say that the poem, particularly the Grendel episode, is concerned with opposites: the hero who comes to save the Danes and the monster who comes to destroy them; the forces of good and the forces of evil; piety and wickedness. Greater effectiveness is gained for the passage if the epithets are chosen to point up this contrast.

The available evidence suggests the meaning "pious-, excellent, noble-minded" for *higeþihtig*. The word *þihtig* is attested three times in all of Old English: in the compound under discussion, uncompounded in *Beowulf* 1558, and in *unðyhtige* from the *Corpus Glossary* (Sweet, *The Oldest English Texts*, p. 107, 2133; W. M. Lindsay, *The Corpus Glossary*, p. 184, 191). In variant spellings *unðyhtige* also occurs in the *Epinal-Erfurt Glossary*, but this is of no consequence. For *þyhtig*, Kemble uses "doughty" in his translation, "validus" in his glossary. This great scholar apparently arrived at his meaning through etymology, but his hesitancy in making the connection with "Nhd. tüchtig. N. E. doughty" indicates his lack of conviction. Grein (*Sprachschatz*) also surmises "validus," perhaps following Kemble. In the *Corpus Glossary*, *unðyhtige egan* glosses *vitiato oculo*. Sweet, possibly influenced by his predecessors, assigned the meaning "weak" to the adjective. B-T follows Sweet in this and then glosses *þyhtig* with "strong, firm." The reasoning at this point seems obvious and has been accepted by all later editors and commentators. As far as I can tell, however, *unðyhtig* does not mean "weak," so *þyhtig* does not necessarily mean "strong."

According to Lindsay, *vitiato oculo* is from Orosius (IV, vi, 38); the OE adjective is used in the gloss because Orosius actually used an adjective, *vitioso*. The past participle was

probably due to the influence of *vitiatum* two lines before
and also from Orosius (IV, pref., 10), which was glossed by
the OE past participle *awerded*. *Vitiatus* means "injured,
corrupted, destroyed, violated"; *awerded* translates it perfectly. A related noun, *vitium*, means "fault, defect, vice."
The adjective *vitiosus* has the same core of meaning and
was used specifically as "sinful" by the medieval Church
Fathers. *Vitioso oculo* appears in one of Orosius' moralizing
passages, and the adjective's sense is "defective, impaired":

> —qui uitioso oculo haec uident atque ideo duplicia illis
> uidentur quae uident et confusi caligine nequitiae in id
> cadunt, ut minus uidendo plus uideant, cum tamen id quod
> est ita ut est uidere non possint; (Karl Zangemeister, ed.
> *Pauli Orosii Historiarum Adversum Paganos, in Corpus Scrip-
> torum Ecclesiasticorum Latinorum*, Vol. V).[2]

The meaning of *vitiosus* in Orosius and the use of *awerded*
to gloss *vitiatus* indicate "sinful, corrupt, faulty, defective"
rather than "weak" as proper translations of *unðyhtig*. Then,
if we follow the accepted line of reasoning, *þyhtig* will mean
"pious, righteous, excellent, perfect." Such a rendering gives
good sense in *Beowulf* 1588: *ealdsweord eotensic ecgum
þyhtig*, "an ancient sword made by giants, excellent in its
edges."

In addition to glosses, etymology is frequently used in
getting at the meaning of OE words. Evidence from this
source supports the suggestion that *þyhtig* be taken to mean
"pious, righteous, excellent, perfect." The adjective *geþyht*
is glossed by B-T as "good, advantageous." The verb *þeon*,
"grow, thrive, prosper," is also etymologically related to
þyhtig. In derivatives and compounds, *þeon* could have easily
been extended in meaning to include the concept of

"strength, might," but there is no evidence it was. The past participle *geþungen* is well attested in the sense of "grown, advanced" but is found more frequently with the meaning "excellent, pious, noble, perfect." For example, in *Beowulf* 624, *mode geþungen* is best taken as "excellent in mind." The same meanings appear in the compounds: *oferþeon*, "excell, surpass"; *heahþungen*, "of high rank, noble, distinguished"; *welþungen*, "able, good, proficient"; *þungenness*, "excellence, virtue."

Neither of the two principal ways of determining meanings for OE words leads to "strong, mighty, firm" for *þyhtig*, but both agree on an area of meaning represented by "pious, excellent, righteous, perfect, good, noble." Selecting those possibilities which I believe contrast most explicitly with Grendel's character, I suggest that *higeþihtig* be translated as "pious-minded, noble-minded." If *rinc* begins a new sentence, *higeþihtigne* must be construed as the object of *nam* and translated as an absolute rather than an attributive, "the one pious in mind, the one noble in mind."

Rinc on ræste: *Rinc* is a nominative, the subject of *ræhte*.[3] The abrupt shift in subject, which occurs if Beowulf is first introduced by *he* in 748b, is eliminated; *rinc* also provides an antecedent for *he*. Since *feond*, an accusative, the object of *ongean*, must now refer to Grendel, it is no longer necessary to point out that *feond* cannot refer to Beowulf; all possible confusion over the meaning of the word is removed. With *rinc* a nominative, a clear contrast between Hondscioh and Beowulf is established, and, reinforced by verbal echoes, this contrast foreshadows the outcome of the fight. Hondscioh, the sleeping warrior (*slæpendne rinc*, 741a), receives the action; he is quickly seized (*gefeng hraþe*) by Grendel and devoured. Beowulf, the warrior in bed but not asleep (*Rinc on ræste*), acts; he quickly seized (*onfeng hraþe*) the monster. Grendel's role in the two encounters is reversed, and Beowulf's triumph is prefigured.

(hine) ræhte ongean: In the MS., at the end of line 6, fol. 131r (new foliation 149r), only traces of letters remain. Zupitza said in a note on the line, "after *ræste* an erasure of some five letters, of which the first seems to have been *h*, the second possibly was *a*." [4] Because of similar smudges at corresponding places on both sides of the preceding leaf (fol. 146; new foliation 148), John C. Pope has concluded that the MS. was accidentally damaged and that restoration was therefore justified; he tentatively offered *him swa* as the original reading. [5] Although *him swa* is certainly possible (but see Klaeber, p. 466), I suggest *hine* as being more likely. The physical evidence points to a four or five letter word beginning with *h*. [6] Stylistically, *hine* is as acceptable as any other proposed restoration, and it makes as much or better sense. Grammatically, *hine* is more satisfactory than a dative because *ongean* usually takes an accusative when used with a verb of motion (see B-T); *feond* becomes a variation of *hine*. Unfortunately, the new photograph of this folio was not made under ultra-violet light and offers no more help with the reading than the old.

he onfeng hraþe: The usual interpretation of *onfeng* as "received" seems both vague and inappropriate. If Beowulf merely "received" Grendel, i.e., accepted the monster's onslaught, "did not flinch or try to avoid the attack" (Wyatt-Chambers, p. 39), *hraþe* is illogical and we are not told that Beowulf got hold of his enemy. At this point, the antagonists are grappling with each other. Grendel had stepped close to the reclining warrior and was trying to take him. As a counter measure, Beowulf reached out and quickly seized his attacker. The natural development of the fight, the contrast between Beowulf and Handscioh, and lines 750–753a, which definitely prove that Beowulf had a grip on Grendel, all require that *onfeng* mean "seized."

inwitþancum: No entirely satisfactory interpretation of this word has ever been proposed. Currently, it is most frequently construed as a noun used adverbially to describe Beowulf's mood when he engaged Grendel: "with hostile intent," but if a noun, it must mean "malicious, wicked, or evil thoughts." Given its proper meaning, *inwitþanc* cannot be applied to Beowulf with propriety even when he is struggling against a relative of Cain. In a second interpretation, it is made the object of *onfeng* and is translated "malicious hostility," "plan of malice," i.e., Grendel's attack. The meaning is again unlikely, and *onfeng* must also be mistranslated. I follow Grein (*Sprachschatz*), Heyne, and Kock (*Anglia*, 45:115) in taking it to be the dative singular of an adjective used absolutely as the object of *onfeng*: "the one malicious, wicked, evil in thought." *Inwitþanc* retains its normal meaning. As a variation of *feond*, it quite appropriately denotes Grendel, and as the perfect antithesis of *higeþihtig*, it emphasizes the contrast between the monster and the hero. This reading, it seems to me, contributes to rather than detracts from the effectiveness of the narrative. Against this interpretation one objection can be raised: *inwitþanc* appears elsewhere in OE poetry only as a noun (Wyatt-Chambers, p. 39).

wið earm gesæt: Nearly everyone agrees on the meaning of *gesæt*: "sat up, came to a sitting position." The progress of the action demands this meaning. In the beginning, Beowulf was lying down (*Rinc on ræste*); in 759b he stood up (*uplang astod*); with *gesæt* he assumed the necessary intermediate position. *Wið earm* presents more of a problem. In the usual interpretation, these words refer to Beowulf: "[he] sat up, leaning against [his own] arm." [7] However, if the arm is Beowulf's, the passage says nothing about how or where Beowulf got hold of Grendel.[8] A better meaning is suggested by the context. Because Beowulf is on the offensive, it is more likely that the arm is Grendel's. The hero appears to have the monster at a disadvantage through the unexpected suddenness of his counterattack. Normal strategy would call for him to press his advantage rather than to lose it by nonchalantly propping himself up with one hand while attempting to hold a foe of Grendel's prowess with the other. The thoughts running through Grendel's mind in lines 750 ff. clearly indicate that Beowulf was serious about his task. In the light of what comes before and after, *wið earm gesæt* gives perfectly good sense if we take it to mean nothing more than that Beowulf sat up while holding on to Grendel's arm. Grendel stepped up to the reclining warrior and extended his arm in an attempt to seize him. Beowulf reacted by reaching for and quickly grasping—perhaps with both hands—the monster's outstretched arm. Then maintaining his grip, the hero moved into a sitting position. With admirable economy, the poet has related the specific way in which Beowulf caught hold of Grendel and has described his second maneuver.

My suggested translation of the entire passage is as follows:

[Grendel] stepped forward, [stepped] nearer, then tried to take the one pious in mind with [his] hand. The warrior in bed reached toward him, [reached toward] the fiend with [his] open palm; he quickly seized the one evil in thought and sat up with (i.e., holding on to) [his] arm.

Lines 745b–749 are thus made to provide more specific details than ever before, and the actions which they describe now fit consistently into the whole episode.

Notes

1. Citations consisting of a person's name only are usually to well-known editions or translations of *Beowulf*; references are to Wyatt-Chambers of 1933 and Klaeber of 1950: Zupitza 2ed is a reissue of the famous *Autotypes* (E.E.T.S. No. 77 [1882]) with new photographs and an introductory note by Norman Davis (E.E.T.S. No. 245 [1959]). Other abbreviated references are B-T for Bosworth-Toller, *An Anglo-Saxon Dictionary* (Oxford, 1882); Grein, *Sprachschatz* for C. W. M. Grein, *Sprachschatz der angelsächsischen Dichter*; Holthausen-Köhler for a re-editing of the preceding by F. Holthausen and J. Köhler (1912).
2. "For these people see these things with defective vision and thus what they see appears double; and being confused as it were by a fog of wickedness, they fall into a condition where by seeing less they see more, since they cannot see things as they are." Irving W. Raymond, trans. *Seven Books Against the Pagans: The Apology of Paulus Orosius*, p. 166.
3. This punctuation has been recommended previously, but for somewhat different reasons, by F. G. Cassidy (*MLN*, L [1935], 88–89); a partial summary of Cassidy's views as well as objections to them and to the punctuation in general is to be found in Dobbie, p. 152.

4. Although a few scholars since Zupitza's time have restored one or more words, most have followed him in considering the lacuna a genuine erasure and have accepted *ræhte ongean* as a full half-line or have emended for reasons of sense or meter.

5. *The Rhythm of Beowulf*, p. 372. The importance of Pope's observation on fol. 131 has apparently been disregarded. Since the appearance of his book, only Holthausen (8ed) and Sune Lindqvist (*Beowulf Dissectus*, pp. 12, 31) have followed him in restoring. Strangely enough, the smudges on fol. 146 have always been thought accidental.

6. At line 6, fol. 146r, *horn* is smudged but legible in both editions of Zupitza; at lines 5 and 6, fol. 146v, editors generally agree on restoring *æthr-* and *he ge-* respectively (see Klaeber's variant readings at 722 and 723). New photographs made under ultra-violet light partially verify the reading at line 5 but *þær a-* is now conjectured for line 6 (see Zupitza 2ed, p. xiii).

7. This widely accepted rendering of *wið earm gesæt* is said to be supported by a parallel from *Christ and Satan* 430–431: *Aras þa anra gehwylc and wið earm gesæt, / hleonade wið handa.* However, there is certainly no possibility that *gesæt* means both "sat up" and "leaning" in *Christ and Satan*, and there is little likelihood that it even means "sat up." *Wið earm gesæt* and *hleonade wið handa* are apparently variations of each other and indicate an action performed after that of *aras*. Because of *hleonade wið handa*, the meaning of *wið earm gesæt* seems clear. I would translate, "Then each one arose and rested against [his] arm, leaned against [his] hand." This meaning of *wið earm gesæt* cannot help with *Beowulf*, where "sat up" is essential.

8. This was pointed out by Calvin S. Brown, Jr., (*PMLA*, LV [1940], 623). Brown constructed an interesting and elaborate explanation of what happened. He believes that Beowulf put

an arm-lock on the monster, and he describes its application and effects in considerable detail. His theory can be neither proved nor disproved, but it seems to make a simple thing unduly complicated.

Langland and the "Canes Muti"

BY ALFRED L. KELLOGG

In the tenth passus of *Piers Plowman* (B 256 et seq.), Clergy defines Dobest as "to be bolde · to blame the gylty," but adds the qualification that the priest, to carry out his duty of just reproof, must himself be blameless: *Si culpare velis · culpabilis esse cauebis.* However, Clergy continues, few are they who obey this injunction, and little are the people benefited by their blind guides:

> Ac it semeth now sothly · to the worldes syght,
> That goddes worde worcheth nauȝte · on lered ne on lewede,
> But in suche a manere as Marke · meneth in the gospel,
> *Dum cecus ducit cecum, ambo in foveam cadunt.*
> Lewed men may likne ȝow thus · that the beem lithe in ȝowre eyghen,
> And the festu is fallen · for ȝowre defaute,
> In alle manere men · thourgh mansed prestes.
> The bible bereth witnesse · that alle the folke of Israel
> Byttere abouȝte the gultes · of two badde prestes,

Offyn and Fynes; · for her coueytise,
Archa dei myshapped · and Ely brake his nekke.
  For-thi, ȝe corectoures, claweth her-on · and corecteth
    fyrst ȝow-seluen,
And thanne mowe ȝe saufly seye · as Dauid made the
    sauter:
Existimasti inique quod ero tui similis: arguam te, et statuam
contra faciem tuam.
And thanne shal borel clerkes ben abasched · to blame
    ȝow or to greue,
And carpen nouȝte as thei carpen now · and calle ȝow
    doumbe houndes,
      Canes non valentes latrare (B X, 274–287) [1]

The significance of the "doumbe houndes" epithet with
which Clergy closes his remarks remains largely unexplored.[2]
It has, of course, long been recognized that the words "canes
muti non valentes latrare" make up a portion of the indictment of the priesthood of Israel found in Isaiah lvi.10:
"Speculatores ejus caeci omnes . . . canes muti non valentes latrare." Beyond this, however, very little of Langland's
allusion has been explained. Why, for instance, are the
secular clergy called "doumbe houndes," and who are the
"borel clerkes" who so accuse them? Finally how are we to
intrepret the passage as a whole? Are we to interpret it as
Langland's delight at the deserved rebuke of the corruption
practiced by the secular clergy, or as his concern over criticism which, if unchecked, might well endanger the existence
of the Church itself?

    The relevance of Isaiah lvi.10 to the secular clergy, Eng-
lish or otherwise, is easily made out. In all the commentaries
the "speculator," watchman, and the "canis," watchdog, are
interpreted as figures of the priest. Of the two, the "canis"
metaphor seems to have been much the more popular. Thus

the *Glossa Ordinaria* says: "Just as it is the duty of dogs to protect a flock, so is it the duty of prelates to protect the people." [3] The failure of the watchdog to bark is the failure of the priest to correct evil when he sees it appear among his flock. Thus in the *Cura Pastoralis* (II.iv), Gregory says:

> Let the spiritual leader (rector) be discreet in silence, useful in word, lest he utter those things which ought to be kept silent, or keep silent those things which ought to be spoken out. For just as incautious speech drags into error, so does indiscreet silence abandon in error those who were capable of being taught. For often improvident leaders (rectores) fearing to lose human favor, tremble to speak out freely those things which are right, and according to the voice of Truth (John x. 12), keep their flocks not with the zeal of shepherds, but in the manner of mercenaries, for when they hide themselves beneath silence, they flee at the approach of the wolf. And thus the Lord reproves them through the mouth of the prophet, saying: "Dumb dogs, not able to bark." [4]

In the British Isles, the Isaiah passage seems to have been as well known as on the continent. It appears first, so far as the present writer is aware, in the famous *De Excidio et Conquestu Britanniae* (6th century), where Gildas speaks of the duty of priests to reprove the sinful, "lest we be 'dumb dogs not able to bark.' " [5] In Anglo-Saxon England, the text is found in the first pastoral letter of Aelfric, and in Wulfstan's brief treatise concerning lazy, timid, and negligent pastors. [6] In the fourteenth century, it appears, amongst other places, in the *Speculum Christiani:* "If he [the curate] es not salt or sauery in wysdom, he es an hounde a-boute the floc of god, but he dryue₃ not a-wey the wolfe with berkynge of prechynge." [7]

From the above references, it is clear that the priest was

expected to be a faithful watchdog, barking vociferously to warn of evil. This warning might be made directly in the form of personal rebuke—as for instance Chaucer's good priest, who would "snybben sharply for the nonys" [8]—or less directly in the form of preaching.[9] It will be noted, however, that in the *Piers Plowman* passage reproduced above, Langland seems to have in mind less an abstract treatment of the duties of the good priest than a specific group or groups—"borel clerkes"—who are calling the secular clergy "doumbe houndes." Who might these be?

No group of Langland's time was more consistent in pointing out the failings of the secular clergy than the friars. Though themselves open to many criticisms, there was one criticism they were not open to, and that was failure to preach. In a curious monitory poem, *De Concordia inter Fratres et Rectores Ecclesiae* (early 15th century), the monk John Audelay contrasts the activity of the preaching friars and the indolence of the parish priests:

> Trule, I trow, þis rewme where chamyd *and* chent
>   Nere þe foreþeryng of þe frerys *and* here prechyng,
> For þe seculars prestis take no*n* entent
>   Bot to here leudnes *and* her lust *and* here lykyng.[10]

What the friars had to say in their sermons about the non-preaching and materially inclined secular clergy is fortunately readily available in the *Summa Predicantium*, the great compilation of preaching material for friars put together not long before 1348 by the Dominican John Bromyarde.[11] Under the head of "Avarice" one finds much relevant material. Here Bromyarde, in his characteristic narrative form, declares that against the avaricious man, in this case evidently the avaricious priest, the three great mas-

ters of deceit, the world, the flesh, and the devil, join forces.
At the beginning of his career, the new priest attacks the
triple temptations facing him with great energy; but the
world, the flesh, and the devil, though duly put to flight by
his eager assault, take care to drop tempting bits in their
precipitous retreat.

> Thus many seek to pursue vigorously, and in this labor begin
> [to attack] the world—that is, sinners living unto the world
> and evilly—by correction; their own flesh by maceration; the
> devil by humiliation. But the world scatters rewards, and while
> they are busy about these, the evil escape . . . . And thus
> they mock the receivers of rewards . . . . These [receivers of
> rewards], made sport of through entreaty and bribe, put off
> their corrections, and about these [corrections] being both
> negligent and timid, permit many to go off to Hell, with
> whom they themselves go for the sake of company. Therefore
> it is said to Moses, Exodus XVIII [21]: "Provide out of all the
> people wise men, able and fearing God, in whom there is
> truth, and who hate avarice . . . ." for they who hate avarice
> and are not busy about rewards, will not permit sinners to go
> off into damnable perdition . . . . Those who give up their
> pursuit because of the aforementioned impediments [i.e., the
> temptations of the world, the flesh, and the devil] are like
> dogs which cease to bark when bread is thrown them by a
> thief, and permit the thief to carry out his intention. Thus
> they are *dumb dogs, not able to bark.*[12]

Another group equally critical of the failings of the secular
clergy and equally devoted to the practice of preaching were
the Lollards. Wyclif's own views on the avariciousness of
the secular clergy and their disinclination to preach are well
enough known to require no further discussion. What is
perhaps more relevant is to examine the kind of popularization of Wyclif's views which might have come to the ears of

Langland. An example of such a popularization is the vast
and discursive tractate *On the Seven Deadly Sins*, thought
to have been written about 1385 by Nicholas Hereford, one
of the best known of Wyclif's followers.[13] Although a few
years too late for the usually accepted date of the B text (ca.
1377), the *Seven Deadly Sins* provides a useful compilation
of typical Lollard opinions, which by the year 1377 were
being actively circulated by Wyclif's "poor priests."[14] Particularly instructive are Hereford's views on preaching. "Þo
moste hye servise þat men have in erthe," says Hereford, "is
to preche Gods worde,"[15] and "herfore Jesus Crist occupyed
hym mooste in þo werke of prechyng, and laft oþer werkes;
and þus diden his apostils, and herfore God loved hom."[16]
But now, continues Hereford,

> no more covetouse men schal men fynde in erthe, ne ferrer
> fro hevenly lif, ne more wrappid wiþ worldly causes. And it
> semes to mony men þat þei gon hedlyngis to helle, and
> drawen men aftir hom þat þei schulden bere to heven . . .
> Ffor prest is a spyere in his castel [Isaiah lvi. 10], to loke ofer
> perels of schepe; and if he be blynde in his soule for pouder of
> temporal goodis . . . and þus perel come to schepe, þo Lord
> þat owis þo schepe by skil schulde dampne hym for negli-
> gense.[17]

The reference to the priest's being a "spyere in his castel" is
of course a reference to the beginning of the text under discussion, "Speculatores ejus caeci omnes . . . canes muti non
valentes latrare" [Isaiah lvi.10]. Given the presence of this
allusion, it is no great surprise to discover elsewhere in
Hereford's text this same image of spiritual blindness merg-
ing into an image of spiritual muteness occasioned by the
devil's casting a highly material bone to the watchdogs:

And as eyne in þo hed reulen al þo body for to go right weyes
and profitable to mon, so prelatis of þo Chirche schulden
lede hit in Gods wey. Bot Crist seis in his Gospel, þat if a
blynde lede a blynde mon in þo wey, þei fallen bothe in þo
dike. And þus þo wey of charite, þat schulde be brood to alle
men, is streyned by envye, and lettis men to sue Crist. And so
þo fend haves cast a boon, and made þese honndes to feght;
and by a bal of talow lettis hom to berke.[18]

It is apparent, I think, that the Dominican Bromyarde and
the Wyclifite Hereford are making essentially the same accusation. Worldly goods have blinded the Church to the needs
of its sheep and made mute the mouths which should warn
the flock of approaching disaster. As a result, the blind pas-
tor accompanies the blind sheep down the road to Hell. In
place of spiritual leaders, there are only blind—and mute—
mouths. All this is to be found in Langland: the covetous-
ness, the blindness, the failure of reproof. However, between
Langland and the two groups whom the present writer takes
to be the "borel clerkes" [19] in question, there is a long and
large difference. Whereas the Wyclifite and the friar either
relished destructive criticism or lacked effective concern
about its consequences, Langland feared what might happen
to the unity of the Church should unbridled criticism be
permitted to gain currency. What Langland hoped to see
was a reform movement within the secular clergy strong
enough to refute, through its own example, the slurs cast
upon it. One of the numerous paradoxes of Langland the
man [20] is that Langland the reformer had a very exact sense
of the dangers of reform:

For-thi I conseil alle creatures · no clergie to dispise,
Ne sette schort be here science · what so thei don
  hemselue.

Take we her wordes at worthe · for here witnesse be
trewe,
And medle we nauȝt muche with hem · to meuen any
wrathe,
Lest cheste chafen vs · to choppe vche man other;
Nolite tangere christos meos, etc.[21]

NOTES

1. All references are to *Piers Plowman*, ed. W. W. Skeat (Oxford, 1886).
2. Brief comments are to be found in Cardinal F. A. Gasquet, *Old English Bible*, 2nd ed. (London, 1908), p. 67, and H. B. Workman, *John Wyclif* (Oxford, 1926), II, 208.
3. "Sicut canes gregem, sic prelati debent custodire plebem" (*Patrologia Latina*, ed. J. P. Migne, CXIII, 1208). Hereafter referred to as *PL*.
4. "Sit rector descretus in silentio, utilis in verbo, ne aut tacenda proferat, aut proferenda reticescat. Nam sicut incauta locutio in errorem pertrahit, ita indiscretum silentium hos qui erudiri poterant, in errore derelinquit. Saepe namque rectores improvidi humanam amittere gratiam formidantes, loqui libere recta pertimescunt; et juxta Veritatis vocem (*Joan* X. 12), nequaquam jam gregis custodiae Pastorum studio, sed mercenariorum vice deserviunt, quia veniente lupo fugiunt, dum se sub silentio abscondunt. Hinc namque eos per prophetam Dominus increpat, dicens: *Canes muti non valentes latrare*" (PL, LXXVII, 30). For this citation I am indebted to the kindness of Professor Morton W. Bloomfield of the Ohio State University.

5. "ne simus 'canes muti non valentes latrare' " ("Gildae Sapientis *De Excidio et Conquestu Britanniae*," in *Monumenta Germaniae Historica* [Berlin, 1898], XIII, 48.)

6. *The Homilies of Wulfstan*, ed. Dorothy Bethurum (Oxford, 1957), p. 240 and note p. 350. These passages were kindly pointed out to me by Professor Rudolph Willard of the University of Texas.

7. *Speculum Christiani*, ed. Gustaf Holmstedt, Early English Text Society, Original Series, No. 182 (London, 1933 [for 1929]), p. 172. Hereafter referred to as "EETS. OS."

8. "General Prologue" to the *Canterbury Tales*, line 523.

9. Preaching seems to have been a very popular interpretation of the hound's bark. In addition to the *Speculum Christiani* passage cited above, see Haymo of Halberstadt, "latratus predicationis" (*PL*, CXVI. 1010); Hervey of Bourg-Dieu, "canes enim dicuntur praedicatores" (*PL*, CLXXXI. 514), and Nicolas of Lyra, "sine voce predicationis" *Biblia Sacra cum Glossa Ordinaria* (Lyons, 1589), IV. 562. The gloss last noted is the interlinear gloss.

10. Lines 599–602 (*The Poems of John Audelay*, ed. E. K. Whiting, EETS. OS. 184.31). It is interesting to observe that the poem seems to be a deliberate imitation of *Piers Plowman*, both in its copying of Langland's alliteration and in its concern with the peril to the unity of the Church posed by the strife between the secular and regular clergy.

11. The *Dictionary of National Biography* (art: "John Bromyarde") puts Bromyarde's period of activity at around 1390. However, recent researches (cf. H. C. Beeching, "The Library of the Cathedral Church of Norwich," *Norfolk Archaeology*, XIX (1915), 72–73) indicate that the *Summa Predicantium* was written certainly before 1352, and that its author probably died in the plague of 1348. For information relative to the dating of the *Summa*, I am indebted to the Rev. James A. Weisheipl, O.P., Dominican House of Studies, River Forest, Illinois, and to the Rev. Leonard E. Boyle, O.P., Collegio San Clemente, Rome. Father Boyle

will shortly publish a definitive article on the date of the *Summa*.

12. "Sic multi conantur fortiter persequi, et hoc opere incipiunt mundum, i.e., peccatores mundialiter et male viuentes correctione; carnem propria[m] maceratione; dyabolum humiliatione. Sed mundus spargit munera, circa que dum intendunt, mali fugiunt . . . . Et sic illudunt receptoribus munerum . . . . Sic illusi prece et precio, correctiones differunt, et circa eas negligentes et timidi, multos ad infernum abire permittu[n]t, cum quibus et ipsimet vadunt ratione societatis. Ideo dicitur ad Moysen (Exodus xviii [21]): *Prouide de omni plebe viros sapientes, potentes, et timentes Deum, in quibus sit veritas, et qui oderint auariciam* . . . quia qui odio habent auariciam, circa munera non intenti, peccatores abire non permittunt in perditionem damnabilem . . . . Propter predicta impedimenta cessantes, canes sunt qui pane sibi a latrone proiecto, latrare cessant, et furem propositum suum persequi permittunt. Sic *canes muti non valentes latrare*" (*Summa Predicantium* [Basel, ca. 1484], Article A xxvii 58). Punctuation has been normalized throughout and Biblical quotations have been italicized. For checking my translation, I am indebted to the Rev. James A. Weisheipl, O.P.

13. The tract is published by Thomas Arnold in *Select English Works of John Wyclif* (Oxford, 1869–71), III, 119–167. Arnold believed the work to be by Wyclif himself, but in 1907, Edmund D. Jones attributed it, on the basis of dialect study, to Nicholas Hereford. See *Anglia*, xxx, 267–268. He is followed in this by Workman (*John Wyclif*, I, 330; II, 135); and H. E. Winn, *Wyclif: Select English Writings* (Oxford, 1929), pp. 146–147. Workman assigns the *Seven Deadly Sins* to about the year of Hereford's return from Rome (1385). See *John Wyclif*, II, 135, and Winn, *Wyclif*, p. 147.

14. Workman finds Wyclif's first reference to the persecution of the "poor priests" in the year 1377 (*John Wyclif*, II, 205).

15. Arnold, *Select English Works*, III, 143.
16. *Ibid.*, III, 144.
17. *Ibid.*, III, 150.
18. *Ibid.*, III, 133. Unlike Bromyarde's hound story, Hereford's occurs under "Envy" and hence the more complicated image of dogs fighting over a bone.
19. "Borel (burel)" is a word of frequent occurrence in Middle English. Numerous examples are to be found in Chaucer, but none in conjunction with "clerk" (see art: "burel" in J. S. P. Tatlock and A. G. Kennedy, *A Concordance to the Complete Works of Geoffrey Chaucer* [Washington, 1927]. Gower, however, in the Prologue to the *Confessio Amantis* (line 52) uses the exact phrase: "Thus I, which am a burel clerk." The *MED*, which cites the Gower passage, interprets the phrase as meaning: "clerk with little learning; ? also, an educated layman" (see art: "burel" in *Middle English Dictionary*, ed. Hans Kurath and Sherman M. Kuhn [Ann Arbor, 1952–]). The word "burel" may of course tend to suggest the garb of Wyclif's "poor priests" (see Workman, *John Wyclif*, II, 203), but it is highly doubtful that Langland could have known much of their activities by the time of the B text (see p. 30 above and n. 14). It seems more likely that "borel clerkes" was used as a simple term of abuse, of which Langland had a considerable store.
20. For the paradoxical nature of Langland's character, see the excellent discussion by E. T. Donaldson, *Piers Plowman: the C-Text and Its Poet* (New Haven, 1949), Chap. VII.
21. B XII, 123–27. The speaker here is Ymagynatyf who in Passus XII answers the doubts set forth by the dreamer in Passus X. He may therefore, I think, be taken as a reliable spokesman for Langland's considered opinions.

The Imagery of Food and Eating in *Coriolanus*

BY MAURICE CHARNEY

The "unsavory figurative language" of *Coriolanus* and its "accumulation of derogatory comment" [1] prompted Oscar James Campbell to classify this play as a "tragical satire" rather than a tragedy. Although we may not accept this new category nor Campbell's extreme judgments on the buffoonery of Menenius and the ridiculousness of Coriolanus, his account of the tone and mood of the play is quite convincing. He shows its affinity with such "disturbing" plays as *Timon of Athens, Troilus and Cressida, Hamlet,* and *Measure for Measure.* This affinity may also be demonstrated in their extensive imagery of food, disease, and animals. These image themes, which form the three dominant motifs in *Coriolanus,* help to establish the peculiarly satirical quality in all of these plays.

The imagery of *Coriolanus* is organized around the conflict between plebeians and patricians, which acts as a negative-positive force: the images that refer to the plebeians are generally pejorative, while those that refer to the patricians are laudatory. But the play is by no means a defense of the old aristocracy. The prevailing tone is harsh and discordant, and the laudatory imagery is very sparse. It is clear that Shakespeare has no love for the plebeians, but it is equally clear that Coriolanus, the chief representative of the patricians, is not a sympathetic character. This makes for a balancing of forces in the play and gives it its tight and paradoxical character.[2]

I shall restrict my discussion of *Coriolanus* to the imagery of food and eating, which is perhaps the most extensive and important motif in the play; the imagery of animals and disease follows a similar pattern. Images of food and eating call attention to the appetitive nature of the plebeians, while the negative (images of temperance and austerity) represents a heroic aristocratic ideal. Another significant aspect of this imagery is the theme of war as a devourer; this develops the sense of "eat" as to devour, to destroy as prey. Shakespeare seems to be deliberately emphasizing this imagery to the exclusion of any talk about usury (there is one reference at I.i.83–84), while in Plutarch usury and dearth of corn are linked as the two chief grievances of the citizens.[3] It has been suggested that Shakespeare's emphasis on food may be related to the enclosure riots in the Midlands in 1607.[4]

The most important and concentrated use of this imagery is in I.i. Like *Julius Caesar*, the play opens with a mob scene: "Enter a company of mutinous *Citizens* with staves, clubs, and other weapons" (I.i. S.D.).[5] It is a violent beginning and a strong statement of the issues of the play, as in the First Citizen's question: "You are all resolv'd rather to die than to famish?" (I.i.4–5). This creates an immediate sense of urgency: it is a matter of life and death that is at stake.

Caius Marcius is "chief enemy to the people" (I.i.8), whom the citizens resolve to kill in order to have "corn at our own price" (I.i.10–11). The propulsive force of the mutiny is checked for a moment by the First Citizen's statement of the case:

> We are accounted poor citizens, the patricians good. What authority surfeits on would relieve us. If they would yield us but the superfluity while it were wholesome, we might guess they relieved us humanely; but they think we are too dear. The leanness that afflicts us, the object of our misery, is as an inventory to particularize their abundance; our sufferance is a gain to them. Let us revenge this with our pikes ere we become rakes; for the gods know I speak this in hunger for bread, not in thirst for revenge.   (I.i.15–25)

In however low esteem Shakespeare's contemporaries regarded the people,[6] "I speak this in hunger for bread, not in thirst for revenge" elicits for the moment our sympathies. The patrician-plebeian class conflict is thus at the outset clearly expressed in terms of food; the one has too much ("surfeits," "superfluity," "abundance"), while the other has too little ("leanness," "misery," "sufferance," "rakes," "hunger"). These opening statements of the play point to an ominous disorder in the body politic of Rome.

When Menenius enters, he acknowledges the citizens' "wants" and "suffering in this dearth" (I.i.68–69), but insists that "The gods, not the patricians, make it" (I.i.75). This does not satisfy the Second Citizen, who states the class conflict again in terms of food; the patricians

> ne'er cared for us yet: suffer us to famish, and their storehouses cramm'd with grain; make edicts for usury, to support usurers; repeal daily any wholesome act established against

the rich, and provide more piercing statutes daily to chain up
and restrain the poor. If the wars eat us not up, they will; and
there's all the love they bear us. (I.i.82–89)

In the last sentence, "eat" is used in the negative sense of
devour or destroy. This is an important aspect of the food
and eating imagery, and it indicates that war and the patricians are both devourers. The image suggests the following
sequence: we who have no food will be made to serve as
food for war; we who have nothing to eat will be eaten by
war, or if we stay at home the patricians will destroy us just
as war does.

It is at this point that Menenius recites his "pretty tale"
(I.i.93) of the belly and the members. Into the disorder of
plebeian mutiny Menenius brings this fable of order, spoken
in the prevailing food idiom. The citizens' grievances are
seen within the larger framework of the idea of the state: it
is a body in which each part must perform its particular and
necessary function in order to maintain health. The immediate purpose of the tale is to still the plebeian mutiny, and it
accomplishes this with great success. The fable begins with
the accusation of the rebellious members against the belly:

> That only like a gulf it did remain
> I' th' midst o' th' body, idle and unactive,
> Still cupboarding the viand, never bearing
> Like labour with the rest . . . .   (I.i.101–04)

This resembles the citizens' complaint that their "leanness
. . . is as an inventory to particularize" the "abundance"
(I.i.20–22) of the patricians. The belly's answer, full of the
commonplaces of Renaissance political theory,[7] is an epit-
ome of the well-ordered state:

> "True is it, my incorporate friends," quoth he,
> "That I receive the general food at first
> Which you do live upon; and fit it is,
> Because I am the storehouse and the shop
> Of the whole body. But, if you do remember,
> I send it through the rivers of your blood
> Even to the court, the heart, to th' seat o' th' brain,
> And, through the cranks and offices of man,
> The strongest nerves and small inferior veins
> From me receive that natural competency
> Whereby they live."   (I.i.134–44)

The belly then is not a tyrannical parasite on the body politic, but the necessary "storehouse and the shop" from which all "receive the flour . . ./ And leave me but the bran!" (I.i.149–50).

The fable is then applied point for point to the situation at hand:

> The senators of Rome are this good belly,
> And you the mutinous members. For, examine
> Their counsels and their cares, digest things rightly
> Touching the weal o' th' common, you shall find
> No public benefit which you receive
> But it proceeds or comes from them to you,
> And no way from yourselves.   (I.i.152–58)

By means of the imagery of body and food—the image literally is of digestion—Menenius states the proper function of patrician and plebeian in the state. The plebeians ("members"), in return for their services to the state, are beneficially ruled by the patricians ("belly"), whose natural function it is to rule. This innocent tale, placed in a commanding position in the first scene, provides a fable of order for the entire play. It is a point of reference for all the later disorder and distemper in the state.

Menenius shows no particular affection for the mob, yet he has earned the reputation of "one that hath always lov'd the people" (I.i.52–53). He is a thoroughly politic figure, shrewd and temperate in his dealings with the plebeians, and acknowledging their vital function in the state. Throughout his speech, the "humorous patrician" (II.i.51) shows all the skill of an Antony in dealing with the mob. Menenius is always conscious of his audience, whom he is able to manipulate with great skill. Notice how, as spokesman for the belly, he directs the tale to his listeners: "Your most grave belly was deliberate,/ Not rash like his accusers . . ." (I.i.132–33). And when he has made sure of his audience at the end of his speech, he thoroughly insults the leader, or "great toe" (I.i.159), of the mob as "one o' th' lowest, basest, poorest/ Of this most wise rebellion . . ." (I.i.161–62). Although some of Menenius' words for the people are almost the same as Coriolanus', the humorous, self-conscious tone in which they are spoken is quite different; he is conciliatory where Marcius is contemptuous.

Compare the opening speeches of the two men. When Menenius enters, the citizens are brandishing "staves, clubs, and other weapons" (I.i. S.D.) and preparing to mutiny; he asks:

> What work's, my countrymen, in hand? Where go you
> With bats and clubs? The matter? Speak, I pray you.
>
> (I.i.56–57)

He very cleverly does not ask them to cease or threaten them with destruction, but proposes to talk the matter over. Marcius, however, enters when the people are already pacified and stirs them up again with angry taunts:

> What's the matter, you dissentious rogues
> That, rubbing the poor itch of your opinion,
> Make yourselves scabs? (I.i.168–70)

This is perhaps a more honest expression of personal belief than Menenius', but it is absolutely wrong at this crisis; the state cannot subsist on the honesty or dishonesty of one's personal feelings. It is precisely the tragic dilemma of Marcius: his hatred of the people springs from a deep conviction of aristocratic worth. He cannot be politic and conciliatory like Menenius without being dishonest to himself, although this brings about his exile from Rome and the demonic revenge that follows.

Marcius' scorn of the people finds expression chiefly in the imagery of food and eating. The plebeians do not act from motives of honor as the patricians do, but merely from the promptings of desire; their

> affections are
> A sick man's appetite, who desires most that
> Which would increase his evil. (I.i.181–83)

It is an image of the changeable and perverse will ruled by a destructive "appetite." Marcius asks the mob contemptuously why

> You cry against the noble Senate, who
> (Under the gods) keep you in awe, which else
> Would feed on one another? (I.i.190–92)

This view of the people is like that of Hobbes (although the *Leviathan* did not appear until the middle of the century): the people would "feed on one another" if not prevented by the Senate's overawing authority, and the patricians are therefore justified in exercising absolute control over their appetitive animal nature.[8] Food and eating imagery is beginning to take on a violent tone, since "feed" here is equivalent to "devour as prey."

Menenius, not tempted to Marcius' choleric vein, says simply that the people's seeking is "For corn at their own rates, whereof they say/ The city is well stor'd" (I.i.193–94). But Marcius scorns their demands, as if it were presumption in them to make demands at all:

> They say there's grain enough?
> Would the nobility lay aside their ruth
> And let me use my sword, I'd make a quarry
> With thousands of these quarter'd slaves as high
> As I could pick my lance.   (I.i.200–04)

This is the direct opposite of Menenius's fable, since Marcius wishes to destroy the organic unity of the state by denying the plebeians any function in it. His report on the troop of people from whom he has just come is another caustic commentary on hunger as the plebeian motive for mutiny:

> They said they were anhungry; sigh'd forth proverbs—
> That hunger broke stone walls, that dogs must eat,
> That meat was made for mouths, that the gods sent not
> Corn for the rich men only. With these shreds
> They vented their complainings . . . .   (I.i.209–13)

As we have seen, the people's hunger is a real grievance, and to scorn it away is an act of human and political folly. Marcius' exaggerated and malicious contempt for the plebeians leaves him here at one of the lowest points in our sympathy; contrary to most of Shakespeare's other tragic protagonists, his first appearance in the play seems to be intended to alienate the audience. And as a Messenger enters to announce that the Volsces are in arms, Marcius adds a final insult: "Go get you home, you fragments!" (I.i.226), a word that means the worthless leftovers after a meal.

From this point through the battle scenes, the themes of the people as food and of war as devourer are especially important. Marcius welcomes the news of war as a "means to vent/ Our musty superfluity" (I.i.229–30). The whole food issue is resolved by war, for the Volscians will either destroy the moldy excess of Rome or provide spoils to satisfy the base plebeian appetite. Marcius calls on the mutinous citizens with utter scorn:

> Nay, let them follow.
> The Volsces have much corn. Take these rats thither
> To gnaw their garners. Worshipful mutiners,
> Your valour puts well forth. Pray follow.   (I.i.252–55)

The stage direction right after reads: "*Citizens steal away*" (I.i.255 S.D.), a strong contrast to their bold entrance at the opening of the scene. This is like the mob scene at the beginning of *Julius Caesar,* where the people "vanish tongue-tied in their guiltiness" (I.i.67). In both plays the seeming docility of the mob carries with it an undercurrent of restive sullenness, shown at the end of the first scene of *Coriolanus* in the Tribune Brutus's reversal of the war as devourer theme: "The present wars devour him! He is grown/ Too proud to be so valiant" (I.i.262–63). It is Marcius, rather than the "musty superfluity" of Rome, who ought to be "vented" (I.i.229–30) in war.

I shall deal more briefly with the food and eating imagery that follows the opening scene. In I.iii Volumnia says that if she had a dozen sons, she would rather have "eleven die nobly for their country than one voluptuously surfeit out of action" (I.iii.27–28). "Surfeit" means intemperate indulgence in food and drink with accompanying ill effects, and this is Volumnia's image for the life of peace, which is represented as very unattractive throughout the play. Food and eating have unpleasant connotations because of their connection with the people, whose indulgence of appetite is the opposite of the aristocratic ideal of honor. The "surfeit" image is used in an opposite sense in IV.i when Cominius says he is "too full/ Of the war's surfeits" (IV.i.45–46) to accompany Coriolanus on his exile. This image is similar to the passage in I.ix where Cominius contrasts the "fusty" (I.ix.7) or moldy plebeians with Marcius' deeds for war the devourer: "Yet cam'st thou to a morsel of this feast,/ Having fully din'd before" (I.ix.10–11). This "feast" (the praise of Marcius' deeds against the Volscians) is merely a "morsel" compared to his former deeds of valor ("fully din'd before"). The destructive sense of food and eating is being used here to indicate the aristocratic virtue of the warrior. Further on in the scene Marcius forswears flattery in the contemptuous imagery of food: "As if I lov'd my little should be dieted/ In praises sauc'd with lies" (I.ix.51–52).

There are a few interesting food images in Menenius' conversation with the Tribunes at the beginning of Act II. He returns a figure in kind when he says that the wolf loves the lamb "to devour him, as the hungry plebeians would the noble Marcius" (II.i.10–11), and he observes satirically that the Tribunes' justice goes awry "if you chance to be pinch'd with the colic" (II.i.82–83)—we are kept unpleasantly aware of the digestive function of the plebeians. But the Tribunes have a remarkable insight into Marcius by which they can work his ruin; they know he considers the people no better than

> camels in the war, who have their provand
> Only for bearing burthens, and sore blows
> For sinking under them.   (II.i.267–69)

It is a paraphrase of Marcius' own words at I.i.253–54: the people are not concerned with honor in battle but only with "provand," a base image of the animal appetite. The contrast is clearly drawn in II.iii where the First Citizen dwells on corn (II.iii.16–18), while Coriolanus in the gown of humility asserts his honor:

> Better it is to die, better to starve,
> Than crave the hire which first we do deserve.
>   (II.iii.120–21)

A noble starvation is infinitely preferable to this base humility of soliciting the plebeians to be consul.

Food imagery becomes fairly important again in III.i, and the corn issue, which was the original cause of the plebeian mutiny, is remembered throughout this scene. Brutus, for example, accuses Coriolanus of opposing the free gift of corn to the people (III.i.43), and this touches off Coriolanus' wrath: "Tell me of corn!" (III.i.61), which he speaks with an explosive emphasis on the final word as if to make an absolute contrast in value between "corn" and "me." Coriolanus agrees that he opposed the free gift of corn (III.i.113–15), but he clearly states the cause:

>   They know the corn
> Was not our recompense, resting well assur'd
> They ne'er did service for't. Being press'd to th' war
> Even when the navel of the state was touch'd,
> They would not thread the gates. This kind of service
> Did not deserve corn gratis.   (III.i.120–25)

The "navel of the state" keeps us unpleasantly aware of the physical reality of the body politic, in which to Coriolanus the formula for distribution can only be: "to each according to his merits."

Besides "corn" there are a number of other food and eating images in III.i. Coriolanus warns the patricians against "mingling" (III.i.72) their authority with the plebeians': "When, both your voices blended, the great'st taste/ Most palates theirs" (III.i.103–04). There is a natural antipathy between plebeian and patrician in Coriolanus' aristocratic order, and this denies Menenius's fable of the organic state. Notice how all words connected with food and eating have taken on negative connotations. The original distribution of corn "nourish'd disobedience, fed/ The ruin of the state" (III.i.117–18). This decree of the Senate was thus an act of self-destruction. It was also a debasing act, which the people will interpret as a sign of weakness:

> How shall this bosom-multiplied [9] digest
> The Senate's courtesy? Let deeds express
> What's like to be their words: "We did request it;
> We are the greater poll, and in true fear
> They gave us our demands." (III.i.131–35)

"Bosome-multiplied" is the Folio reading for line 131, and in this context "digest" not only means "interpret," but also literally refers to the digestion of food, a repeated theme for the people. They are imagined collectively as a great digestive mechanism, a "bosom-multiplied," that suggests an aspect of the Hydra monster.

These tirades arouse the immediate demand for Coriolanus' death. Menenius tries to pacify the people lest Rome, "like an unnatural dam/ Should now eat up her own!" (III.i.293–94). "Eat" means "destroy" here, with Senecan overtones—the "hungry plebeians" (II.i.10–11) of Rome are threatening to devour their chief defender. Finally in this scene, Menenius uses food imagery to apologize for Coriolanus' rash words; he is a soldier

> ill-school'd
> In bolted language; meal and bran together
> He throws without distinction. (III.i.321–23)

The pejorative food images are meant to define Coriolanus' virtue; he is not at all to be associated with such base plebeian matters. There is another example of this in his defiance of the people at the end of III.iii. He would not "buy/ Their mercy" (III.iii.90–91) with flattery even if he were "pent to linger/ But with a grain a day . . ." (III.iii.89–90). The "grain a day" is the ascetic strain in the aristocratic ideal of honor.

The depreciative and violent tone of the food imagery grows more pronounced with Coriolanus' exile. Volumnia will not dine with Menenius because "Anger's my meat. I sup upon myself,/ And so shall starve with feeding" (IV. ii.50–51). Her anger at her son's banishment is self-consuming. Food is also one of the images of worthlessness in Coriolanus' soliloquy at Antium: "Fellest foes" (IV.iv.18) grow dear friends by "Some trick not worth an egg . . ." (IV.iv.21). In the next scene a strong contrast is made between Coriolanus "in mean apparel, disguis'd and muffled" (IV.iv. S.D.) and the sound and bustle of the feast going on off-stage in the house of Aufidius. Coriolanus addresses the plebeian servants in food imagery filled with contempt: "Follow your function, go and batten on cold bits" (IV.v. 35–36). As he tells Aufidius, only his name "Coriolanus"

remains, for the "hungry plebeians" (II.i.10–11) of Rome
"hath devour'd the rest" (IV.v.5.81). The last food images
of this scene are those the servants use to indicate Coriolanus' superiority to Aufidius:

> 1. *Serv.* Before Corioles he scotch'd him and notch'd him
> like a carbonado.
> 2. *Serv.* An he had been cannibally given, he might have
> boil'd [10] and eaten him too.   (IV.v.197–200)

A "carbonado" was a piece of meat scored by the cook for
roasting on the coals, and both images develop the violence
of the war as devourer theme.

The news of Coriolanus' approach to Rome with a Vol-
scian army pricks the bubble of optimism blown up at the
beginning of IV.vi. The Tribunes' petty empire of "Our
tradesmen singing in their shops and going/ About their
functions friendly" (IV.vi.8–9) crumbles before an overwhelming force. It was "The breath of garlic-eaters" (IV.vi.
98) that banished Coriolanus, and retribution is now coming for it, as Menenius forebodes in his repeated refrain,
"You have made good work" (IV.vi.95, 100, 117, 118, 146–
47, and V.i.15).

Aufidius's own revenge on his rival is being prepared in
the next scene (IV.vii), where a Lieutenant tells him what
he himself knows only too well about Coriolanus:

> Your soldiers use him as the grace fore meat,
> Their talk at table, and their thanks at end;
> And you are dark'ned in this action, sir,
> Even by your own.   (IV.vii.3–6)

The association of Coriolanus and eating is curiously positive here, something we have not noticed before. It is per-

haps part of the twisted values in these scenes of revenge.

The food imagery of V.i echoes the corn issue at the beginning of the play. Cominius's mission to Coriolanus has been a failure, and he reports his unsuccess to Menenius and the Tribunes:

> I offered to awaken his regard
> For's private friends. His answer to me was,
> He could not stay to pick them in a pile
> Of noisome musty chaff. He said 'twas folly,
> For one poor grain or two, to leave unburnt
> And still to nose th' offence.   (V.i.23–28)

Coriolanus now sees all Rome in the food imagery of the plebeians—not even food, but "a pile/ Of noisome musty chaff." The "poor grain or two" is absolutely lost in this evil-smelling heap and must burn with it. Menenius cannot believe this inhumanity:

> For one poor grain or two?
> I am one of those! his mother, wife, his child,
> And this brave fellow too—we are the grains . . . .
> (V.i.28–30)

And he accuses the Tribunes of being responsible for the present catastrophe:

> You are the musty chaff, and you are smelt
> Above the moon. We must be burnt for you!
> (V.i.31–32)

As we soon see, these poor grains become the test of Coriolanus' mercy, for he has already condemned the chaff of the plebeians out of hand.

Menenius uses a curious, extended food image as he pre-

pares to visit Coriolanus; he attributes Cominius's failure
to trivial matters:

> He was not taken well; he had not din'd.
> The veins unfill'd, our blood is cold, and then
> We pout upon the morning, are unapt
> To give or to forgive; but when we have stuff'd
> These pipes and these conveyances of our blood
> With wine and feeding, we have suppler souls
> Than in our priest-like fasts. Therefore I'll watch him
> Till he be dieted to my request,
> And then I'll set upon him.   (V.i.50–58)

The hypothetic image of Coriolanus "stuff'd . . . With
wine and feeding" is almost impossible to conceive—"priest-
like fasts" would be more typical of him. This is one of the
few places in the play where Coriolanus is favorably associated with eating (cf. IV.vii.3–6). I suspect a note of strong
irony in Menenius's tone here. It is a desperate attempt to
explain away Cominius's refusal by irrelevant reasons, a way
of trying to avert the impending disaster and make ready for
his own possible rejection. He continues in this vein in V.ii
when he asks the First Watchman: "Has he din'd, canst
thou tell? For I would not speak with him till after dinner"
(V.ii.36–37). There is a real desperation in this, which is
only increased by the guards' humiliation of Menenius; his
appeal to them is only "the palsied intercession" of "a decay'd dotant" (V.ii.46–47).

    These are the last significant food images in the play, and
it is perhaps a comment on the character of this imagery
that it is excluded from the climax in V.iii. There are actually only two places in the play (I.i and III.i) where it is
used with much sense of a deliberate effect, yet in both these
places it is of crucial importance. Elsewhere, the repeated

images of food and eating serve as a commentary on the plebeian-patrician conflict and on the function of war as a devourer. Although any particular example of this imagery may seem trivial in itself, the cumulative effect of all the examples, taken together with the imagery of disease and animals, is very strong. These image themes make only a few points about the tragedy of *Coriolanus,* but they make them so often that they cannot possibly be overlooked, and they do much to create the harsh and satirical tone of the play.

Notes

1. Oscar James Campbell, *Shakespeare's Satire* (New York, 1943), pp. 200 and 208.
2. See Willard Farnham, *Shakespeare's Tragic Frontier* (Berkeley, Calif., 1950), Ch. V. *Coriolanus* offers one of the best examples of Farnham's thesis, while *Antony and Cleopatra* seems somewhat constrained by it. See also the excellent essay by D. J. Enright, "*Coriolanus*: Tragedy or Debate?" *Essays in Criticism,* IV (1954), 1–19.
3. Plutarch speaks of the rebellion against "the sore oppression of usurers" as if it were justified (*Four Chapters of North's Plutarch,* ed. F. A. Leo [London, 1878], p. 237). The later corn insurrection, however, was stirred up by the flatterers of the people "without any new occasion, or iust matter offered of complaint" (p. 241). Shakespeare completely recasts the sequence and import of these events in Plutarch.
4. See Sidney Shanker, "Some Clues for *Coriolanus,*" SAB, XXIV (1949), 209–13; Brents Stirling, *The Populace in Shakespeare* (New York, 1949), pp. 42, 126, 127; and E. C. Pettet, "*Coriolanus* and the Midlands Insurrection of 1607," *Shakespeare Survey* 3 (Cambridge, 1950), pp. 34–42.

5. All references to Shakespeare are from George Lyman Kittredge's edition, *The Complete Works of Shakespeare* (Boston, 1936).
6. See Frederick Tupper, Jr., "The Shaksperean Mob," *PMLA*, XXVII (1912), 486–523; Frederick T. Wood, "Shakespeare and the Plebs," *Essays and Studies by Members of the English Association*, XVIII (1932), 53–73; and Stirling, *The Populace in Shakespeare*.
7. See James Emerson Phillips, Jr., *The State in Shakespeare's Greek and Roman Plays* (New York, 1940), Ch. VIII and pp. 6–10. See also the interesting analogues noted by Kenneth Muir in "Menenius's Fable," *Notes and Queries*, CXCVIII (1953), 240–42.
8. "Awe" is a favorite word of Hobbes for the sovereign authority in his state, as in the following passage: "men have no pleasure, but on the contrary a great deal of grief, in keeping company, where there is no power able to over-awe them all" (*Leviathan*, ed. Michael Oakeshott [Oxford, 1946], p. 81); or in the passage where he speaks of war as "necessarily consequent . . . to the natural passions of men, when there is no visible power to keep them in awe . . ." (p. 109). R. W. Chambers sees a similarity in doctrine at this point between *Coriolanus* and the 147 lines of *Sir Thomas More* that seem to be in Shakespeare's hand, especially the passage describing the anarchy of rebellion: "men lyke rauenous fishes / Woold feed on one another" ("The Expression of Ideas—Particularly Political Ideas—in the Three Pages, and in Shakespeare," in *Shakespeare's Hand in the Play of Sir Thomas More*, [Cambridge, 1923], pp. 142–87). But this was also a commonplace image—see the examples given in F. P. Wilson, "Shakespeare's Reading," *Shakespeare Survey 3* (Cambridge, 1950), pp. 19–20.
9. Kittredge's "beesom multitude" follows an emendation first proposed as "bisson multitude" by Collier. The Folio reading makes good sense if interpreted metaphorically. A. E. Brae notes that the image behind this passage is that of the

body politic, which the belly-members fable has established as a "prevailing metaphor." Thus "digest" completes the metaphor of food and eating in "bosom-multiplied," as well as the metaphor of "nourish'd" and "fed" above (III.i.117) (*The Tragedie of Coriolanus*, ed. Horace Howard Furness, Jr., A New Variorum edition [Philadelphia, 1928], Vol. XX, 300–04, esp. 301).

10. The Folio reads "boyld," which Kittredge, following Pope, changes to "broil'd" for the sake of consistency with "carbonado." But these two speeches need have no logical connection.

Cleopatra's Immolation Scene

BY DONALD J. MCGINN

The tragedy of *Antony and Cleopatra* is unique in the Shakespearean canon in that what editors generally designate as the final act [1] is entirely devoted to the heroine, the hero having been disposed of in the preceding act. Shakespeare's Antony, indeed, does not differ markedly from the Antonies of the other Elizabethan dramatists, but his Cleopatra is incomparable. The dramatic purpose of the closing scene is to add the finishing touches to the portrait of the famous Egyptian Queen, whom Enobarbus, seeming to speak for the playwright, calls "a wonderful piece of work" whose "infinite variety" neither age can wither nor custom stale. J. Dover Wilson terms this scene "a coda to the tragedy of Antony which many consider the most wonderful movement in any of his great symphonies." [2]

Yet editors and critics have been troubled by a seeming inconsistency between these final moments of sublimity and the actions of the Queen in the earlier part of the play. Maurice R. Ridley, for example, fears that the "light and

colour" displayed by Cleopatra at the end of the play may
dazzle our eyes so that we forget Shakespeare's earlier "un-
sparing picture of the professional courtesan." [3] And A. C.
Bradley considers her sacrifice merely the result of vanity
rather than proof of her unselfish love of Antony.[4] While
conceding that after Antony's death the Queen emerges as
"a tragic figure for the first time," Harley Granville-Barker
feels that she has lost "none of her pristine quality" and has
gained little dignity in her new role.[5]

Her only champion seems to be Wilson, who attempts to
refute "the charge by Bradley and others, including Granville-Barker, which now seems generally accepted, that she
shrinks from following Antony 'after the high Roman
fashion.' " [6] Wilson maintains that from her first expression
of determination to follow Antony in death until the application of the deadly asps to her bosom her resolution remains constant and unwavering. Though Ridley recognizes
that she becomes a better woman at the end, he accuses
Wilson of ignoring the "awkward interval" between Antony's death and the interview with Caesar, when it appears
that Cleopatra "would make terms with Caesar if she could
make her own." [7] In short, for her hostile critics the main
stumbling block seems to be her hesitation to "rush into the
secret house of death" with her Antony.

Perhaps, however, there is a middle position between the
derogatory views of Bradley, Granville-Barker, and to some
extent Ridley, on the one hand, and Wilson's overidealiza-
tion, on the other. Certainly at the end of the play Shakespeare implies that Cleopatra is transformed into a nobler
person than she earlier appears. Nevertheless she does not
immediately, nor even entirely, cast off her sensuality; indeed, only her knowledge of the shame awaiting her in
Rome forces her to rise above her natural fear of pain and

death. Yet her eventual triumph is another vindication of Shakespeare's conviction expressed in *Hamlet* and *King Lear* that human nature may be purified through suffering.

Before the Battle of Actium Cleopatra is portrayed as a royal courtesan. Hence, Ridley advises that we select as "the best description of her . . . Enobarbus's simple 'a wonderful piece of work'" and thereby avoid "any idle questionings as to the morality or immorality of Antony and Cleopatra." [8] Yet Shakespeare himself in the very first scene places her destructive passion for Antony in a hostile frame of reference. This scene opens and closes with the moralist's viewpoint expressed by the two disapproving Romans, Philo and Demetrius, who scornfully call Antony a "strumpet's fool," his love "dotage," and hers "a gipsy's lust." Within this moral framework, which prevents the audience from actively sympathizing with the guilty pair, Shakespeare sets the picture of their passion, intense and interesting. In defiance of the moralists, Antony eloquently expresses the lovers' viewpoint as contrasted with that of ambitious Caesar:

> Let Rome in Tiber melt, and the wide arch
> Of the rang'd empire fall! Here is my space.
> Kingdoms are clay; our dungy earth alike
> Feeds beast as man; the nobleness of life
> Is to do thus, when such a mutual pair
> And such a twain can do't, in which I bind,
> On pain of punishment, the world to weet
> We stand up peerless. (I.i.33–40) [9]

But no sooner has this ringing eloquence faded on our ear than we enter the corrupt Alexandrian Court, where, as Granville-Barker comments, "we have a taste of the chattering, shiftless, sensual, credulous Court, with its trulls and wizards and effeminates," [10] and we realize that we have been gazing at a sordid love affair through the doting eyes of one of its participants.

In subsequent scenes Shakespeare pitilessly exposes Antony's loss of judgment. A few minutes after challenging the world to question the propriety of giving up his kingdom for the woman he loves, he hears of the loss of his Asiatic empire and ruefully tells himself:

> These strong Egyptian fetters I must break
> Or lose myself in dotage.   (I.ii.119–20)

Then, apprised of the death of Fulvia, his wife, he repeats this conviction:

> I must from this enchanting queen break off:
> Ten thousand harms, more than the ills I know,
> My idleness doth hatch.   (I.ii.131–33)

Later, in his apology to Caesar in Rome, he refers to his time lost in Alexandria as "poison'd hours" (II.ii.94) which have infected his reason. Thus Shakespeare informs his audience that Antony is fully aware of the immorality of his union and its inevitable consequences.

Nor in this unsentimental portrayal is Cleopatra spared. The destructive effect of her influence on Antony she not only knows but boasts of. Imagining what he, absent from her in Rome, is thinking of, she speculates:

> He's speaking now
> Or murmuring, "Where's my serpent of old Nile?"
> For so he calls me.   (I.v.24–6)

At Actium she ignores the protests of Enobarbus and as

"president" of her kingdom insists upon directing the action of her "sixty sails" (III.vii.17, 49) herself. Her unwillingness to accept the advice of an experienced soldier undoubtedly stems from her great vanity. Always the actress, she delights in staging spectacles with her own person the center of all eyes and then in her imagination standing off and enjoying the effect on her dazzled audiences. For example, in order to flatter Antony at their first meeting on the river Cydnus, she arrays herself as the Roman goddess Venus. Indeed, she puts on such a scene that all the city turns out to behold her and leaves the conqueror "enthron'd i' the market-place . . . whistling to the air" (II.ii. 220–21). When, after the departure of Octavia, he returns to Egypt, Cleopatra "in the habiliments of the goddess Isis" appears "publicly en-thron'd" with him "on a tribunal silver'd . . . in chairs of gold" (III.vi.3ff.). Perhaps her stubborn foolhardy deter-mination to command the admiral ship, the "Antoniad," at Actium may have been the result of one of her fantasies in which she pictured herself as a goddess of war.

As might be expected, therefore, in all her actions she is constantly aware of the impression that she makes on the people around her. When Antony first mentions returning to Rome, Enobarbus warns him that Cleopatra upon hear-ing the news will pretend to faint:

Cleopatra, catching but the least noise of this, dies instantly; I have seen her die twenty times upon far poorer moment. I do think there is mettle in death which commits some lov-ing act upon her, she hath such a celerity in dying.

(I.ii.143–47)

At Antony's first words, true to Enobarbus's prediction, she exclaims, "Cut my lace, Charmian, come." Then, because she immediately decides on another reaction more dramatically effective, she changes her tactics with, "But let it be," and disarms Antony with a bit of flattery:

> I am quickly ill, and well,
> So Antony loves.   (I.iii.71–3)

Again, when the messenger from Rome tells her of Antony's marriage to Octavia, she exclaims, "I am pale, Charmian!" (II.v.59). Later, after the hapless fellow, terrified by her temper, obviously underrates the beauty of her Roman rival, she accepts his distorted description with a complacent self-compliment, "The man hath seen some majesty, and should know" (III.iii.42).

Along with her intense personal vanity she is a voluptuary who has devoted herself to a life of pleasure, and she makes no attempt to conceal this side of her personality. Impatient with boredom induced by Antony's absence she exclaims:

> Give me some music; music, moody food
> *Of us that trade in love.*   (II.v.1–2) [11]

With no sense of shame she interrupts her ecstatic description of the absent Antony with a recollection of her earlier conquests:

>   Broad-fronted Caesar,
> When thou wast here above the ground I was
> A morsel for a monarch, and great Pompey
> Would stand and make his eyes grow in my brow;
> There would he anchor his aspect and die
> With looking on his life.   (I.v.29–34)

Similarly, a few lines further on, after praising Antony's

"well-divided disposition" and vowing to write him daily, she asks:

> Did I, Charmian,
> Ever love Caesar so?   (I.v.66 ff.)

When Charmian playfully assures her that she did, she attributes to youth her earlier protestations of affection:

> My salad days,
> When I was green in judgment, cold in blood,
> To say as I said then!

Thus Shakespeare avoids romantic sentimentality by constantly reminding his audience that Antony is only one in a series of amours.

As might be expected of a person thus addicted to sensual pleasure, Cleopatra is terribly afraid of pain. After her death Octavius Caesar accepts the verdict of suicide resulting from the venom of the asp because, as he puts it—

> She hath pursu'd conclusions infinite
> Of easy ways to die.   (V.ii.352–53)

With this foreknowledge of her temperamental weaknesses we could hardly expect her to lose her "other elements" of "baser life," as she eventually comes to regard them, immediately after Antony's death.

Yet even before this extremity Shakespeare provides intimations of the heights to which her love for Antony will elevate her, once she has purged herself of vanity and self-love. This initial development progresses through a series of indecisions. Her first opportunity to vacillate in her affections occurs when, after the defeat at Actium, Caesar begins his machinations to entrap her for his triumph in Rome. He sends the eloquent and cunning Thyreus to hoodwink her into believing that she is to be pardoned. Just before Thyreus appears before her, Euphronius tells Antony that Caesar has refused mercy to him but has promised leniency to Cleopatra if she—as Caesar bluntly puts it—

> From Egypt drive her all-disgraced friend
> Or take his life there.   (III.x.22–3)

Thinking to test her, Antony says to her:

> To the boy Caesar send this grizzled head,
> And he will fill thy wishes to the brim
> With principalities.   (III.xi.17–9)

With her simple, but obviously sincere, reply, "That head, my lord," Antony is temporarily satisfied, for he immediately returns to the conqueror a biting taunt and a challenge.

Yet a few minutes later at Thyreus' crafty hint that Caesar believes her relations with Antony to be the result of compulsion, she, faced with the flattering thought of perhaps ensnaring another world conqueror, merely utters a surprised, irresolute "O!" And when Thyreus repeats his absurd statement, Cleopatra, swept off her feet by temptation, hesitates:

> He is a god, and knows
> What is most right. Mine honour was not yielded,
> But conquered merely.   (III.xi.57 ff.)

Continuing to temporize, she sweetly asks Thyreus his name and bids him convey her obeisance to his master. Feeling emboldened by her flattery, Thyreus asks to kiss her hand

just as Enobarbus walks Antony in. After Antony has ordered Thyreus flogged and has berated Cleopatra for cheap-
ening her favors, he plaintively asks:

> To flatter Caesar, would you mingle eyes
> With one that ties his points?

Again her simple question, "Not know me yet," transforms
his wrath into a reproach: "Cold-hearted toward me?" Her
answer reveals no trace of dissimulation:

> Ah! dear, if I be so,
> From my cold heart let heaven engender hail,
> And poison it in the source; and the first stone
> Drop in my neck: as it determines, so
> Dissolve my life. The next Caesarion smite,
> Till by degrees the memory of my womb,
> Together with my brave Egyptians all,
> By the discandying of this pelleted storm
> Lie graveless, till the flies and gnats of Nile
> Have buried them for prey!

Her eloquent protest, in which she weighs her love for
Antony with all that she holds dearest in life—beginning, as
might be expected, with herself—he accepts without further
question: "I am satisfied." In this way Cleopatra rejects the
first two opportunities to abandon Antony to his fate.

The third, and last, opportunity—if it may be called that—
comes after the Battle of Alexandria, Antony's last encounter with Octavius Caesar. At the sight of his deserting
fleet he furiously accuses Cleopatra of treachery:

> All is lost!
> This foul Egyptian hath betrayed me;
> My fleet hath yielded to the foe, and yonder

> They cast their caps up and carouse together
> Like friends long lost. Triple-turn'd whore! 'tis thou
> Hast sold me to this novice, and my heart
> Makes only wars on thee . . .
>   Betray'd I am.
> O this false soul of Egypt! this grave charm,
> Whose eyes beck'd forth my wars, and call'd them home,
> Whose bosom was my crownet, my chief end,
> Like a right gipsy, hath, at fast and loose
> Beguil'd me to the very heart of loss. (IV.x.22 ff.)

His desperate attempt to place the responsibility for his ruin on Cleopatra, however, should not be taken as evidence of her faithlessness. Earlier, after the defeat at Actium, Shakespeare pointedly exonerates her from all blame for that disaster. To her question, "Is Antony or we in fault for this," Enobarbus, who frequently serves as the "voice" of the playwright, replies:

> Antony only, that would make his will
> Lord of his reason. (III.xi.2–4)

Now, at the nadir of his fortunes, when his dearest friends have left him, why should the Egyptian and Phoenician mercenaries sacrifice themselves for him? Moreover, in a significant parenthesis in Cleopatra's message brought him by Mardian as he lies dying Shakespeare again denies complicity:

>   . . . for when she saw—
> *Which never shall be found*—you did suspect
> She had dispos'd with Caesar, and that your rage
> Would not be purg'd, she sent you word she was dead.[12]
>   (IV.xii.121–24)

Indeed, had Shakespeare intended his audience to believe that Cleopatra ordered the fleet to surrender to Caesar, he doubtless would have shown her either informing her navy or communicating with Caesar himself. Then later she certainly would have referred to this valuable service in her negotiations with Caesar.

On the contrary, the dramatic purpose of Antony's suspicion seems to be to accentuate the pathos of his reversal of fortune from the time when he amused himself with "half the bulk o' the world" (III.ix.64). His willingness to blame Cleopatra for his own mistakes, in grim contrast with his gallantry on a similar occasion after the Battle of Actium when he had comforted the penitent Queen with—

> Fall not a tear, I say; one of them rates
> All that is won and lost—   (III.ix.69–70)

indicates his degeneration through despair. Now, as he shifts the responsibility of failure from his shoulders to hers, he spitefully paints a frightening picture of the disgrace that Caesar plans for her in Rome:

> Let him take thee,
> And hoist thee up to the shouting plebeians;
> Follow his chariot, like the greatest spot
> Of all thy sex; most monster-like, be shown
> For poor'st diminutives, for doits; and let
> Patient Octavia plough thy visage up
> With her prepared nails.   (IV.xii.46–52)

These threats, seared into her memory, eventually will serve to goad her "to do that thing that ends all other deeds."

Convinced that Antony has abandoned her to her fate, she takes it upon herself to ascertain Caesar's "intents" and for that purpose dispatches the faithful "Egyptian" to Caesar's camp.[13] In the meantime, Antony, who has received the false report of her death, attempts suicide. Weak from loss of blood, he is carried to the Monument, where he expires in Cleopatra's arms.

Her grief at his death is obviously sincere; furthermore, it is realistically portrayed. When she sees his head fall back, she is well aware that now would be the ideal moment for a rhetorical outburst in her old manner. But she has reached the crisis in her character: brought face to face with stark reality, she completely surprises her women by fainting. Upon recovering, she acknowledges that her earlier self-deification was mere pretense:

> No more, but e'en a woman, and commanded
> By such poor passion as the maid that milks
> And does the meanest chares.

For the first time she dares to raise the question of suicide:

> . . . then is it sin
> To rush into the secret house of death
> Ere death dare come to us?   (IV.xiii.73 ff.)

And in her pathetic attempts to comfort her terrified women she partially forgets herself. Finally she resolves to die.

Scarcely has she formulated her resolution when Caesar's men are upon her. Even as she is expressing her awareness of the beginning of her self-purification—

> My desolation does begin to make
> A better life—   (V.ii.1–2)

Proculeius appears.[14] Named by Antony as the only one of

Caesar's men whom Cleopatra should trust, Proculeius may
have been a sycophant of Antony's before Actium just as he
now is of the conquering Caesar. Doubtless extremely per-
sonable, he has been selected, whether he knows it or not, as
a decoy to distract the attention of the Queen while Gallus
overpowers her guards.[15] After Proculeius delivers Caesar's
message, Cleopatra states her terms with a dignity quite different from her easy manner with Caesar's first messenger,
Thyreus. Assuring her that Caesar would outdo himself in
kindness to her, Proculeius urges her to beg for clemency.
Thus encouraged, she requests a personal interview with the
conqueror. Consenting to transmit this request, Proculeius
reiterates his confidence in Caesar's leniency. Hardly has he
uttered these soothing promises when Gallus and his guard
break in behind the Queen. With triumphant egotism the
bully exclaims:

> Proculeius,
> You see how easily she may be surpris'd
> Guard her till Caesar come.[16]

Iras warningly cries, "Royal Queen," and Charmian, "Oh,
Cleopatra, thou art taken, Queen!" Cleopatra tries to stab
herself, but Proculeius seizes her hand:

> Hold, worthy lady, hold:
> Do not yourself such wrong, who are in this
> Reliev'd but not betray'd.

While he is endeavoring to calm her terror, the gallant but
conceited Dolabella enters and takes command. Now she
must exercise all her ingenuity in order to outwit her cap-
tors. Easily winning over Dolabella, whose first words of
greeting, "Most noble Empress, you have heard of me,"

show his high opinion of himself, she asks him whether or not he knows what Caesar intends to do with her. As Dolabella hesitates, she puts the words in his mouth, "He'll lead me then in triumph?" And Dolabella replies, "Madam, he will, I know't." [17]

At once she sets about to deceive the conqueror into thinking that she trusts his promises. With the aid of her loyal Egyptians she first makes arrangements for the asps. Then, always a consummate actress, she decides to play the scene that will influence Caesar to relax the guard so that the asps can be smuggled in.[18] For this purpose she instructs her loyal treasurer what his part will be. Upon learning— doubtless from Dolabella—the exact time for the interview that she has requested of Caesar through Proculeius, she dresses herself and her women in garments of humility so that they all look alike,[19] and at the Emperor's entrance they are lying prone on the floor. Thus at the offset she confuses him and wins the initial advantage. Completely disconcerted, he asks, "Which is the Queen of Egypt?" Dolabella gives the signal to Cleopatra, "It is the Emperor, madam," at which she rises to her knees. This initial submission actually shocks Caesar, who commands, "Arise, you shall not kneel." And when she does not move, he entreats her, "I pray you, rise." Finally, thoroughly impressed, he magnanimously adds—and the ruthless conqueror loves to play the generous man—"Rise, Egypt." But Cleopatra remains on her knees and in a meek voice whispers:

> Sir, the gods
> Will have it thus; my master and my lord
> (*bowing to the floor*)
> I must obey.

Quite taken in by her mock humility, he promises to forget all the "injuries" done him, provided that she does not take "Antony's course." Then, turning to the guard, "You shall advise me in all for Cleopatra," he is about to leave. But he has not reckoned with Cleopatra, who has not yet reached the high point of her performance. Jumping to her feet, she hands him a "brief of money, plate, and jewels," a false inventory of her possessions, and summons her treasurer who has been stationed where he can hear her cue, "Where's Seleucus?" Introducing him to Caesar—

> This is my treasurer; let him speak, my lord,
> Upon his peril, that I have reserv'd
> To myself nothing—

she prompts him, "Speak the truth, Seleucus." Scarcely has he uttered his opening lines—

> Madam,
> I had rather seal my lips, than, to my peril,
> Speak that which is not—

than she anticipates—an almost certain indication that Shakespeare intends us to regard this episode as a clever trick on her part—what he has been rehearsed to say *but has not yet said*, "What have I kept back?" At his seeming disclosure of her duplicity she, always the perfect actress, begins to blush furiously. Caesar, however, is delighted with what he regards as her acquiescence. Accordingly, when in a feigned fury she leaps at Seleucus as if to claw out his eyes, the conqueror smilingly intervenes: "Good Queen, let us entreat you."

Continuing in her role of mock humility, she thanks him

for condescending to visit her, all the time fully aware that
she herself has requested him to come:

> O Caesar! what a wounding shame is this,
> That thou, vouchsafing here to visit me,
> Doing the honor of thy lordliness
> To one so meek, that mine own servant should
> Parcel the sum of my disgraces by
> Addition of his envy.

Then, in what is intended to impress Caesar as feminine
vanity, she excuses her seeming deceit by saying that she has
reserved "some lady trifles," "immoment toys," for her host-
esses in Rome, including Livia and Octavia, whose "sober
eye" we know she has sworn never to meet. Again, as her
feigned anger seems to flare up at the thought of her treasurer's ingratitude, Caesar with an amused tolerance requests
Seleucus to withdraw, and with a grand bow he hands back
her list with the assurance that he has no intention of appro-
priating anything that is hers. Since he wants her to look her
best for the exhibition in Rome, he advises her to "feed and
sleep" and reassures her of his "friendship." In all outward
appearance Cleopatra is submission itself as she again kneels
before the conqueror and murmurs, "My master, and my
lord."

Hardly has he gone out of the door when she leaps to her
feet and scornfully exclaims:

> He words me, girls, he words me, that I should not
> Be noble to myself.

Again she has won. Caesar, convinced that he has nothing to
fear, orders the guard relaxed so that Cleopatra will show no

traces of captivity when she plays the leading part in his triumphal procession in Rome.

Then Cleopatra goes into action. She first sends Charmian for the asps, for which arrangements already have been made. As Charmian is leaving, Dolabella hastily brushes by her but stops short as he sees the three women identically dressed. "Where is the Queen?" he asks. Charmian merely gestures, "Behold, sir," and goes out. To Cleopatra's anxious query he replies that in accordance with his promise made her during their brief friendship he must now inform her that Caesar "within three days" intends to remove her to Rome. She thanks this latest victim of her charms and bids him farewell. In the interval of Charmian's absence she recounts to Iras the horrors of captivity in order to steel herself. At Charmian's re-entrance the Queen merely asks, "Now, Charmian?" As Charmian nods assent, Cleopatra orders herself made ready for her last and greatest appearance—this time as "Cleopatra, Queen of Egypt":

> Show me, my women, like a queen; go fetch
> My best attires; I am again for Cydnus
> To meet Mark Antony.

Sending Iras, apparently not strong enough to face the terrible actuality of death, for her royal robes, jewels, and crown, she discloses her intention to Charmian:

> Now, noble Charmian, we'll dispatch indeed;
> And when thou hast done this chare, I'll give thee leave
> To play till doomsday.

At this point the guard ushers in a "rural fellow" bringing the basket of figs containing the asps. After a bit of comic relief that tends to heighten the effect of the catastrophe Cleopatra dismisses her benefactor. As soon as Iras returns, the two women array their mistress for the last time. As they move about her, she expresses her feeling of transfiguration:

> Give me my robe, put on my crown; I have
> Immortal longings in me; now no more
> The juice of Egypt's grape shall moist this lip.
> Yare, yare, good Iras; quick. Methinks I hear
> Antony call; I see him rouse himself
> To praise my noble act; I hear him mock
> The luck of Caesar, which the gods give men
> To excuse their after wrath: husband, I come:
> Now to that name my courage prove my title!
> I am fire and air; my other elements
> I give to baser life.

She is convinced that the imminent "noble act," contradicting as it does all that life has hitherto meant for her, will purify her love for Antony and win her the title of his wife.

When her women have put the last touches on the adornment of her person, she bids them farewell. Iras's instant death from heartbreak is Shakespeare's way of intensifying the tragic effect. As Cleopatra applies the asp to her breast, Charmian begins to wail, "O eastern star," but Cleopatra quickly silences her with a metaphor, the calmness of which strangely contrasts with the terrible actuality:

> Peace, peace!
> Dost thou not see my baby at my breast,
> That sucks the nurse asleep?

While Charmian bids her own heart break, Cleopatra describes the druglike effect of the venom, "As sweet as balm, as soft as air, as gentle." Then, breaking off, she applies a second asp to her arm. But the poison already is overcoming her. Half-whispering, "What—should—I—stay—," her head falls forward in death.

Completing her mistress's half-finished question, "In this vile world," Charmian straightens Cleopatra's head, closes her eyes, and steps backward to survey the effect. Noting that Cleopatra's crown is "awry," she is adjusting it as the guard rushes in to announce Caesar's command. Cleopatra has been just in time. Moving and speaking deliberately so as not to arouse suspicion, Charmian applies the asp to her own person. When the guard, examining the dead Queen, asks, "Charmian, is this well done," she glances at her beloved mistress, wonderfully beautiful in death, and replies:

> It is well done, and fitting for a princess
> Descended of so many royal kings.

And with a sigh, "Ah! soldier," she drops at Cleopatra's feet.

The guards summon Dolabella, quickly followed by Caesar, who, realizing that he has been outwitted, gracefully accepts defeat:

> Bravest at the last,
> She levell'd at our purposes, and, being royal,
> Took her own way.

While Dolabella questions the guard, Caesar, gazing at the Queen, is impressed by her beauty:

> . . . she looks like sleep,
> As she would catch another Antony
> In her strong toil of grace.

How Cleopatra would have enjoyed this tribute! And, ordering her buried beside her Antony, Caesar seems to express what has been Shakespeare's interest throughout the play:

No grave upon the earth shall clip in it
A *pair so famous.*

Thus, when the Cleopatra of the final scene is compared
with her counterpart in the rest of the play, Shakespeare's
consistency in portrayal becomes clear. The change in character wrought by Antony's death no longer seems impossible. Her final transformation is achieved, not through a
romantic love like Juliet's, but realistically through her
grief at her loss of Antony and her determination never to
be disgraced by Caesar. And what her love for Antony is not
strong enough to impel her to do her love for herself finally
accomplishes.

Notes

1. The text in the First Folio, our only source, has no act or
   scene divisions beyond "Actus Primus, Scœna Prima," following the title piece. H. Granville-Barker convincingly
   demonstrates the absurdity of the act and scene divisions
   established in the eighteenth century and followed by most
   editors of the play—*Prefaces to Shakespeare* (Princeton,
   1951), I, 379 ff.
2. *Antony and Cleopatra,* The New Shakespeare (Cambridge,
   1954), p. xxxii.
3. *Antony and Cleopatra,* Arden ed. (London, 1956), p. lv.
4. *Oxford Lectures on Poetry* (London, 1909), pp. 301–302.
5. Granville-Barker, *op. cit.,* i. 444 ff.
6. Wilson, *op. cit.,* p. xxxiv.
7. Ridley, *op. cit.,* pp. xlvii ff.
8. *Ibid.,* p. liii.
9. The modern edition to which reference is made in this essay

is that of W. J. Craig, *The Tragedies of Shakespeare* (New York, 1924).

10. Granville-Barker, *op. cit.*, i. 372
11. The italics are mine.
12. The italics are mine.
13. Ridley erroneously assumes that during the "awkward interval" which he accuses Wilson of ignoring (*op. cit.*, p. xlvi), namely, that between Antony's death and the interview with Caesar, Cleopatra sends this Egyptian to Caesar. A careful examination of the circumstances of Antony's death precludes this interpretation. In Act IV, Scene xii (according to the traditional scene division) Antony falls on his sword. One of his followers, Dercetas, finds him dying, snatches up the sword, and sets out for Caesar's camp in order to ingratiate himself with the conqueror. Antony then orders himself carried to Cleopatra's Monument, where in Scene xiii he dies. In the next scene, Act V, Scene i, Dercetas arrives at Caesar's camp with the fatal sword and surrenders himself. Even while Caesar, completely taken by surprise, is hypocritically expressing his grief at the news of his rival's death, the Egyptian, obviously unaware of Antony's suicide, enters and delivers Cleopatra's message. As soon as the messenger departs, Caesar sends Proculeius and Gallus to capture the Queen. His celerity, already repeatedly stressed (III.vi.19–23, 30–31; vii.20–25, 56–7, 74–7), serves him in good stead, for Proculeius arrives at the Monument as Cleopatra is recovering from the shock of Antony's death. Evidently, then, Shakespeare considered Act IV, Scene xiii, and Act V, Scene i, as concurrent. When thus viewed, the awkwardness of the interval disappears.
14. Since in the preceding scene Caesar has sent Gallus to "second" Proculeius, most editors, except Wilson and Ridley, include Gallus with Proculeius. The Folio, however, mentions only Proculeius.
15. Unfortunately the Folio has no stage direction indicating the manner of Cleopatra's capture. Nevertheless, most edi-

tors assume that somehow or other it was effected by Gallus (e.g., cf. Wilson, *op. cit.*, pp. 110, 235). The most convincing plan to date for restaging the capture in terms of the Elizabethan theatre, effective from the standpoint both of dramatic surprise and of economy of setting and action, is that of Ridley (*op. cit.*, pp. 253 ff.). After reviewing the schemes of Granville-Barker and others who use either the upper or the lower inner stage and also of Wilson, who favors a temporary wooden structure simulating the Monument, Ridley makes what he calls the "heterodox suggestion" that the entire action in the final scene take place on the "whole stage" now representing the Monument. He then would have Gallus and the guard "break in from behind, either through the curtain or ordinary doors." Thus he would eliminate the awkward climbing necessary if the upper stage or a temporary structure were used as the Monument.

16. In the Folio these last two lines, strongly contrasting with the honeyed words preceding, are also marked "*Pro.*" Attributing this "muddled speech-heading" to the compositor, who transferred the proper name from the text to the speech-heading, Ridley suggests the solution that I have here adopted. Since not only speech-headings but all proper names in the original text are italicized, this emendation seems reasonable enough.

17. At this point in the original text appears what Dr. Joseph Q. Adams, first Director of the Folger Shakespeare Library, in his lectures some thirty years ago at Cornell University used to call "a bit of stage-manager's cement": "*Flourish. Enter Proculeius, Caesar, Gallus, Mecenas, and others of his Traine. All. Make way there Caesar.*" For while it is generally agreed that the manuscript in the hands of the compositor of the First Folio was either Shakespeare's own or one very close to it—W. W. Greg, *The Editorial Problem in Shakespeare* (Oxford, 1942), p. 148; Wilson, *op. cit.*, pp. 124, 127; Ridley, *op. cit.*, p. xvi—it also seems evident that this manuscript was in the process of being revised and

abridged, by either Shakespeare or someone else (Wilson, *op. cit.*, pp. 127 ff.; Ridley, *op. cit.*, p. xix.; Granville-Barker, *op. cit.*, pp. 372n., 400, 405). Apparently two scenes have been cut (cf. Wilson, *op. cit.*, pp. xxxv, 239). In the first of these Cleopatra requests Dolabella to let her know exactly when Caesar plans to send her to Rome, and in the second Cleopatra arranges for the asps to be brought to her. Later, after the interview with Caesar, Dolabella enters and with greater familiarity than he has hitherto shown—suggesting an acquaintance of some length—informs her of Caesar's departure with obvious reference to a previous conversation not now in the text (V.ii.197–203). Just before his entrance Cleopatra whispers in Charmian's ear; whereupon, though nothing has yet been said of the asps, Iras, as if recalling an earlier conversation, immediately infers that they are discussing suicide. Cleopatra then refers to arrangements previously made (V.ii.192–95). *Only a lapse of time between her capture and her interview with Caesar* would have permitted these activities.

18. Ridley questions Wilson's interpretation of this episode as "a cunning and entirely successful device to 'unpolicy' Caesar, make an 'ass' of him, to put him off the scent by persuading him that she has no intention of committing suicide since she discovers herself busy trying to save the best part of her treasure for life in the future" (Wilson, *op. cit.*, xxxiv). Ridley points out that "there is as yet, so far as we know, no guard through whom the bearer of the asps has to be brought in, and so nothing in the world to prevent her arranging for his arrival when she chooses" (Ridley, *op. cit.*, pp. xlviii–xlix). He thus disregards his own stage direction "Enter Gallus *and* guard," Gallus's order "*Guard* her till Caesar come," Dolabella's dismissal of Proculeius "For the Queen, I'll take her to my *guard*," not to mention the *guard* who admits the "rural fellow" with the asps and also the *guards* who come "rustling in" after Cleopatra dies.

19. Only this manner of dress can explain Caesar's inability to

distinguish which of the three women is Cleopatra. Though Wilson regards Caesar's question, "Which is the Queen of Egypt," as the "opening shot in the duel of wits" (*op. cit.*, p. 237), this explanation will not account for Dolabella's similar confusion, when, coming in after Caesar's departure, he asks, "Where is the Queen?" Even though he has just spoken to her in Caesar's presence, he is unable to recognize her until Charmian with a wave of the hand says, "Behold, sir." Cleopatra then identifies herself by pronouncing his name. Perhaps this disguise is Shakespeare's way of rendering more palatable Plutarch's distasteful description of Cleopatra's appearance in his account of the same interview: "Cleo., being laid upon a little low bed in poor estate (when she saw Caes. come into her chamber), she suddenly rose up, naked in her smock, and fell down at his feet marvellously disfigured: both for that she had plucked her hair from her head, as also for that she had martyred all her face with her nails; and besides, her voice was small and trembling, her eyes sunk into her head with continual blubbering; and moreover, they might see the most part of her stomach torn in sunder. To be short, her body was not much better than her mind: yet her good grace and comeliness and the force of her beauty was not altogether defaced. But notwithstanding this ugly and pitiful state of hers, yet she shewed herself within, by her outward looks and countenance" (*ibid.*, p. 219).

Three Additional *Much Ado* Sources

BY JOHN J. O'CONNOR

To someone who believes that source hunting is a useless
pastime, a mark of the static mind—Professor Saintsbury
thought it only a degree above hunting cats—Shakespeare's
Much Ado might be taken as a case in point. The fullest
scholarly treatment of the play, Professor Charles T. Prouty's
Sources of Much Ado About Nothing, mentions eighteen
versions of the Hero-Claudio plot written during the sixteenth century prior to Shakespeare's play.[1] Although no
sane scholar would suggest that Shakespeare knew all the
available versions of the Hero-Claudio story, most of the
commentators on *Much Ado* seem to believe that he knew
at least Bandello and a version of Ariosto's tale of Ariodant
and Genevra or that he knew a play, now lost, in which the
Bandello-Ariosto versions were combined. Since a non-
existent play can scarcely be expected to shed any light upon
Shakespeare's dramatic methods, most scholars have been
forced to make a choice from among the relatively large
number of possible sources. Such are the intangibles of

source hunting and such is the genius of Shakespeare that it is sometimes more hazardous to assert he could not have been inspired by a given work than that he did indeed use it. At any rate, the number of possible sources has remained fairly large, and most scholars play safe by offering a variety of possibilities.[2] Perhaps unfortunately, the number of sources can be enlarged somewhat further. Overlooked by modern scholarship, there are three additional analogues, any one of which Shakespeare might have used as a source for his Hero-Claudio plot. Since two of them were available in English at the time *Much Ado* was written, they ought to be resurrected from obscurity.[3]

The analogues are all to be found deep-buried in the chivalric underbrush of *The Mirror of Knighthood*, a vast episodic Spanish romance which had a considerable vogue in Elizabethan England. As befits so unwieldy a work, the history of its publication is somewhat complex. It was begun by Diego Ortuñez de Calahorra, who published the three books of part one in 1562. Apparently exhausted by his labors,[4] he gave way to Pedro de la Sierra, who continued the work by publishing in 1581 a second part in two books. In 1589 a third author, Marcos Martinez, brought the romance to a stop—though not to a conclusion, for he promises a further continuation—by adding a third and a fourth part, each of two books, to those already in print.

The task of Englishing *The Mirror of Knighthood* required as many translators as it had authors. It was begun by Margaret Tyler, who completed the first book in 1580. The translation was then taken over by R. P. (probably Robert Parry), who was in turn succeeded by L. A. The three translators turned out a total of nine books comprising 3200-odd pages of English black letter—an inky monument to man's doggedness and uncertain taste.

The three analogues are to be found in widely scattered portions of *The Mirror of Knighthood*. Each of the three authors has a version. The first, by Diego Ortuñez de Cala-horra, occurs in *The Third Part of the First Booke of the Mirrour of Knighthood* (1586?). In Chapter 43—mistakenly written Chapter 21 in the Huntington Library copy which I used—Rosicleer meets a damsel riding as fast as her palfrey will carry her. She is looking for help, and from her recital and the facts later disclosed by the author the following tale emerges:

> The damsel is one of two waiting women who serve Poli-sena, one of the fairest at the court of King Tiberio of Hun-garia. Polisena has been courted by many, but loves only the gallant Lusiano, Prince of Suevia. In the presence of her two waiting women she and Lusiano plight their troth but decide to keep their relationship secret. Unaware that Polisena is already pledged, a rival lover, Roberto, Duke of Saxony, comes to court and woos her. When he sees he is making no progress, he plots to force her to be his wife. He first learns which of Polisena's waiting women is "basest of linage & poorest." He then tries to seduce her with gifts and promises, and "in the end he brought her vnto the bent of his bow, and hauing her at his commandement, & as he would wish, vpon a night, at such time as the Moone did shine most cleerest, hee practised with her, that she should apparell her selfe with the same apparell & attire of her head, that the Dutches her Ladie did weare the daie before, & being so attired shee shoulde come forth into a gallant fresh garden, which was vnder the window of the Dutches . . . , & being there, she should present her selfe to be the faire *Polisena*, and hee would meete with her in the sayd garden, whereas betwixt them they would plight their faith & troth of matrimonie, & how that he would take her into his armes, as though she were his spouse and lawfull wife." Meanwhile Roberto has

been boasting to three of the most respected knights of the court how much he has been favored by Polisena. He explains, however, that she keeps postponing a public announcement of their engagement. On the night he arranges to meet the waiting woman, he asks the three knights to accompany him so that they may be witnesses in the event Polisena attempts a further postponement. At midnight Roberto goes with the trio to the walled garden outside Polisena's lodging. There the witnesses see and hear all that passes between him and the waiting woman whom they take to be Polisena. They see and hear the plighting of troth. Later Roberto and the damsel move away from the witnesses so that they can no longer see, and "there the Duke did accomplish his will with the Damsell." Soon after the events of this night Roberto complains to King Tiberio that he and Polisena have been made sure together but that she denies the contract. He asks that Tiberio command Polisena to marry him. Polisena denies his story, but in the presence of Lusiano Roberto produces his three witnesses, who swear that Roberto and Polisena "were made sure together, in so ample maner, as man and wife ought to be, and how that ouer and aboue all this, they had bene together . . . ." When Tiberio orders Polisena to marry Roberto, Lusiano can contain himself no longer. He accuses the three witnesses of lying and says he is Polisena's spouse. When Polisena admits to the king that Lusiano is right, Tiberio orders her imprisoned because he thinks she has promised both suitors. He stipulates that the matter be settled by a duel: Roberto and his three knights against Lusiano and any three knights he can find to help him. The date of the combat is set a month hence, but because of the prowess of Roberto and his knights and their reputation as men of honor Lusiano is unable to find anyone, until Rosicleer appears on the scene, willing to risk his life in what seems an unjust cause.[5]

The second of the *Much Ado* analogues, this one written
by Pedro de la Sierra, occurs in Chapter 17 of *The Second
Part of the Mirror of Knighthood* (1583). Here the Knight
of the Sun and Tefereo meet a damsel on a palfrey. She asks
their help and tells the story of the fair lady Artalanda, "who
is accused by the greatest and falsest treason that euer was
inuented in the worlde":

Artalanda, daughter of the King of France, is wooed by
Dalior, son of the Prince of Scotland, and by Lidiarte, son of
the Duke of Guyan. Lidiarte perceives that Artalanda favors
his rival and as a result "waxed verie leane, and his face became yelow and wan . . . ." He puts away his gay clothing
and dresses somberly. Tarfina, Artalanda's waiting woman, in
love with Lidiarte, is upset by the change in his appearance.
Now "the diuell put into her head, a meruaylous & wicked
inuention." To comfort Lidiarte, she tells him that Artalanda
wishes to meet him secretly at midnight. At the appointed
hour she herself lets down a piece of timber so that he can
climb the wall of the enclosed garden near Artalanda's lodging. Then she asks him to wait while she notifies her mistress
that he has come. She dresses in the "same garments which
her Lady the Princesse had worn the daye before" and returns
to the waiting lover. In the darkness Lidiarte is completely
gulled. He falls on his knees before her "and so both of them
by great pollicie and deceite, and with exceeding ioye, did fulfill their desires, and tooke their leaue each of other . . . ."
Next day Lidiarte dresses again in his gayest finery, comes
early to the court, boldly enters Artalanda's chamber while
she is at her prayers, and, encouraged by his memories of last
night "spake vnto her certaine louing and amorous words,
throwing his armes about her neck, and ioyning his face vnto
the face of the Princesse." Startled, her prayer book falling
from her hands, she shrieks. Dalior appears, draws his sword,

and lunges. Lidiarte avoids the thrust and, drawing his own weapon, kills him. The irate king orders Lidiarte hanged immediately, and the distraught Tarfina commits suicide. But Lidiarte's relatives are certain that chicanery is involved. Three of them appear and publicly accuse Artalanda of responsibility in Lidiarte's death. She is given fifteen days in which to find champions to take her part in the combat which honor decrees must follow.[6]

The third of the analogues, by Marcos Martinez, is to be found in Chapter 2 of *The Ninth Book of the Mirror of Knighthood*. There the Prince of Tinacria is told a story by a damsel who is seeking help for a lady condemned to death. The lady is Celibella, only daughter of the King of Samogacia, and the story is as follows:

Celibella is wooed by two brothers, sons of the King of Podolia, but favors the younger, Rosaner. Her kinswoman and confidante Felina falls in love with the older, Daristeo, but he has eyes only for Celibella. Meanwhile the princess seems unable to make Rosaner understand that she loves him, nor can she discourage Daristeo. While matters are in this indecisive state, Furiander, the bastard son of the King of Podolia, comes to court, where he makes a very favorable impression. Her unrequited love for Daristeo finally drives Felina to a rash expedient. She tells him Celibella wishes to meet him secretly at night in the garden. At the arranged time Felina, dressed in Celibella's clothing and counterfeiting Celibella's voice, speaks out Celibella's window to Daristeo. Rosaner happens upon them and overhears Felina, whom he like his brother takes to be Celibella, tell Daristeo she loves him. In the darkness Rosaner does not recognize his brother and attacks him. In the fight both are killed. Felina screams and, distraught, leaps from the window to her death. In the ensuing uproar at court Furiander blames Celibella for the deaths of his brothers. Since both of them have confided to him their feelings for her, he thinks she has procured their deaths to be rid of their importunities. He therefore formally charges her and so by law makes her bound to answer. She is imprisoned and given four months to find a champion to fight Furiander, "for it was ye kings law held inuiolably, (although very rigorous) that whatsoeuer person were accused of an offence cōmitted within the palace, that doeth not either of himself, or some knight for him answere the challenge, within the time lymitted in the challenge, shall be condemned to be burnt; the most cruell thing that euer was heard." [7]

All three episodes described above clearly derive from Ariosto's tale of Ariodant and Genevra. All center upon the deception by which a woman, usually a dependent, dresses in another's clothing and meets a lover at night—as Margaret meets Borachio. All three episodes, therefore, qualify as possible sources for the Hero-Claudio plot. The Polisena-Lusiano story develops the deception at greater length and more closely resembles *Much Ado* in such details as the multiple, and obviously upright, witnesses, but either of the other analogues might as easily have given Shakespeare the idea of incorporating the deception scene into his play. The third analogue seems less probable only because it did not appear in English translation until 1601, and the dramatist would therefore have had to read it in its original language. But Shakespeare, who Professor Prouty believes could read French and Italian, might no less plausibly be assumed to have read Spanish—Is not the source of *The Two Gentlemen of Verona* commonly assumed to be Montemayor's *Diana?*—and so not even the third analogue can be safely omitted from consideration. If we follow Professor Prouty's arithmetic, we must add three, or perhaps five, sources to the *Much Ado* tally sheet. [8]

Admittedly the addition of three sources to an already
long list does not seem to bring the scholar much closer to
an understanding of *Much Ado*. It is not my intention to
argue that Shakespeare must have read *The Mirror of
Knighthood*, or that any of the three analogues described
above are closer to the deception scene of *Much Ado* than,
say, Spenser's or Beverley's version of the Ariodant-Genevra
tale. It is vain to argue about priority among sources which
are all variants of the same story, especially when one is
dealing with such a variable as Shakespeare's creative imagination.

Though this paper has few certainties to offer, only the
dullest of source hunters—the kind who might believe that
the bastard Furiander is the model for Don John—will be
disappointed. The recognition of three more sources at least
re-emphasizes certain ideas. In the first place the three episodes from *The Mirror of Knighthood* generally fit easily
into the framework of Professor Prouty's admirable and provocative discussion of the play. Some of his generalizations
would have to undergo minor changes. For instance, the
clause "whereas hitherto the deception plot has been put in
motion by a rival lover, usually a friend of the hero" would
have to be revised in the light of the second and third episodes, in both of which the plot is initiated by a woman.
Second, the episodes in *The Mirror of Knighthood* help to
underline one of Professor Prouty's main theses: the vitality
of Ariosto and the Renaissance impulse, in adapting him, to
"wade further." That there should be in this chivalric romance three such different versions of the same basic story
is to be accounted for only partially by the fact that they
were written by three different authors. In its ardent striving
after "Infinite riches in a little room," the Renaissance mind
welcomed a clever plot whose every rift could be loaded with

ore. Since the rifts in the Hero-Claudio plot glitter with
Benedick and Beatrice and with Dogberry and Verges, we
should be content that Ariosto was so well "imitated."

NOTES

1. (New Haven, Conn., 1950), p. 5.
2. In his *Shakespeare's Sources: I. Comedies and Tragedies*
   (London, 1957), Kenneth Muir suggests as the primary
   source of *Much Ado* a "lost play" but offers several secondary sources.

   Geoffrey Bullough in his *Narrative and Dramatic Sources
   of Shakespeare* (London, 1958), Vol. II, reprints selections
   from Bandello, Ariosto, and Spenser as the sources of the
   Hero-Claudio plot, but, like Professor Prouty, he lists eighteen sources and analogues.
3. I speak of "resurrection" because the three analogues I am
   about to describe in detail were first pointed out in print
   more than fifty years ago but have, in a way comprehensible
   only to those who are aware of the mass of twentieth-century scholarship, been buried in the slough of Shakespeare
   bibliography. Although I came across the analogues in *The
   Mirror of Knighthood* independently, they were originally
   remarked upon by Joseph de Perott in an article entitled
   "The Probable Source of the Plot of Shakespeare's *Tempest*," which appeared in the *Publications of the Clark University Library*, Vol. I (1905). Since de Perott was interested
   primarily in showing that Shakespeare had found his source
   for *The Tempest* in *The Mirror of Knighthood*, he mentioned the *Much Ado* analogues only in passing. He made
   no substantial effort to prove his case about *Much Ado*, and
   his comments have been apparently not taken seriously.

Perhaps they were considered as fantastic as his ideas about *The Tempest*, which were savagely criticized.

The *Much Ado* suggestions have not been totally disregarded, for in his *Spanish and Portuguese Romances of Chivalry* (Cambridge, 1920), p. 277, Sir Henry Thomas, while attacking de Perott's ideas on *The Tempest*, admits there is "perhaps more to be said for the suggestion that an essential incident in the plot of *Much Ado about Nothing* (1600), Margaret's impersonation of Hero at the chamber window was borrowed from the Spanish romance." Moreover, Selma Guttman's handy book, *The Foreign Sources of Shakespeare's Works* (New York, 1947), p. 128, has a brief account of de Perott's article. Nevertheless, there has been no general recognition of the validity of de Perott's incidental comment, and no reference to *The Mirror of Knighthood* in connection with *Much Ado* is to be found in the works already cited of Prouty, Muir, or Bullough. The state of Shakespeare bibliographical studies being what it is, de Perott's article has been almost as lost as "the matter of Panecia."

4. In the latter stages of the third book of part one (fols. 176ᵛ–177ᵛ in the English translation) he refers in considerable detail to his weariness, the enormity of his task, and his intention to leave off after he has concluded the third book.

5. This episode begins on fol. 222ᵛ and goes on to fol. 233ᵛ, where the traitorous waiting-woman is slain by her lover: "And this is the reward that all such ought to looke for, for although there be many that would profit themselues of the treason, yet in conclusion (by great fortune) there are few traitors that doe escape their reward . . . ."

6. The episode begins on fol. 94 and ends on fol. 98 in the 1583 edition.

7. This tale begins on sig. B2 and continues to sig. C2ᵛ in the edition of 1601.

8. Professor Prouty includes in his tally translations and adaptations. If we count both Spanish and English versions of

The Mirror of Knighthood in print before 1598, omitting only the 1601 English translation of the Celibella-Rosaner story, we would have a total of five. It is, of course, not very likely that in the case of a chivalric romance an Elizabethan dramatist would be so scholarly as to go to the original when a translation was available.

The Right Vein of Rochester's *Satyr*

BY C. F. MAIN

John Aubrey records an interesting contemporary opinion of the Earl of Rochester as a satirist. Andrew Marvell, he tells us, was wont to say that Rochester "was the best English Satyrist and had the right vein." [1] If modern commentators on Rochester never fail to quote Marvell's opinion, they also never fail to leave it unexplained. Clearly Marvell had in mind some sort of contrast between Rochester's satires and other people's, including his own. It is equally clear that at least one of Rochester's satires, *A Satyr against Mankind*, is indeed quite unlike Marvell's political pasquils, Butler's burlesque narratives, or Cleveland's lampoons on the Puritans. When the label *satire* is applied to these representative English works, it refers to a mode or an attitude; when Marvell applies it to Rochester's poem, it refers to a classical genre, the formal verse satire or *satura*. Rochester's *Satyr* breaks with the native tradition. Its closest contemporary affinities are not with English satire but with French, especially with Boileau's *Satire VIII*. In fact, its resemblance to

Boileau's *Satire* (1667) and its later date (ca. 1675) have led some critics, including Johnson, to regard it as a mere pendant to the earlier poem. But Rochester's and Boileau's satires are independent works, as John F. Moore has demonstrated; they have only a "broad structural similarity." [2] They are structurally similar, Moore might have added, because they are both in a vein derived from the Roman *satura*. When Marvell calls this vein the right one, he commends as a critic and a classical scholar certain conventions of satire that he ignores as a practicing satirist. His position is like Dryden's, since the *Discourse concerning the Original and Progress of Satire* (1693) describes and praises the kind of formal verse satire that Juvenal, Persius, and Boileau wrote, but that Dryden himself never attempted except in translation. Formal verse satire is so rare in English that Rochester's brilliant and early specimen in the kind deserves a closer study than it has yet received.

A formal verse satire is a quasi-dramatic poem in which a voice is heard arraigning one particular vice and commending its opposite virtue. Though sometimes the first portion of the poem contains the arraignment and the last the commendation, a formal verse satire never splits into two distinct pieces because the virtue is always present, if not overtly then at least by implication. Thus a formal satire has two main parts in the way that a balance has them: one part will not function without the other. The satirist's "negative" denunciations always imply "positive" standards of some sort, usually a "dominant rationalistic philosophy" of the time.[3] The positive-negative contrast gives the satire its framework, within which a great variety of rhetorical and dramatic devices may be used. At times this "medley" (an etymological meaning of *satura*) of devices may give an impression of disorder and would indeed render the satire quite formless, were it not for the bipartite structure. As a formal satirist Rochester uses several of the conventions: the unpleasant satirical *persona*, the *adversarius* who interrupts him, the partial retraction at the end of the poem. But let us first look at the structure, and first within the structure at the "negative side."

In his *Discourse* Dryden insists that a perfect satire "ought only to treat of one subject; to be confined to one particular theme; or at least, to one principally. If other vices occur in the management of the chief, they should only be transiently lashed." [4] Rochester's practice conforms with the theory that Dryden deduced from the ancient satirists. The *Satyr* lashes one principal vice: pride. Instead of attacking proud individuals, the formal satirist attacks pride itself, the generic pride that mankind assumes from the mere fact of its humanity. The speaker of the satire (a discussion of the nature of this speaker must be postponed until we look at the "positive side") begins by saying that he would rather be a dog, a monkey, or a bear,

> Or any thing but that vain *Animal*,
> Who is so proud of being rational.[5]
> (lines 6–7)

The important word here is *proud*, not *rational*; at least the reader who seizes on the latter and ignores the former is bound to ignore the design of the poem. Thomas H. Fujimura, for instance, has recently attempted to define the "precise objects" of Rochester's satire by "distinguishing between the epistemological first portion and the moral satire of the second." [6] This view leaves the poem in two distinct pieces because it overlooks the fact that *all* of a satire must be moral—that is, concerned with judging human attitudes and conduct. Pride, not epistemology, is the error satirized throughout.

At climactic points the satirist arraigns pride by name. After denouncing pride founded on the mistaken notion that man has a rational faculty unique to himself (lines 1–28), the satirist paints this grim picture of man *in extremis*:

> Hudled in dirt, the reas'ning *Engine* lyes,
> Who was so proud, so witty, and so wise.
> *Pride* drew him in, as *Cheats*, their *Bubbles*, catch,
> And made him venture, to be made a W*re[t]ch*.
> (lines 29–32)

Then follows (lines 33–45) an account of a typical figure, the witty man whose pride in his own wit causes his downfall. A couplet (lines 46–47) introduces another speaker in the manner of French satire (in Roman satire the *adversarius* interrupts more abruptly). The other speaker defends all of humanity except wits and justifies human pride by asserting that man is made in God's image (lines 48–71). To silence him, the satirist renews his attack on pride in learning (lines 72–113) and in a triplet clinches his indictment:

> For all his Pride, and his Philosophy,
> 'Tis evident, *Beasts* are in their degree,
> As wise at least, and better far than he.
> (lines 114–116)

Having disposed of pride in wisdom, the satirist now demolishes pride in accomplishment (lines 117–173). Man, he says, owes his entire civilization—his moral code, his "Projects," the very government that protects him from his fellows—to his innate fear. Consequently man can no more rightly be proud of what he does than of what he knows. The satire proper ends with these lines:

> All this with indignation I have hurl'd
> At the pretending part of the proud World,
> Who swolne with selfish vanity, devise,
> False freedomes, holy Cheats, and formal Lyes
> Over their fellow *Slaves* to tyrranize.
>
> (lines 174–178)

The poem ends with a partial retraction, a common feature in formal verse satire. This retraction (lines 179–224) was probably not prompted by the writers who answered Rochester's *Satyr*, as Vivian de Sola Pinto suggests;[7] Rochester hardly needed crude rejoinders to remind him of the satirical conventions. The rejoinders to the *Satyr* may help us to discover how the poem was received, but not how it was composed. Despite the versions in which the retraction is labeled "Postcript," it is an integral part of the *Satyr*. It consists, first, of three brief satirical characters. The character of the courtier and that of the clergyman both mention pride, and that of the foppish councilman plainly implies it. In addition, other vices besides pride are, in Dryden's words, "transiently lashed." A succinct commendation of the "meek humble man" follows the characters and ends the poem. Having praised humility, though ever so perfunctorily, the satirist has evaded the charge of complete virulence.

Negatively considered, then, the *Satyr* is an attack on humanity's chief sin. The aristocratic libertine has chosen the most hoary of subjects for his satire, and the most traditional of satirical forms. Yet, or perhaps therefore, he has created an original work. Behind him lies the weight of centuries of sermonizing on pride, sermonizing that he pointedly ignores because his grounds are very different from those of Christian clergymen. The final admonition to be humble is the logical conclusion of an unorthodox view of man that runs through the poem alongside the denunciation of pride.

One must beware of taking the "positive side" of the *Satyr* as Rochester's personal credo, of reading the poem as though it were *The Prelude*. The classical satirist is not "expressing himself." Convention requires him to assume a mask and strike a pose, to be insincere. Nothing, therefore, could be more incorrect than this typical opinion of the *Satyr*: "Browning might have written just such a poem in his *Men and Women*, dramatically; but Rochester is speaking for himself." [8] This comment is incorrect because it implies, among other things, that the darling of Charles's court actually wished to change places with his pet monkey. "That Rochester regarded men as knaves, fools, and animals," another critic remarks, "there can be no doubt; it is the main argument of his satirical masterpiece, 'A Satire Against Mankind.'" [9] Although it is always disastrous to re-create the historical poet from the dramatic poem, commentators on Rochester seem irresistibly tempted to do so, perhaps because the poet's life itself was so luridly theatrical. Rochester loved to appear what he was not. "In all his frolicksome Disguises," says the author of the *Memoir* attributed wrongly to Saint-Évremond, "he so truly personated the Thing he would seem, that his most intimate Acquaintance could not discover the Imposture." [10] The man who in real life successfully impersonated a woman on one occasion and a mountebank on another must, surely, be permitted to invent a satirical *persona*. Whatever the positive doctrine of a man contained in the *Satyr* may be, we have no evidence that it is Rochester's private philosophy of life.

Several scholars have canvassed the sources of this doctrine. J. F. Crocker, for instance, traces the *Satyr* to Montaigne's *Apologie de Raimond Sebond*. "There is scarcely an idea of major or minor importance in Rochester," he concludes, with more assurance than proof, "that is not present in Montaigne." [11] Were the parallels that Crocker cites at all close, his conclusion would still be unconvincing because the *Satyr* and the *Apologie* discredit human reason for very different purposes. Montaigne and his fellow skeptics question man's ability to reason in order to stress his need to have faith in divine revelation. The main speaker of Rochester's poem is not skeptical in this sense; he makes no claim for faith. He does not even offer a choice between reason and faith, as Dryden does in *Religio Laici*; instead, he sets up reason and sense as opposites. Man, he says at the beginning of the poem, is inferior to the beasts because he prefers reason to "certain instinct," and because he leaves the "light of Nature, sense, behind" (lines 10–13). The skeptics, in contrast, have no such confidence in the senses. According to Thomas Stanley's *History of Philosophy*, they hold that "the Senses are so far from guiding the Intellect to comprehension, that they contradict one another." [12] Rochester may have known Stanley's *History*, but if he did know it, he drew on its account of epicureanism, as Ronald Crane suggests,[13] rather than on its account of skepticism. Crane also cites some convincing parallels between the theriophilic ideas in the poem and in ancient writers; yet his helpful notes are not intended to be a coherent account of the poem. Moore, who demonstrates Rochester's independence of Boileau, is equally inconclusive: "A single source for the content of the *Satyr* will be difficult to accept," [14] he says. Finally, and most recently, Fujimura finds in the satire a "naturalistic creed," Hobbist in the main but with significant departures from Hobbes (p. 588). None of these investigators considers the dramatic convention of the satirical genre.

Rochester creates a speaker, who for convenience will be referred to simply as the "satirist," of the sort that will give the maximum amount of offense to godly and conventional people in his audience, the same people whom he affronted when he had the famous portrait painted in which he is elegantly placing a laurel wreath on a monkey. The satirist commits his first offense against conventional morality in the passage denouncing pride in reason. The lines are as interesting for what they leave unsaid as for what they say:

> The senses are too gross, and he'll contrive
> A Sixth, to contradict the other Five;
> And before certain instinct, will preferr
> *Reason,* which Fifty times for one does err.
> *Reason,* an *Ignis fatuus,* in the *Mind,*
> Which leaving light of Nature, sense behind;
> Pathless and dang'rous wandring ways it takes,
> Through errors, Fenny-*Boggs,* and Thorny *Brakes;*
> Whilst the misguided follower, climbs with pain,
> *Mountains* of Whimseys, heap'd in his own *Brain:*
> Stumbling from thought to thought, falls headlong down,
> Into doubts boundless Sea, where like to drown,
> Books bear him up awhile, and makes him try,
> To swim with Bladders of *Philosophy;*
> In hopes still t'oretake the'escaping light,
> The *Vapour* dances in his dazl[ed] sight,
> Till spent, it leaves him to eternal Night.
> Then Old Age, and experience, hand in hand,
> Lead him to death, and make him understand,

> After a search so painful, and so long,
> That all his Life he has been in the wrong;
> Hudled in dirt, the reas'ning *Engine* lyes,
> Who was so proud, so witty, and so wise.
>
> (lines 8–30)

In this bitter attack on intellectual pride the satirist has ignored sin and has thus implied a heterodox view of man. With such extremists as Calvin he agrees that man is a worm five feet long, but he fails to give the orthodox reason for that view: man is a fallen creature, worthy only of such merit as God's grace may confer on him. The rejoinders to the *Satyr* call attention to the satirist's failure to mention sin. For instance, Richard Pocock, or whoever wrote *An Answer to the Satyr against Mankind*, agrees that mankind now has little to be proud of, but he argues that original sin deprived the race of merit:

> Must the first draught of Man be vilify'd,
> Scorn'd and contemn'd, 'cause Man himself hath stray'd?
> Or did not *Eve* sufficiently transgress,
> And Bastardise Posterity? unless
> Man, little as he is, be made much less.[15]

The Christian view always leaves man with more than a few rags of pride. Rochester's satirist, in contrast, strips from man even the dignity of having fallen from grace. By indicting the race for stupidity rather than for sinfulness, he commits an outrage against conventional morality.

When the satirist argues that "Sense" should take priority over "Reason," he apparently wishes to appear as a disciple of the most conspicuous contemporary bugbear, Thomas Hobbes. His term *reason*, as Fujimura shows, is synonymous with Hobbes's "abstruse philosophy," the speculations of

schoolmen which produce nothing but rigmaroles and ver-
biage; and his emphasis on sense is reminiscent of the opening chapter of *Leviathan.* Yet the passage in the *Satyr* must
not be taken as an adequate summary of Hobbes's epistemology. Hobbes obviously lacked the satirist's complete
confidence in sense; he relied rather on what he thought of
as geometric logic, on reasoning deductively from self-evi-
dent axioms in which the terms had been meticulously de-
fined. Sense, after all, can provide data only about the secondary qualities of matter. In *The Questions concerning
Liberty, Necessity, and Chance* (1656) Hobbes compared
man and beast with results very different from the satirist's:

> There be beasts that see better, others that hear better, and
> others that exceed mankind in other senses. Man excelleth
> beasts only in making rules to himself, that is to say, in re-
> membering, and in reasoning aright upon that which he
> remembereth. They which do, deserve an honor above brute
> beasts . . . . So that it is not merely the nature of man, that
> makes him worthier than other living creatures, but the
> knowledge that he acquires by meditation, and by the right
> of use of reason in making good rules of his future actions.[16]

The satirist speaks, then, as a quasi Hobbist. By echoing the
famous statement about sense in *Leviathan* and by adopting
Hobbes's ridicule of inspiration and speculation, he associates himself with the alleged atheism, materialism, and
licentiousness of Hobbes.

The satirist takes full advantage of the convention that
obliges him to be inconsistent and unfair when he calls the
inspired philosopher a "reas'ning *Engine*" (line 29). There
is nothing "mechanical" about this philosopher's view of
man; on the contrary, "engine" is an epithet more properly
applied to the naturalistic satirist himself. Bishop Bramhall

accused Hobbes of picturing man as a "wooden top" (V, 55), or a "tennis-ball (V, 278), or "a watch which is wound up by God" (V, 203)—that is, as a temporary aggregate of material in motion. The satirist, conscious of his audience, forestalls a similar accusation by making it himself. With more boldness than truth, he annoys the supernaturalists by calling them "reasoning engines."

Having made this telling point, the satirist offers some bait to his auditory in the form of what seems to be an attack on wit. His *adversarius*, a "formal Band and Beard," rises to the bait, agrees that wit should be lashed, but finds man in general worthy of more praise than censure:

> *What rage ferments in your degen'rate mind,*
> *To make you rail at Reason, and Mankind?*
> *Blest glorious Man! to whom alone kind Heav'n,*
> *An everlasting Soul has freely giv'n;*
> *Whom his great Maker took such care to make,*
> *That from himself he did the Image take;*
> *And this fair frame, in shining Reason drest,*
> *To dignifie his Nature, above Beast.*
> *Reason, by whose aspiring influence,*
> *We take a flight beyond material sense,*
> *Dive into Mysteries, then soaring pierce,*
> *The flaming limits of the Universe.*
> *Search Heav'n and Hell, find out what's acted there,*
> *And give the World true grounds of hope and fear.*
>
> (lines 58–71)

In this utterance the *adversarius* reveals his character. He is a smug prelate, a self-styled idealist of the kind that regards all satirists as degenerates. He believes in the dignity of man, in man's essential difference from the beasts, and in man's ability to pierce the infinite and thereby attain ultimate knowledge. These notions are the commonplaces of Renaissance optimism, but never in the Renaissance were they mouthed so complacently and so glibly. The *adversarius* is a proud man defending Pride, a mock Christian who has conveniently forgotten the Fall. Again Rochester has offended the pious by making this facile optimist their spokesman.

It is easy to demolish such a straw man, and the satirist does so by comparing him with three tenth-rate writers: Nathaniel Ingelo, Simon Patrick, and Richard Sibbes. The lines that follow the interruption show that the satirist shares Hobbes's notorious anticlerical bias, his prejudice against "Those Reverend Bedlams, *Colledges* and Schools" (line 83), and his distrust of "reason":

> Borne on whose Wings, each heavy *Sot* can pierce,
> The limits of the boundless Universe.
> So charming Oyntments, make an Old *Witch* flie,
> And bear a Crippled Carcass through the Skie.
> (lines 84–87)

The satirist's "heavy Sot" resembles Hobbes's dogmatic man, who takes "*the habitual discourse of the tongue for ratiocination*" (IV, 73).

In opposition to this kind of reason, for which a better name would be "revelation," the satirist sets up his own "right reason":

> Thus, whilst 'gainst false reas'ning I inveigh,
> I own right *Reason*, which I wou'd obey:
> That *Reason* that distinguishes by sense,
> And gives us *Rules*, of good, and ill from thence:
> That bounds desires, with a reforming Will,
> To keep 'em more in vigour, not to kill.

> Your *Reason* hinders, mine helps t'enjoy,
> Renewing Appetites, yours wou'd destroy.
> My Reason is my *Friend*, yours is a *Cheat*,
> Hunger call's out, my Reason bids me eat;
> Perversely yours, your Appetite does mock,
> This asks for Food, that answers what's a Clock?
> This plain distinction Sir your doubt secures,
> 'Tis not true Reason I despise but yours.
> Thus I think Reason righted.   (lines 98–112)

This definition of "right reason" is perhaps the most outrageous thing in the poem, for it vastly reduces the meaning that that venerable term had carried for several generations of Christian humanists. Traditionally, right reason signifies the "immutable coalescence of truth and goodness whose source is God and whose formative cosmic role is manifested in all the workings of nature." [17] As the term is used in the *Satyr*, it obviously lacks all its former grandeur. Hobbes might be thought responsible for this particular deflation, since he let the wind out of so many terms, if he had not described right reason as "the natural, moral, and divine law" (II, 166), and if he had not said, "When a man *reasoneth* from *principles* that are found indubitable by experience, all deceptions of sense and equivocation of words avoided, the conclusion he maketh is said to be *according to right reason*" (IV, 24). The satirist and Hobbes clearly use the terms differently.

In fact, to find parallels with the *Satyr* one must descend from the philosophers to the dramatists. Don John, the hero of Shadwell's *The Libertine* (1675), agrees with the satirist that sense is the proper guide of reason:

> Nature gave us our Senses, which we please:
> Nor does our Reason war against our Sense.

By Natures order, Sense should guide our Reason,
Since to the mind all objects Sense conveys.
But Fools for shaddows lose substantial pleasures,
For idle tales abandon true delight,
And solid joys of day, for empty dreams at night.[18]

Similarly Deidamia, the lustful queen of Sparta in Otway's *Alcibiades* (1675), speaks of "sense" as man's "God." [19] Finally, in Rochester's own unproduced *Valentinian* the chaste Claudia says:

Each man I meet I fancy will devour me;
And sway'd by Rules not natural but affected
I hate Mankind for fear of being lov'd.

To which Marcellina, a much frailer creature, replies:

Prithee reform; what Nature prompts us to,
And Reason seconds, why should we avoid? [20]

In founding reason on sense, or rather in confounding reason with sense, the satirist associates himself with scandalous personages currently being represented on the stage. Like them he overturns the traditional hierarchy in which reason is the master rather than the servant of appetite. No clocks—no external regulators—keep the satirist from satisfying his appetites and thus achieving the ends for which he and the animals were created:

Those *Creatures*, are the wisest who attain,
By surest means, the ends at which they aim.
(lines 118–119)

This couplet leads from the attack on pride in philosophy

to the attack on pride in accomplishment. To discredit human accomplishment, the satirist discredits human motivation. Here his "positive" doctrine of man seems entirely derived from Hobbes, whose emphasis on fear as a motive is so well known that it hardly needs rehearsing. Fujimura has recently challenged this traditional view of the *Satyr;* he finds that "the emphasis on fear in the poem is . . . a basic departure from Hobbes" (p. 585). The departure, however, is due to the conventions of satire rather than to divergent philosophies. The satirist does simplify Hobbes's complex analysis of human motivation, as Fujimura indicates, not because he disagrees with it but because satire must always be simpler than philosophy. Here Rochester has a precedent in Persius, who used only those parts of an elaborate philosophical system that were relevant to his purposes. The very act of attacking only one vice in a satire is a kind of simplification. Again, Fujimura finds "absolute" values in the *Satyr,* "relativistic" ones in Hobbes; and he remarks parenthetically, "I shall not try to explain why Rochester is not relativistic like Hobbes" (p. 588). The question whether Hobbes is a relativist does not concern us here. But we must expect a satirist to assume absolute standards, since satire always measures man against a fixed scale and always finds him short of the mark. In the latter part of the poem the standard is furnished by animals, who, according to Hobbes, live in "good order and government for their common benefit" and are "free from sedition and war amongst themselves." Nor, among animals, is there any "question of precedence in their own species, nor strife about honor, or acknowledgment of one another's wisdom, as there is amongst men" (IV, 120). Animals, in sum, lack pride and fear.

Here, as earlier in the poem, the satirist argues from a naturalistic rather than a Christian bias. After contrasting man with animal, he invites his audience to

> Look to the bottom, of his vast design,
> Wherein *Mans* Wisdom, Pow'r, and Glory joyn;
> The good he acts, the ill he does endure,
> 'Tis all for fear, to make himself secure.
> Meerly for safety, after Fame we thirst,
> For all Men, wou'd be *Cowards* if they durst.
>   (lines 153–158)

And again a passage in the *Satyr* is notable for what it omits. Thomas Lessee of Wadham College, who penned some doggerel to reprove the satirist and his mentor, has an explanation of man's fearfulness:

> And first the fear y^t trouble's him within,
> Proceed's not from his nature but his sin.
> Which like pale Ghosts, while they their
>   murderers haunt,
> Doe's cramp his soule, and all his courage daunt.
> .   .   .   .
> For lately 'tis evinc't all creatures are
> Noe less y^n man in the wild state of warr,
> Which long agoe, ye weary Emperour knew,
> Who hostile flyes with princely valour slew.
> Is he alone? he startle's when he see's
> His moving shadow, & his shadow flee's,
> ffor who can evidence but that may bee
> No meere privation, but any Enemy.
> So when alone the tim'rous wretch is scar'd,
> And when hee's not, hee's fearfull of his guard.
> What shall he doe, or whether shall he fly,

> Who durst not live, and yet he dare's not dye.
> Say you, who er'e have felt those painefull stabs,
> Say wretched Nero, or thou more wretched Hobbs.
> Guilt is of all, and alwayes is afraid,
> From fear to fear successively betray'd.
> Ti's guilt alone breeds cowardice & distrust,
> For all men would be valiant, if they durst.[21]

Notwithstanding the *ad hominem* argument, Lessee's ethic is the traditional one.

The satirist's ethic—his "positive" doctrine of man derived from a "dominant rationalistic philosophy of the time" —is a compound of Hobbesean materialism and naturalism with tinctures of epicureanism and libertinism. This doctrine provides a much more effective basis for an attack on pride than either the stoicism of the ancient satirists or the modified stoicism of the Elizabethan, for the stoic himself can always be charged wtih the vice that he attacks. Hobbism is not a philosophy that glorifies man, either collectively or individually. Hobbes's very exposition of human nature seemed libelous to many of his contemporaries: "If men had sprung up from the earth in a night," complained Bramhall, "like mushrooms or excrescences, without all sense of honour, justice, conscience, or gratitude, he could not have vilified the human nature more than he doth" (IV, 288). And the same doctrine, when calmly set forth in a poem, is more damaging to man's ego than any direct assault.

That Rochester's satirist is calm and self-controlled may be perceived by comparing him with the angry *personae* created by the Elizabethan satirical poets. Unlike the "satyrs" of Hall and Marston, he does not lose his temper, become frenzied, wallow in filth—and thereby discredit everything he says. He is so much in control that he can afford to sneer at misanthropy itself, as he does when he glances at Diogenes, the "Whimsical *Philosopher*" who preferred his tub to "the spacious *World*" (lines 90–91). The satirist, quite at home in the world, is no outraged idealist; he is a sublunary man whose soul is sense. His tone is weary rather than angry, for he does not expect much of the human race except conduct commensurate with the race's limitations. What is unique about the *Satyr*, then, is that the standard it sets is very low, and that man still falls short. The poem derives its extraordinary force from the cooperation between the "positive" doctrine and the "negative" attack. In addition to being a remarkably successful work of art, the *Satyr against Mankind* documents the change in man's view of himself that took place in the seventeenth century. Pride, once a deadly sin, has become a gross absurdity.

I have not tried to document Rochester's own personal views from the *Satyr*, to incorporate the dramatic poem into the morality play that Rochester's biographers make of his life. The numerous ways in which Pope—to mention only one maligned satirist—has been misrepresented stand as a permanent warning against the practice of assuming that the "I" in every poem represents the poet. The analysis has had another purpose: to uncover the true vein of Rochester's masterpiece and to demonstrate that it heads the list of Augustan formal verse satires. With the possible exception of Donne, who escaped the customary Elizabethan confusion between *satyr* and *satura* and thus was able to imitate the spirit of ancient satire more closely than any of his contemporaries,[22] Rochester wrote the first formal verse satire in English.

NOTES

1. "John Wilmot: Earl of Rochester," *Brief Lives*, ed. O. L. Dick (London, 1950), p. 321.
2. John F. Moore, "The Originality of Rochester's *Satyr against Mankind*," PMLA, LVIII (1943), 401.
3. The terms in quotation marks, as well as the gist of my whole paragraph, are taken from Mary Claire Randolph, "The Structural Design of the Formal Verse Satire," *PQ*, XXI (1942), 368–384.
4. *Essays of John Dryden*, ed. W. P. Ker (Oxford, 1926), II, 102.
5. *Poems by John Wilmot, Earl of Rochester*, ed. Vivian de Sola Pinto (Cambridge, Mass., 1953), p. 118. All quotations from the *Satyr* are taken from this edition.
6. Thomas J. Fujimura, "Rochester's 'Satyr against Mankind': An Analysis," SP, LV (1958), 590. Subsequent references will be given in the text.
7. *Poems by John Wilmot*, p. 215.
8. Oliver Elton, *The English Muse* (London, 1933), p. 252.
9. George Williamson, "The Restoration Petronius," *The University of California Chronicle*, XXIX (1927), 275.
10. John Wilmot, *Poetical Works*, ed. Quilter Johns (Halifax, England, 1933), p. xxx.
11. "Rochester's *Satire against Mankind*," *West Virginia University Studies: III. Philological Papers*, II (1937), 73.
12. Thomas Stanley, *The History of Philosophy* (London, 1660), sig. 4F2ᵛ.
13. Ronald Crane, *A Collection of English Poems, 1660–1800* (New York, 1932), p. 1198.
14. Moore, *op. cit.*, p. 401.
15. (London, *ca.* 1675), p. 2. Wing P2664. I quote from the copy in the Harvard College Library.

16. *The English Works of Thomas Hobbes*, ed. Sir William Molesworth, 5 vols. (London, 1841), V, 186. Subsequent references will be given in the text.

17. Herschel Baker, *The Wars of Truth* (Cambridge, Mass., 1952), p. 92.

18. *The Complete Works of Thomas Shadwell*, ed. Montague Summers (London, 1927), III, 26.

19. *The Complete Works of Thomas Otway*, ed. Montague Summers (London, 1926), I, 21.

20. *Collected Works of John Wilmot, Earl of Rochester*, ed. John Hayward (London, 1926), pp. 191–192. With these libertine arguments cf. a "licentious" suppressed stanza of Alexander Pope's "The Universal Prayer" (*Minor Poems*, ed. Norman Ault and John Butt [London, 1954], p. 147) that Pope quite innocently penned and canceled apparently when his friends showed him its implications:

> Can Sins of Moments claim ye Rod
> Of Everlasting Fires?
> Can those be Sins wth Natures God
> W^{ch} Natures selfe inspires?

21. "A Satyre, in answer to my Ld Rochesters," British Museum MS. Sloane 1485, fol. 44. Another version of this poem, more than twice as long, is printed among the "Miscellanea" appended to Jane Barker's *Poetical Recreations*, 1688, sigs. 2F2–2G1^v.

22. The ablest discussion of this confusion is chapter three of Alvin Kernan's *The Cankered Muse* (New Haven, 1959).

The Frailty of Lemuel Gulliver

BY PAUL FUSSELL, JR.

"... I was bred a Surgeon, whose Trade it is to cure Wounds and Hurts in the Body, got by Accident or Violence."

Because it provides its age with a lively image of a representative man, Gulliver's *Travels into Several Remote Nations of the World* is at once both the *Hamlet* and the *Faust* of its time. And like these analogous humanist masterpieces that precede and follow it, it has been found perplexing both in theme and in method. As with *Hamlet* or *Faust*, no single, exclusive interpretative procedure can render an account of *Gulliver's Travels* at all adequate to its rich complications. But by employing one necessarily limited analytical procedure at a time, we can unravel and detach for examination certain important techniques and themes. I should like to begin, therefore, by disregarding the rest of the book for a moment in order to observe closely Gulliver the man and the sailor. This pathetically diminished Enlightenment Odysseus is, after all, the one constant in the four voyages: he is forever before us. Although the satire and the polemic and the intellectual comedy wax and wane, we constantly hear Gulliver's voice and feel his postures and gestures. We are always aware of both his present action as narrator and his past action as protagonist. And he is, we find, equally an object of pity in each role.

Gulliver can be considered a sort of post-Renaissance New Man, and to compare him to Robinson Crusoe is to perceive at once a part of his meaning. Crusoe the Dissenter is a personification of religious awareness, however coarse. He is concerned with conscience; he experiences visions; he devotes himself to Bible study, to Christian good works in the conversion of Friday, to prayer and divine meditation. He is conscious of an "invisible world," a world of spirits. He recognizes the psychological inadequacy of a purely mechanical explanation of phenomena, and the word "Providence" is often on his lips. But when we bring Gulliver next to Crusoe, not to mention other loquacious sailors like Odysseus, Coleridge's Mariner, Melville's Ishmael, or Conrad's Marlow, nothing is more striking than Gulliver's complacent materialism, his lack of a critical sense, his naïve absence of interest in any other kind of experience than that in which he is immersed by his senses. Unlike Crusoe, Gulliver appears as a personification of religious unawareness. He is an eighteenth-century rationalistic naturalist with an incurable itch for mere exploration, inquiry, and reportage. Had he been conceived a century later, he would have joined with enthusiasm the team of Bouvard and Pécuchet. He embodies the very spirit of the Royal Society; he is a figure whose choices are motivated by that violent and rapid reaction against medieval and Renaissance values known as the scientific revolution. And his sufferings, I suggest, constitute in large part a passionate, almost Burkean critique of that earlier revolution.

II

During his four voyages, Gulliver undergoes countless profound intellectual and psychological humiliations, from the cumulative impact of which his morose, self-righteous, self-pitying state of mind at the end of the fourth voyage is an almost predictable result. The man who, devoted now to merely intellectual "systems," finally comes to prefer the company of two young stallions and their groom to the presence of his own human family is a man whose initial conviction of rational self-sufficiency has been gravely injured, and a man who has been left without means for the restoration of his dignity but outrageous expressions of a mad (and, to a humanist, sublimely comical) self-regard.

Although *Gulliver's Travels* is a series of variations on the theme of intellectual and psychological pride, the expression of this theme (as we see when we focus on the physical Gulliver) is accomplished less by direct revelation of Gulliver's mental attitudes than by a characteristically Swiftian employment of particularized physical emblems and correlatives. Throughout his career Swift makes it clear that he is uninterested in merely describing and reacting to the states of mind which he is anatomizing: instead, he thrusts into the reader's face some concrete physical emblem of a corrupted mind or psyche. The squalor of Chloe's mind, for example, finds its emblem in filthy towels; the Æolists express their meager, gaseous intellectual matter by belching through their noses; the spider emits his self-manufactured nastiness from his own behind. And in *Gulliver's Travels*, Swift's method of inventing vivid physical correlatives for moral circumstances results in an important recurring motif of physical injury, damage, pain, and loss. This motif is expressive of extreme physical frailty and vulnerability, of the pathetic likelihood of damage to weak and unassisted things, whether minds, eyes, limbs, or even hats and breeches. The physical damage which Gulliver either undergoes or fears becomes, through concrete, muscular rendering, a uniquely naturalistic emblem of the damage wrought by experience on Gulliver's presumably self-sufficient mind. It is this motif of physical injury, damage, and loss that I now wish to explore in an attempt to point to an important theme in *Gulliver's Travels*, and, at the same time, in an attempt to define Swift's most characteristic method of imagination.

III

From the beginning to the end of his travels (with time out now and then, of course, for standard touristic inquiries), Gulliver generally suffers rather than acts. Crusoe, once cast away, acts, and he acts with great vigor and stubbornness, but Gulliver is the archetypal victim. He anticipates the modern victim-protagonist in the work of Kafka or in the early works of Hemingway, the man whom things are done to. Most obviously, Gulliver is cast away four times, and each time in a more outrageous manner than the last. Even though, as a surgeon, he is more likely than most to dwell obsessively on his own physical injuries, and even though his commitment to the scientific ideals of the Royal Society impels him to deliver his narrative with a comically detailed circumstantiality, he records a really startling number of hurts. In the voyage to Lilliput, for example, his hair is painfully pulled, and his hands and face are blistered by needle-like arrows. During his visit among the people of Brobdingnag, Gulliver is battered so badly that we are tempted to regard him as strangely accident-prone: his flesh is punctured by wheat beards; twice his sides are painfully crushed; he is shaken up and bruised in a box; his nose and forehead are grievously stung by flies the size of larks; he suffers painful contusions from a shower of gigantic hailstones; he "breaks" his shin on a snailshell; and he is pummeled about the head and body by a linnet's wings.

In the third voyage Gulliver is given a respite: his experiences here are primarily intellectual, and he is permitted for a brief period to behave as curious tourist rather than universal sufferer. But the final voyage, the voyage to the land of the Houyhnhnms, brings Gulliver again into dire physical jeopardy. His last series of physical ordeals begins as his hand is painfully squeezed by a horse. And finally, as he leaves Houyhnhnmland to return to England, he is made to suffer a serious and wholly gratuitous arrow wound on the inside of his left knee ("I shall carry the Mark to my Grave"). Looking back on the whole extent of Gulliver's foreign experiences before his final return to his own country, we are hardly surprised that Gulliver's intellectuals have come unhinged: for years his body has been beaten, dropped, squeezed, lacerated, and punctured. When all is said, his transforming experiences have been as largely physical as intellectual and psychological. So powerfully does Swift reveal Gulliver's purely mental difficulties at the end of the fourth voyage that we tend to forget that Gulliver has also been made to undergo the sorest physical trials: during the four voyages he has been hurt so badly that, although he is normally a taciturn, unemotional, "Roman" kind of person, he has wept three times; so severely has he been injured at various times that at least twenty-four of his total traveling days he has been forced to spend recuperating in bed.

In addition to these actual emblematic injuries which Gulliver endures, he also experiences a large number of narrow escapes, potential injuries, and pathetic fears of physical hurt. In Lilliput, the vulnerability of his eyes is unremittingly insisted upon: an arrow barely misses his left eye, and only his spectacles prevent the loss of both his eyes as he works on the Blefuscan fleet. Furthermore, one of the Lilliputian punishments decreed for Quinbus Flestrin is that his eyes be put out.

And in the voyage to Brobdingnag, Gulliver's experience is one of an almost continuous narrow escape. He almost falls from the hand of the farmer and off the edge of the table. Stumbling over a crust, he falls flat on his face, barely escaping injury. After being held in a child's mouth, he is dropped, and he is saved only by being almost miraculously caught in a woman's apron. He is tossed into a bowl of cream, knocked down but not badly hurt by a shower of falling apples, and clutched dangerously between a spaniel's teeth. He is lucky to escape serious injury during a nasty fall into a mole hill. An agonizing fall of forty feet seems to bode ill for Gulliver, but no—his breeches catch on the point of a pin, and again he is wonderfully saved from destruction. In the same way, during the sojourn at Laputa, Gulliver is afraid of some "hurt" befalling him during the episode of the magician. And likewise in the fourth voyage Gulliver is frequently conscious of potential injury.

But Gulliver, this physically vulnerable ur-Boswell on the Grand Tour, is not the only one in the book who suffers or who fears injury: the creatures he is thrown among also endure strange catastrophes of pain and damage, often

peculiarly particularized by Swift. Thus, in Lilliput, two or
three of the rope-dancing practitioners break their limbs in
falls. A horse, falling part way through Gulliver's handker-
chief, strains a shoulder. The grandfather of the Lilliputian
monarch, it is reported, as a result of breaking his egg upon
the larger end suffered a cut finger. In the same way, the
fourth voyage is full of what seem to be gratuitous images
of injury and pain: for example, Gulliver carefully tells us
that an elderly Houyhnhnm "of Quality" alighted from his
Yahoo-drawn sledge "with his Hind-feet forward, having
by Accident got a Hurt in his Left Fore-foot."

Nor are all these injuries confined to the bodies of Gulliver and his hosts. Gulliver's clothing and personal prop-
erty are perpetually suffering damage, and, when they are
not actually being damaged, Gulliver is worrying that, at
any moment, they may be. Of course, mindful of Crusoe's
pathetic situation, we are not surprised that a shipwrecked
mariner suffers damage to his clothing and personal effects.
But we may be surprised to hear Gulliver go out of his way
to call careful attention to the damages and losses he suffers. In the first voyage, for example, Gulliver circumstan-
tially lets us know that his scimitar has rusted, that his hat
has been sorely damaged by being hauled through the dust
all the way from the sea to the capital, and that his breeches
have suffered an embarrassing rent. The boat in which Gulliver escapes to Blefuscu is, we are carefully told, "but little
damaged." Once off the islands and, we might suppose,
secure from losses and accidents until his next voyage, Gulliver loses one of his tiny souvenir sheep—it is destroyed by
a rat aboard ship.

Presumably outfitted anew, Gulliver arrives ashore in
Brobdingnag with his effects intact, but the old familiar

process of damage and deterioration now begins all over again. Wheat beards rip his clothes; a fall into a bowl of milk utterly spoils Gulliver's suit; his stockings and breeches are soiled when he is thrust into the marrow bone which the queen has been enjoying at dinner; his clothes are again damaged by his tumble into the mole hill; and his suit (what's left of it) is further ruined by being daubed by frog slime and "bemired" with cow dung. Likewise, in the third voyage, our attention is called to the fact that Gulliver's hat has again worn out, and in the fourth voyage we are informed yet again by Gulliver that his clothes are "in a declining Condition."

At times, in fact, Gulliver's clothes and personal effects seem to be Gulliver himself: this is the apparent state of things which fascinates the observing Houyhnhnm before whom Gulliver undresses, and this ironic suggestion of an equation between Gulliver and his clothing, reminding us of the ironic "clothes philosophy" of Section II of A Tale of a Tub, Swift exploits to emphasize that damage to Gulliver's naturalistic garments is really damage to the naturalistic Gulliver. The vulnerability of Gulliver's clothing, that is, is a symbol three degrees removed from what it signifies: damage to Gulliver's clothes is symbolic of damage to Gulliver's body, which, in turn, is emblematic of damage to Gulliver's self-esteem.

These incidents of injury and destruction are thus pervasive in Gulliver's travels, as one is reminded by the recurrence, very striking when one is attuned to it, of words such as "hurt," "injury," "damage," "accident," "mischief," "misfortune," and "spoiled." Once his attention is aroused to what is going on physically in Gulliver's Travels, the reader senses the oblique appearance of this pervading vulnerability motif even in passages which really focus on something quite different. For example: "His Majesty [the Emperor of Blefuscu] presented me . . . with his Picture at full length, which I put immediately into one of my Gloves, to keep it from being hurt." In *Gulliver's Travels* Swift never allows us to forget that there is a pathetic fragility in his objects, both animate and inanimate. Swift's conception of Gulliver reminds us of Pope's sense of the vulnerability of the china jar which is Belinda's virtue. The Augustan mind in one of its most significant moods senses man thus as a little delicate cage of bones and skin constantly, if not always consciously, trembling before the likelihood of accidental damage or destruction. This is an image which we encounter increasingly following the impact of the philosophic naturalism of the Renaissance. Sir John Davies, still writing early enough to retain a feeling for man's essential dignity, expresses the idea this way:

> I know I am one of Nature's little Kings,
> Yet to the least and vilest things am thrall.

Pope in his more formal, oratorical moments is similarly possessed by a sense that, although man is the "Great Lord of all things," he is yet paradoxically "a prey to all" because, like Gulliver fearing for his eyes in Lilliput and for his body in Brobdingnag, he is "so weak, so little, and so blind." Even John Gay, satirizing a lady's passion for old china, moralizes in the same strain:

> If all that's frail we must despise,
> No human view or scheme is wise.

This conservative consciousness of the limitations of man persists in the eighteenth century up through serious humanists like Johnson and Burke. Johnson, for all his massive insistence on the freedom of the will and for all his own passionate personal incarnation of the Promethean spirit, reminds Boswell that "There is nothing . . . too little for so little a creature as man." And Burke insists on the necessity to human life of "superadded ideas" (ideas of an hereditary nobility, for example) "to cover the defects of our naked, shivering nature." Burke's figure reminds us of the image of Gulliver stripped and thus forlorn before the puzzled Houyhnhnm. The repeated variations on this theme of the inadequacy of secularized man throughout that body of eighteenth-century literature which derives its primary vision most clearly from Renaissance humanism (I am speaking mainly of the work of Pope, Swift, Johnson, Burke, and Gibbon) present us with the eighteenth-century version of Shakespeare's consciousness, as expressed in *King Lear*, of the vast spiritual embarrassment implicit in the idea of a wholly naturalistic, "unaccommodated" man. And yet, participating also in a Newtonian, Lockian, naturalistic view of things (Swift, for one, constantly betrays his predicament by his instinctively materialistic images, which suggest his debt to Newtonian physics and optics), none of these major humanists of the English eighteenth century is able to find a wholly satisfactory principle for redeeming, or even ameliorating, human vulnerability. Hence, perhaps, the violence of the aged Swift, the masochistic spiritual agonizings of the aged Johnson. Gulliver's pride is mocked by the liability of his own frail person to the degradation of injury. Gulliver's intellectual vainglory becomes the more ironically empty the more his body, which is regarded as intimately allied to his almost material soul, reveals its fragility.

IV

Swift seems to have provided within the text of *Gulliver's Travels* materials for some further speculations about these pervasive concrete reminders of the vulnerability of man and the fragility of the physical objects with which he is fond of associating himself. In the voyage of Brobdingnag, we are told in a voice which sounds perhaps more Swiftian than Gulliverian of a "little old Treatise" treasured now only by elderly women and the more credulous vulgar, a copy of which Glumdalclitch has been given by her governess. The burden of this mysterious little book, we are told, is precisely the theme of the physical vulnerability of man: the book shows "how diminutive, contemptible, and helpless an Animal . . . [is] Man in his own Nature." It emphasizes, like Johnson's version of Juvenal in *London*, man's inability to defend himself against the accidents of injury, and argues that "the very Laws of Nature absolutely required we should have been made in the Beginning, of a Size more large and robust, not so liable to Destruction from every little Accident of a Tile falling from an House, or a Stone cast from the Hand of a Boy, or of being drowned in a little Brook." Here we might say that Swift avails himself of the humanist myth of The Decay of Nature just because the traditional formulation of The Fall no longer impels instinctive acceptance. In other words, Swift is making philosophic use of the myth of The Decay of Nature as a surrogate for a Christian explanation of human frailty which is no longer, in Swift's age, artistically employable. Although, as Miss Kathleen Williams reminds us, Godfrey Goodman's *The Fall of Man, or the Corruption of Nature*

(1616) is perhaps the kind of "little old Treatise" Swift has in mind, I think we shall not go far wrong if we associate (even though we do not identify) Glumdalclitch's conservative little book with the Bible itself.

In the fourth voyage Swift returns to the theme expressed in this "little old Treatise" and characteristically again embodies it in the most physical, even fleshly terms: Gulliver proudly strips himself to demonstrate to the Houyhnhnm master the wonders of human clothing, and then hastens to dress again, for, as he explains, "I was shuddering with Cold." The naked but nevertheless warm and comfortable horse, in the following chapter, emphasizes the permanent flaw in the human situation by commenting that something must be gravely wrong with Gulliver's body, which requires "a Fence against Heat and Cold, which [Gulliver says] I was forced to put on and off every Day with Tediousness and Trouble." One way for the conviction of a deep, permanent flaw in human nature to find expression is through myths of The Fall; another way for the same conviction to find expression is through these Swiftian myths of The Decay of Nature and the consequent physical vulnerability of man. Swift's choice of this physical imagery suggests his profound artistic awareness of the inaccessibility to his largely secularized audience of traditional Christian symbols and modes of thought. Earlier in his career, in the allegory of the three brothers and their clothing (like Gulliver's, subject to shocking damage), Swift had demonstrated that his favorite literary action was the articulation of late seventeenth-century Church of England commonplaces with a new physical immediacy which the Lockian age demanded. He is doing just this in his most notorious poems. And in *Gulliver's Travels* we see him doing the same sort of thing as in A *Tale of a Tub* and poems like

"The Progress of Beauty," and doing it still by means of the same fundamental method. The happy physical violence of the imagery in A *Tale of a Tub*, the obvious glee with which Swift depicts coats being ripped and Jack crashing into posts: these destructive physical immediacies anticipate the meaty empirical destructions of *Gulliver's Travels*, the images of painful abrasions, shocking contusions, blisters and arrow wounds, ruined hats and coats and breeches. These are the concrete particulars of fiction, not the abstractions and constructions of exhortation and polemic, and it is here that we can see most clearly that Swift was only secondarily a satirist: he was primarily a maker of fiction.

The vulnerability motif, then, realized by this empirical, emblematic method, is Swift's way of incarnating Gulliver's spiritual embarrassment. By these means Swift realizes in *Gulliver's Travels* his quasi-Christian theme: the theme of the inadequacy of an unassisted self-esteem in redeeming Everyman from his own essential frailties. By these means Swift treats Gulliver the naturalist from a traditional Christian-Humanist point of view: what is done to Gulliver physically during his voyages constitutes Swift's major assault on progressivist naturalism.

But Swift finds that he cannot bruise and wound Gulliver without suffering himself some of Gulliver's agonies, and a suggestion of the sympathetic pain which Swift experiences lies in the pathos of many of these injuries. What we discover when we probe into some of the means by which *Gulliver's Travels* creates the illusion of life is what we are now learning to recognize in everything Swift wrote—his quick sympathetic humanity.

Recent Byron Scholarship *

BY LESLIE A. MARCHAND

Scholarship and criticism in the past thirty years have substantially increased our knowledge and widened our understanding of Byron. Scholars in this period have had the advantage of an impressive amount of new biographical material brought to light in the twenties when the centennial of Byron's death (1924) encouraged a spurt of interest in the poet. That fruitful decade saw the publication of *Astarte* (1921), with letters not in the 1905 private printing, and the two volumes of *Lord Byron's Correspondence* (1922), containing the extremely revealing and valuable letters to Lady Melbourne, Hobhouse, and Kinnaird (edited, and considerably bowdlerized, without indication of omissions, by the fourth John Murray). These volumes compelled drastic reappraisal in both the biographical and critical fields. The centennial year itself saw the publication

* Parts of this article have been published in the *English Miscellany*, No. 3, Rome, 1952. They are reprinted here, with some revisions, with the kind permission of the Editor, Professor Mario Praz.

of Ethel Mayne's revised life of Byron, and Harold Nicolson's perceptive *Byron: The Last Journey*, a detached analysis of the confusion and discord of Byron's last days that tender-minded Byron admirers have often regarded as cynical. This was followed by John Drinkwater's warmhearted but somewhat soft-headed *The Pilgrim of Eternity* (1925). At the end of the decade appeared the life of Lady Byron by Ethel Mayne (1929), enriched by a vast quantity of unpublished letters and other documents from the Lovelace collection (though she was restricted in the use of that material by Lady Lovelace), and finally the suave and on the whole keenly discerning biography by André Maurois (1930).

Despite the errors resulting from a not sufficiently close study of sources or weighing of conflicting evidence, despite the omissions and the liberties taken with chronology for the sake of dramatic impact, and despite the scanty attention granted Byron's poetry, Maurois's biography revealed a rational appreciation, a tolerance for Byron's moral aberrations, and a psychological acuteness which stimulated interest in the complex personality of the man and set the tone of Byron studies in the years that followed. With all its shortcomings Maurois's volume encouraged a turning from apologetics and narrow controversy over the poet's sins to a frank acceptance of Byron's eighteenth-century and Regency outlook and conduct as a part of the whole man— an attitude which did not lessen esteem for his poetic accomplishment nor darken his character.

In biography and the materials of biography the Byron scholarship of the past thirty years has been unexpectedly fruitful, chiefly because of the appearance of large numbers of letters and other documents in public and private collections. It was commonly thought, after the revelations of the Lovelace papers in *Astarte* and the publication of the letters in the Dorchester collection in the two-volume Murray edition of the *Correspondence*, that the last important biographical sources had been tapped. But careful scholars were aware that much remained partly or wholly unexplored in widely scattered collections. Byron letters and Byroniana in considerable quantity have become available for study in American libraries during recent years, notably in the Morgan Library, the Berg Collection of the New York Public Library, the Huntington, and in the university libraries of Texas, Yale, and Harvard. Most of the Byron letters in the Ashley Library, now in the British Museum, were published in the pretentious two-volume bibliography which T. J. Wise launched in 1932 and 1933. And through the generosity of the Murrays, the greatest Byron collection of all, that in the famous publishing house at 50 Albemarle Street, has yielded to scholars in recent years many unused and valuable manuscript sources.

In Italy Count Gamba, after having withheld them for many years, finally made accessible the papers of the Countess Teresa Guiccioli, including 156 letters and notes of Byron written in Italian to the Countess, and her own unpublished manuscript "Vie de Lord Byron en Italie." (These papers are now in the Biblioteca Classense in Ravenna.) The Byron letters in this collection were published first in Maria Borgese's posthumous *L'Appassionata di Byron* (1949) in the Italian text with innumerable errors of transcription and some omissions, and in the same year in excellent English translation by the Marchesa Iris Origo in her *The Last Attachment*, with the correct and complete Italian text in an appendix.

In the following year the house of Murray published a two-volume selection of Byron's letters bearing the title

Byron: A Self-Portrait. Peter Quennell, the editor, announced in his foreword that the edition included fifty-six hitherto unprinted letters and thirty-six in which passages omitted in earlier publication had been restored. Some of the scholarly shortcomings of these volumes have already been pointed out in reviews (for example, in Samuel C. Chew's critique in the New York *Herald Tribune Book Review,* April 15, 1950, page 6, and my own in the New York *Times Book Review,* June 4, 1950, page 17). Quennell's notes are negligible in quantity and sometimes in error, and often they gloss the most obvious things, leaving without comment names or allusions needing some explanation. Six of the letters starred as previously unpublished had already appeared in part or whole, five being in Prothero's edition published fifty years previously. Two more are forgeries of the self-styled Major Byron, according to his biographer, T. G. Ehrsam. Many of the letters were published from earlier printed texts, when suppressed passages might have been restored from the extant and now easily available holographs. Nevertheless, the new letters in the edition have a biographical significance which makes their publication a boon to Byron scholarship.

Quennell had previously written two biographical studies of the poet. In 1935 he attempted in his *Byron: The Years of Fame* to reinterpret Byron's meteoric London career against the background of the picturesque Regency social and political life and to cast light upon the paradoxes of the Byronic temperament. Quennell ranged freely among the letters and journals already published, and with little respect for chronology quoted and paraphrased striking phrases and characteristic pronouncements with a brilliance which lends persuasiveness to his interpretations. Many of his observations on Byron's character are shrewd enough, but often he is betrayed into a generalization which a closer study of biographical detail would controvert or qualify.

Although he had access to the Murray files, Quennell used surprisingly little that was new in documentary source material. He did, however, quote some significant passages (already printed by Maurois) from Hobhouse's marginalia in a copy of Moore's *Life*. From Hobhouse's hints, and from other sources not indicated, Quennell drew some discerning conclusions about Byron's sexual ambivalence which no previous biographer had stated so specifically.

Quennell's sequel, *Byron in Italy* (1941), more diffuse in its speculative analysis and more sketchy in its narrative, achieved added scintillation by the quotation of Byron's own immensely entertaining letters from Italy already published in the *Letters and Journals* and the *Correspondence*. But the author made even less use than in the earlier volume of unpublished sources available to him.

Two careful biographical studies of Byron's early years were published in 1948. Willis W. Pratt's *Byron at Southwell* traced the details of Byron's holidays spent at Burgage Manor and Newstead during his Harrow and Cambridge years, with particular stress on the composition and publication of his early poems. The retreading of familiar ground is justified by the inclusion of some new letters and poems and the correction of others from the manuscript collections of the University of Texas. Richer in background and more illuminating in interpretation is William A. Borst's *Lord Byron's First Pilgrimage*. Borst made a wider survey of the political and personal attitudes which colored Byron's reactions to his exotic experiences than had ever been made before. Particularly valuable is the light thrown on the first two cantos of *Childe Harold* and on the gradual molding of the Philhellenism which helped make Byron a "Citizen of the World" and continued to color his cosmopolitan distaste for the narrower prejudices of the "tight little island." The author's extensive and judicious study of contemporary travels, memoirs, and records compensates for the fact that he lacked access to the unpublished portions of the Hobhouse diary which fill in many details of the journey.

Doris Langley Moore's "The Burning of Byron's Memoirs" (*Cornhill*, Winter, 1958–59) recounts the oft-told tale with the aid of new documentary material from the Lovelace papers, the Hobhouse diary, the Murray collection, and other sources, and shows that although Murray and Hobhouse were the prime movers in the affair, Lady Byron, without ever expressing an overt wish, exerted a subtle influence on events, partly because she was not eager for Byron's story of the marriage and separation to get abroad.

By far the most important contribution to Byron biography in recent years, however, is the illumination of the fascinating and productive Italian period, and particularly the clarification of Byron's relations with the Countess Teresa Guiccioli. Austin K. Gray's *Teresa or Her Demon Lover* (1945), in spite of its lurid subtitle (changed in the English edition to *The Story of Byron's Last Mistress*) and despite the sometimes disconcerting fictionized style, was written after several years of careful research. Although he added depth to the picture of the love affair which colored all Byron's activities in Italy during his last years, Gray was seriously handicapped, as Quennell had been, by not having seen the Gamba papers.

It was fortunate that these papers should have come into the hands of the Marchesa Iris Origo, who with scholarly acumen and imaginative insight molded them into the most revealing biographical study of Byron which has appeared in many years: *The Last Attachment* (1949). Her exhaustive research brought together pertinent letters and documents from the secret archives of the Vatican and the libraries and state archives of half a dozen Italian cities, as well as unpublished letters from American and English collections.

With a scholar's objectivity the Marchesa Origo has told in a lively and unaffected style the intricate and often painful story of Byron's liaison—practically a marriage—with Teresa Guiccioli, showing how Byron's love for Teresa, at first a genuine passion, faded into a conjugal fondness when his loyalty survived his outworn emotions. With equal care and realism she traced Byron's political sympathies and affiliations in Italy, revealing how completely he entered into the life of the people of Ravenna. The cumulative evidence of his important Italian years gives new glimpses into the mind of the Byron who created *Beppo* and *Don Juan* as well as the more tortured and melancholy poems of his later moods.

My *PMLA* article "Lord Byron and Count Alborghetti" (Vol. LXIV, Dec., 1949) gives additional details concerning Byron's Ravenna associations and his curious friendship with the Secretary General of the Lower Romagna.

A substantial contribution to an understanding of Byron's complex relations with his Pisan circle and particularly of the far-reaching repercussions of the affray with the dragoon is made by C. L. Cline in his *Byron, Shelley, and Their Pisan Circle* (1952). Cline has delved into Byron's correspondence with the British Chargé d'Affaires, Edward Dawkins, and a great mass of court records and letters in the State Archives of Pisa, Florence, and Lucca. Centering upon this one event, the study reaches out to include a comprehensive consideration of the whole drama of Byron's life in Tuscany.

An ambitious compendium of contemporary records of Byron is to be found in *His Very Self and Voice: Collected Conversations of Lord Byron*, edited by Ernest J. Lovell, Jr. (1954). Although it arbitrarily omits two of the most famous reports of Byron's conversation, those of Medwin and Lady Blessington, on the ground that they will be edited separately, and although its chronological arrangement tends to make for disjointed fragmentation of some unified contemporary records, it is a valuable gathering of material, some of which is now difficult of access. The editor has added a few items from unpublished manuscript sources including some passages of John Cam Hobhouse's diary and Teresa Guiccioli's "*Vie de Lord Byron en Italie.*" These contemporary accounts (the editor has gone beyond his original intention to include much that is not a simple record of conversations) reveal that Byron never had his proper Boswell. Moore's transcriptions hardly give the colloquial flavor. The Countess Guiccioli, to use the Marchesa Origo's phrase, "has no ear for any style but her own." Hobhouse merely paraphrases or summarizes the sense of Byron's conversations. Medwin (not here included) comes nearest to capturing the racy flavor of Byron's talk.

G. Wilson Knight's *Lord Byron's Marriage* (1956) uses the key of two bawdy poems, written after Byron's death by someone (Knight attributes them with less than conclusive arguments to George Colman the Younger) who apparently knew a great deal about Byron's private life, to unlock the mystery of the Byron separation. Knight's thesis is that the innocent Lady Byron, having indiscreetly revealed to her family and friends her husband's homosexual propensities, was persuaded to leave him. But the purpose of the book is not merely to offer a solution to the Byron mystery. It attempts to assemble overwhelming proof of the strength of the homosexual inclination in Byron and to show the extent to which it dominated his life. It is unfortunate, however, that the now abundant evidence of these tendencies should have been brought before the public in a book that combines demonstrable facts and patent errors, shrewd guesses and absurd distortions. Professor Knight has weakened his case by the manner in which he has tortured evidence to fit a thesis. The author's *idée fixe* has driven him to some ridiculous conclusions. His desire to discount Byron's heterosexual experience has led him to suggest that the poet's relations with Caroline Lamb and Teresa Guiccioli were only platonic, and to attempt to upset the strong evidence of the poet's liaison with his half-sister Augusta by bringing in the undocumented nonsense of the late Richard Edgcumbe. In spite of all its faults, however, Knight's book is likely to make a mark in Byron studies just as did *Astarte*, which was equally lopsided in presentation, but which gave new dimensions to the study of Byron's life and character. In like manner, Knight's one-track thesis and cavalier handling of biographical evidence is offset by imaginative hunches which may illuminate facets of Byron's personality that have not been thoroughly explored—such, for example, as the feminine traits observed by many of his contemporaries.

My own *Byron: A Biography* (3 vols., 1957) has made the fullest use of material published and unpublished and is deeply indebted to all of the works mentioned above. As I said in the preface, it was my aim "to evaluate my source materials, old and new, as if they were all new, and not to give undue weight to some document merely because it has not been used before." The principal new sources are unpublished portions of the Hobhouse diaries, letters of Byron and to Byron in the Murray collection, the Gamba papers, including the manuscript *"Vie de Lord Byron en Italie"* by Teresa Guiccioli, documents from the Archives of the State in Italy and Greece, and miscellaneous manuscript evidence from the Byron collections in the British Museum and in American libraries.

Several collateral studies and publications containing source material are of particular importance to Byron biography. Iris Origo's *Allegra* (1935—revised in the light of recently discovered documents and letters and published in her *A Measure of Love*, 1957) tells the pathetic story of Byron's unhappy relations with Claire Clairmont and the illegitimate daughter she bore him.

R. Glynn Grylls (Lady Mander) in her *Claire Clairmont* (1939) brought together much information about that unfortunate and irritating mistress of Byron, some of it newly published from the Shelley papers in the long inaccessible collection of Lord Abinger. Unfortunately not much of the new material touches directly upon Claire's relations with Byron.

A richer storehouse for the biographer is the selection from the vast number of letters from women to Byron in the Murray collection published by George Paston (Miss E. M. Symonds) in the *Cornhill Magazine* in 1934 (later added to and printed in book form by Peter Quennell with the title *To Lord Byron*, 1939). These letters, though sometimes carelessly transcribed, reveal the fanatic devotion inspired by Byron not only in the women with whom he was closely involved, such as Lady Caroline Lamb, Lady Frances Webster, Mary Chaworth, and Claire Clairmont, but also in such relative strangers as Lady Falkland, Henrietta D'Ussières, and Harriette Wilson, the famous courtesan of the Regency.

Michael Joyce's *My Friend H: John Cam Hobhouse* (1948) is valuable for its inclusion of some of Hobhouse's letters to Byron in the Murray collection and some of the unpublished portions of the Hobhouse diary, the most interesting being the detailed account of how Hobhouse prevented Byron from eloping with Caroline Lamb.

David Cecil in *The Young Melbourne* (1939) has devoted a chapter to Caroline Lamb's relations with Byron. Adding some facts from a number of unpublished family papers to the already familiar sources in contemporary memoirs and letters, he has set the episode against the light of the varied personalities and the Regency background. Dame Una Pope-Hennessy in "The Byrons at Seaham" in her *Durham Company* (1941) has added little to Ethel Mayne's account of the marriage and honeymoon of Byron.

The complete and accurate text of the journal of Edward E. Williams, the friend of Shelley and Byron at Pisa, edited from the manuscript in the British Museum by Frederick L. Jones (1951), indicates, what was not clear in Richard Garnett's curtailed edition of 1902, that Williams was much closer to Byron and more devoted to him than has commonly been supposed. Of great service to Byron biography also are Jones's *The Letters of Mary W. Shelley* (1944) and *Mary Shelley's Journal* (1947).

Of other publications contributing fresh facts of peripheral interest may be mentioned *Byron, Hobhouse, and Foscolo* (1949) by E. R. Vincent, which concerns Byron's indirect relations with Foscolo, the unacknowledged supplier of facts for Hobhouse's *Historical Illustrations of the Fourth Canto of Childe Harold*. *Les Philhellènes et la Guerre de l'Indépendance*, edited by Eugène Dalleggio for

138 ❦ LESLIE A. MARCHAND

the Institut Français d'Athènes (1949), contains a few letters from the Greek Deputies to Byron and others to members of the Greek Committee in London. "A Greek Folk-
song Copied for Lord Byron," by C. M. Dawson and A. E.
Raubitschek (*Hesperia,* 1945), concerns Byron's relations
with the residents of Athens in 1810 and 1811. And C. G.
Brouzas' studies of Teresa Macri, the "Maid of Athens"
(*Byron's Maid of Athens: Her Family and Surroundings,*
West Virginia University, 1949) and all her relations and
descendants, though they are in many points pedantic and
inaccurate, add substantial bits to the sparse knowledge of
Byron's Athenian adventures.

In the realm of interpretation of the Byronic mind, two
books first published on the Continent, one in Italy and one
in France, have had their chief impact in English translations. Both were stimulated by the new and startling biographical sources in *Astarte* and the *Correspondence.* Mario
Praz's *The Romantic Agony* (first published in Italy, 1930;
in England, 1933; second English edition, 1951) examines
Byron's satanism, his embodiment of the ideal of *l'homme
fatal,* and his conception of the *caractère maudit.* Praz, who
ranges at will through most of the literatures of Europe, has
made a useful comparative study of these significant and
compelling traits of the romantic mind and has pointed out
sources and far-reaching influences of Byron in European
literature.

Charles du Bos in *Byron and the Need of Fatality* (Paris,
1929; London, 1932) has ridden the dark horse of Byron's
fatalistic creed over the familiar biographical ground. Along
the way, however, he occasionally transcends his too-rigid
thesis and gives a psychological interpretation which is exceptionally keen. Thus he says: "The Byronic basis is, in
very truth, that inborn melancholy, due perhaps to a heart

. . . essentially static, which could not feel its own pulsations unless they were accelerated to fever-point." But this generalization of du Bos, easily supported by Byron's own pronouncement: "The great object of life is sensation—to feel that we exist, even though in pain," takes into account only one side of the Byronic temperament.

C. E. Vulliamy's *Byron: With a View of the Kingdom of Cant and a Dissection of the Byronic Ego* (1948) seeks to explain Byron in terms of a "temperamental dualism," looking first at "The dark frustrated hero and rebel," and then at "the rollicking sensualist and adventurer." The aphoristic style of the book is tiring after a few chapters, and most readers will conclude that it tends to run into critical ranting divorced from biographical reality.

A number of recent studies have focused attention upon the less strained and more natural Byron of the satires and particularly of *Don Juan*. Two full-length critiques of that poem appeared in 1945. Paul G. Trueblood's *The Flowering of Byron's Genius*, somewhat too solemn in its systematic analysis to catch the overtones of humor and caprice in Byron's volatile nature, contends that the later cantos of the satire reveal a progressively serious purpose and a growing "inclination toward social satire and revolutionary indoctrination." The evidence is selective and hardly convincing to anyone acquainted with the manifold moods of the poet.

A more penetrating critique is Elizabeth F. Boyd's *Byron's Don Juan*. With closer study and richer understanding of the varied personal and literary ingredients of that "versified Aurora Borealis," Miss Boyd has illuminated every facet of Byron's epic satire without advancing a categorical thesis. Particularly valuable is her analysis of the literary background of the poem. But she has not been blinded by her own impressive array of literary sources, and remains aware that Byron's "intense personal experience" has dominated the literary material.

E. D. H. Johnson in "Don Juan in England" (*English Literary History*, June, 1944) has emphasized how completely Byron misjudged the moral temper of his middle-class readers in making his accusations of cant and hypocrisy apply to all Englishmen, whereas they were pertinent only to the Regency society he had known most intimately. And T. G. Steffan in "The Token-Web, the Sea-Sodom, and Canto I of *Don Juan*" (*Studies in English*, University of Texas, 1947) has traced the circumstances of Byron's personal history and examined the Venetian environment which contributed to the realistic transference of experience to the beginning of *Don Juan*.

Mark Van Doren, in a half-epigrammatic, half-paradoxical style, has tried *Don Juan* by the touchstone of the comic spirit (in *The Noble Voice*, 1946) and has found it lacking, though he admits that Byron "flounders brilliantly," "has missed the heart of comedy at which he aimed" only by a margin, and contributes untiringly to our amusement. "Long though *Don Juan* is, it grows steadily fresher," he says. "We never quite decide that he is wasting our time. . . . Only a poet of tremendous powers could endure as he does, lacking proper food."

"Irony and Image in Byron's *Don Juan*," by Ernest J. Lovell, Jr., an essay included in *The Major English Romantic Poets: A Symposium in Reappraisal*, edited by Clarence D. Thorpe, *et al* (1957), stresses the thematic unity of the poem—"the basically ironic theme of appearance versus reality." Lovell maintains that Byron's irony "is neither shallow, cynical, insincere, incidental, nor typically romantic. . . . It is, instead, ordinarily the precise, necessary, fully orchestrated, and artistically functional expression of his own hard-won point of view. . . ." In the last section he shows how, by the standards of the new critics themselves, many of whom are inclined to belittle or neglect Byron, he belongs to the "age of Irony and Ambiguity, the Period of the Poetic Paradox."

Willis W. Pratt's article, "Byron and Some Current Patterns of Thought," in the same volume, examines the reasons for the adverse judgments of Eliot and others on Byron's poetry and finds the answer partly in the fact that he is too often judged by his adolescent, sentimental, and cheaply rhetorical work. But, Pratt maintains, Byron has been condemned for qualities which should link him with the thought of modern poets: the duality of his character which sprang from confusions and disenchantments of life no different in kind from those that shaped an Auden or a Pound; his scorn of metaphysical speculation, which formed a part of his distaste for obscurity of thought; his skepticism of systems; his inability to make up his mind, which stemmed from a restless desire to range widely in his thinking and not to stop at comfortable conclusions.

My own short essay in the same volume, "Byron and the Modern Spirit," stresses Byron's hard-headedness, his refusal to believe that the romantic dream was other than of the mind's creation, and yet his clinging to the dream as an acknowledged part of man's life. "His agnostic humility touches more sympathetic chords in our time than the philosophic certainties of other men."

The most impressive contribution to the study of *Don Juan*, however, is the four-volume Variorum edited by Truman Guy Steffan and Willis W. Pratt (1957). The first volume, *The Making of a Masterpiece*, is a gathering of Steffan's several thorough studies of the background, composition, and revisions of the poem. Beginning with an attempt to bring together all that Byron "thought, felt, did, and said about the writing and publishing of Don Juan," he proceeds in "The Anvil of Composition" to analyze the poet's additions and emendations and the motives that led him to digressive stanzas. In this he demonstrates that, despite Byron's claim that he could not furbish ("I am like the Tiger; if I miss the first spring, I go growling back to my Jungle again; but if I *do hit*, it is crushing"), he was not less eager than other poets to avoid the cliché and to find the right word.

The editors joined labors in establishing the text (volumes II and III), starting with the first editions and showing all the variants, additions, and cancellations from extant manuscripts, including every word that Byron wrote and then deleted. Pratt's notes in the fourth volume include those of Moore and others in the 1833 edition and those of E. H. Coleridge in the Murray edition of 1898 to 1904 (identified) and his own additional clarifications and more precise identifications and translations. He has also given some biographical information hitherto suppressed or not known. It may seem to scholars that the annotation extends to the obvious, but it is a most useful reference work for any further study of the poem. (For a detailed analysis and some emendations of the Don Juan Variorum see the review by Carl R. Woodring in The Journal of English and Germanic Philology, Vol. LVII, No. 2, April, 1958.)

Alan Lang Strout, in an excellent critical edition of John Bull's Letter to the Right Honorable Lord Byron, an anonymous contemporary critique of the first two cantos of Don Juan, demonstrates that the author was John G. Lockhart, sketches in the background of the critical climate in England at the time the poem was published, and summarizes the whole treatment of Byron in *Blackwood's Magazine*.

No critic of modern times has been so completely swept away by Byron and by his own rhetoric as G. Wilson Knight, who, in his essay on the poet in *The Burning Oracle* (1939), has made use of all the superlatives in the language to make Byron the equal of Shakespeare, even in his dramas. Knight's lack of critical balance makes a burlesque of his judgments, even when they have some reasonable basis. The same lack of perspective is apparent in his *Byron: Christian Virtues* (1952), wherein he goes almost as far as Teresa Guiccioli in endowing the poet with angelic wings.

The curious dichotomy of Byron's literary aims and accomplishments is analyzed with clarity and acuteness in W. J. Calvert's *Byron: Romantic Paradox* (1935). Calvert sees Byron's allegiance to classicism in his "constant emphasis on the immediate reality," his hatred of humbug, and his "conscientious and consistent dwelling with the certainty of facts." But though his most compelling literary inspiration, to find relief for the intensity of his feelings, drove him in another direction, his respect for fact and reality clung to him and in the end brought him back to "the sober light of the reasonable" in *Don Juan*, which is classic in spirit if not in form.

The best, clearest, and most detailed account of Byron's political interests, affiliations, and activities in England is given in three articles by David V. Erdman. "Lord Byron and the Genteel Reformers" (*PMLA*, December, 1941) stresses the influence of Lady Oxford and her radical Whig friends in directing into practical politics Byron's native rebelliousness, and examines the subtleties of personal ambition, altruistic motives, and social forces which governed the behavior of a "radical aristocrat" in Regency England. "Lord Byron as Rinaldo" (*PMLA*, March, 1942) follows in further detail the parliamentary career and ambitions of Byron and stresses two significant and neglected facts: Byron evinced greater interest in political activities than he later pretended, seeing the goal of statesman and orator as the most attractive for his own personal success. And his earnestness and the spirit of opposition carried him farther to the left than was approved by most of his Whig friends and won him the approbation of the extreme radicals, with whom his aristocratic sensibilities, however, would not permit him to associate without reserve. In "Byron and Revolt in England" (*Science and Society*, Summer, 1947), Erdman has made a penetrating study of Byron's attitude toward and influence on the revolutionary spirit in England during the post-Napoleonic unrest.

Byron's attitudes toward religion have been the subjects of two rather extensive recent studies. E. W. Marjarum's *Byron as Skeptic and Believer* (1938) views the shifting course of the poet's speculations and instinctive reactions to doctrinal Christianity; his skepticism arising from his reading in rationalistic literature and from a desire to escape the fears of an ingrained Calvinism; his tentative acceptance of "Natural Religion," partly under the influence of Rousseau and Shelley; and his toying with Catholicism because of its emotional and picturesque appeal rather than because he had any conviction of the truth of its dogmas. Marjarum insists that though Byron once called himself a deist, his "agitated denial and brooding depression," a heritage of his Calvinistic training, differentiated him markedly from Voltaire and the English rationalists.

In his chapter on Byron in the third volume of his *Reli-*

gious Trends in English Poetry (1949) Hoxie Fairchild has made a keen analysis of the egocentric Byronic temper, "frustrated not only by external reality but by inward division." The "illusion of infinite self-expansion," which in Fairchild's view is the quintessential fallacy of Romanticism, is blocked in Byron by his inability to deceive himself. That self-honesty, however, Fairchild ascribes to the weakness of a disintegrated personality rather than to strength, finding that in Byron the craving for self-deification, the core of romantic religion, "is short-circuited by the very blatancy of his egotism," and that he ends by betraying Romanticism "in deriding his own bluster." As Fairchild said memorably in his earlier book *The Romantic Quest*, Byron's is "the history of a mind too idealistic to refrain from blowing bubbles, and too realistic to refrain from pricking them." Examining Byron's specific religious attitudes, Fairchild concludes: "This realistic sense of human limitation and human evil, combined with the superstitious strain in his character, prevented him from denying that Christianity which he was never able to accept." Sentimental deism, he finds, "was the only positive form of belief to which he [Byron] could lay claim."

On the whole there is a remarkable clarity and objectivity in Fairchild's account which contrasts with the treatment of the subject by nineteenth-century apologists who felt constrained to prove that Byron was basically a Christian. The author's Anglo-Catholic convictions, however, do inevitably color his interpretation of Byron's character and limit his appreciation of the poet's speculative thinking in *Don Juan* and elsewhere. It is a temptation to put beside Fairchild's judgments here, shaped by his present faith, his equally cogent remarks in *The Romantic Quest* (1931): "But one may justly be irritated by the common assumption that a man who refrains from believing in lofty and inspiring ideas for which there is no evidence whatever necessarily has an inferior mind. Although no one would undertake to prove that Byron was a profound thinker, he possessed a quality which many supposedly profound thinkers lack—a sense of the toughness of facts and an inability to dupe himself about them. . . . Beneath all his protective histrionism, his mind possessed a certain desperate integrity which should command respect."

Several recent attempts to relate Byron's life and works to the modern world are of particular interest. Bertrand Russell in his essay "Byron and the Modern World" (*Journal of the History of Ideas*, January, 1940; included, slightly abridged, as a chapter in his *History of Western Philosophy*, 1945) has emphasized the far-reaching European reputation and influence of Byron, the aristocratic rebel whose potent support of the "revolt of solitary instincts against social bonds" has been a boon to freedom, but, interpreted in terms of Nietzschean self-realization, has encouraged the lawless ego and hindered social cooperation.

But of greater significance, after a period when the sensational aspects of Byron's life overshadowed interest in his work, is the unapologetic return of several acute critics to a reconsideration of his poetry in terms of modern values. It is not surprising that Harold Nicolson, the constant Byron enthusiast, should have found even in *Childe Harold*, which he admits to be one of the most artificial of Byron's poems, "a central fibre of sincerity" (*The Poetry of Byron*, 1943). More unexpected, in a poet and critic who in precept and practice has magnified the virtues of compactness and richness of symbolic meaning wholly lacking in Byron, is T. S.

Eliot's almost rapturous praise of *Don Juan*, particularly the satire on English society, for its expression of a genuine emotion, its hatred of hypocrisy, and its "reckless raffish honesty" ("Byron," in Bonamy Dobrée's *From Anne to Victoria*, 1937). It is true that Eliot prefaced this enthusiasm with some disparagement of Byron's "sonorous affirmations of the commonplace." Another English poet, Ronald Bottrall, in discussing "Byron and the Colloquial Tradition in English Poetry" (*The Criterion*, January, 1939), is even more enthusiastic, finding *Don Juan* "the greatest long poem in English since *The Dunciad*." Taking exception to Eliot's strictures on Byron's "imperceptiveness to the word" and "schoolboy command of language," Bottrall maintains that "Byron by bringing to his verse the colloquial force of his prose vivified and renewed the English poetic tradition."

Herbert Read's monograph on Byron (1951) concludes that at the base of all Byron's work is "an essential sanity, a hatred of sham and humbug, generous impulses and manly courage." Finally, he says, Byron was "a free spirit, and if we cannot all be free spirits, at least it is good that once at least in a generation there should be a poet who rises above the daily conflict of vice and virtue to view the spectacle with cynical humour."

Ernest J. Lovell's analysis of Byron's concept and treatment of nature (*Byron: The Record of a Quest*, 1949) concludes with a critical postscript on "The Contemporaneousness of Byron" which in a sense elaborates Herbert Read's concept of "a free spirit." His very "mobility" enabled Byron to do justice as no one had done before to the complicated aspects of the world within and without him. "Nowhere," the author says, "is Byron so modern as here, where he sets up a state of tension between the complexities of several points of view." In short, Byron did not "suppress nine-tenths of his awareness of the world around him." To demonstrate that is perhaps the best service of modern scholarship to the study of Byron.

The Troubled Sleep of Arthur Gordon Pym

BY WALTER E. BEZANSON

The Southern Literary Messenger for January, 1837, gave most of four pages to an episode called "Arthur Gordon Pym. No. 1." It was unsigned, but the table of contents on the inside of the blue wrapper noted that this piece, along with two poems, four reviews, and a brief statement of his resignation as editor, was "By E. A. Poe." The following month a second installment appeared, and that was all. Some eighteen months later Harper and Brothers issued an anonymous book of 198 pages. It was Pym again, but under a new guise. What Poe was now up to is best conveyed by the full original title, not reprinted in modern editions:

*THE NARRATIVE OF ARTHUR GORDON PYM
OF NANTUCKET:*

COMPRISING THE DETAILS OF A MUTINY AND ATROCIOUS BUTCH-
ERY ON BOARD THE AMERICAN BRIG GRAMPUS, ON HER WAY TO
THE SOUTH SEAS, IN THE MONTH OF JUNE, 1827. WITH AN AC-
COUNT OF THE RECAPTURE OF THE VESSEL BY THE SURVIVERS;
THEIR SHIPWRECK AND SUBSEQUENT HORRIBLE SUFFERINGS FROM

FAMINE; THEIR DELIVERANCE BY MEANS OF THE BRITISH SCHOONER
JANE GUY; THE BRIEF CRUISE OF THIS LATTER VESSEL IN THE ANT-
ARCTIC OCEAN; HER CAPTURE, AND THE MASSACRE OF HER CREW
AMONG A GROUP OF ISLANDS IN THE EIGHTY-FOURTH PARALLEL
OF SOUTHERN LATITUDE; TOGETHER WITH THE INCREDIBLE AD-
VENTURES AND DISCOVERIES STILL FARTHER SOUTH TO WHICH
THAT DISTRESSING CALAMITY GAVE RISE.

Clearly Poe and Harper were exploiting the contemporary
tradition of the cheaply printed record of disasters at sea.
Americans of the thirties belonged to a seafaring nation;
accounts of voyages by whalers, traders, and explorers were
standard fare. A special fillip of the Pym narrative was the
Antarctic section: no one had been further than 74°S., there
was much speculation as to what might be found there, and
the American Congress was about to underwrite a major
exploration—the famous Wilkes Expedition of 1840. Ex-
cited by the plan of trying to hoax his contemporaries, Poe
had been plundering voyage literature and boning up on
things nautical.[1] He was after the popular market, not the
literati. He offered a shocker and wanted it believed.

"A d----d lie!" cried William Burton in *The Gentle-
man's Magazine*, comparing his mood to that of an Indian
who had tried to scalp a Tory wearing a peruke. Even a
Philadelphia editor could spot the nautical errors, the "various discrepancies," the events "outraging possibility"; Burton's reply to the hoax was "to throw it away in contempt." [2]
Even assuming he had not seen the two original installments
of *Pym*, the intricate rationalizations of the Preface, in
which "Pym" acknowledged those printings and tried to
explain them away, gave Burton a tip-off to the whole
shenanigan; he was furious. It seems not to have occurred
to him that if *Pym* could not be taken as fact it might be
taken as fiction. One winces at Poe's capitulation to Burton

two years later: "You once wrote in your magazine a sharp critique upon a book of mine—a very silly book—*Pym*. . . . Your criticism was essentially correct . . . although severe. . . ." [3]

Modern criticism has dealt more kindly with *Pym,* so much so that the chief intention of the present essay is to suggest that its literary worth depends almost entirely on Poe's central technique of dream recital. In such a study one is naturally indebted first to Marie Bonaparte's professional psychiatric study of Poe, in which her concern, as Freud says in a brief Foreword to his pupil's book, is with "the life and work of a great writer with pathological trends," with Poe's personality and "how that personality derived from intense emotional fixations and painful infantile experiences." Mme. Bonaparte, a specialized reader of great integrity, views *Pym* as one of Poe's major Tales of the Mother. Her aim is properly at the latent content of its episodes, as this essay's properly is not; this difference in quarry is a minor theme in what follows. The present essay is also an extension of Patrick Quinn's extremely able, generalized argument, following the French line, that Poe's genius was for dream symbolism and morbid fantasies; it accepts, but does not extend, Quinn's thesis that revolt, deceit, and self-destruction are the primary themes in *Pym*. It profits also from Harry Levin's graceful commentary in which, through examining sources, color symbolism, and subliminal themes, he places *Pym* in that dark corner of the American imagination which is Levin's subject. Finally the essay, by implication rather than by argument, takes issue with Edward Davidson's recent view that *Pym* is an account of a "moral being" engaged in "a quest for understanding" and maturity. [4]

The modern reader takes *Pym* as acknowledged fiction. The problem of verisimilitude therefore has a different cast for us: the air of reality will amuse or dismay according to the skill or obviousness of a given passage. Hoaxing or not, Poe enjoyed few things more than engaging the reader in a surface game of credibility, and at its best this gives much of his work what might be called a secondary charm. His ability to particularize, to play the role of expert, to anticipate disbelief, are all part of the game in most of his fiction, and especially here. At the same time, it is very hard to take *that* aspect of his art very seriously. What we can take seriously, however, is the apocalyptic strain, the boldly ejaculated dream forms that rise from the artifice of plot at frequent intervals.

As *Pym* really consists of three stories, it will be useful first to see clearly the relationship of the separate voyages to one another, and the proportions each occupies in the narrative as a whole:

[Editorial preliminaries—Preface by Pym: 3 pp.]
PROLOGUE: The *Ariel* incident (ch. I: 12 pp.)
PART I: The Wreck of the *Grampus* (chs. II–XIII: 131 pp.)
    Pym in the hold (chs. II–III)
    Story of the mutiny and Pym's rescue (chs. IV–V)
    Recapture of the ship (chs. VI–VIII)
    Adrift on the wreck (chs. IX–XIII)
PART II: The Voyage of the *Jane Guy* (chs. XIV–XXV: 95 pp.)
    Cruising south (chs. XIV–XVI)
    Through the ice-barrier (ch. XVII)
    The strange island of Tsalal (chs. XVIII–XXIV)
    Into the Unknown (ch. XXV)
EPILOGUE: The Chasms of Darkness (Note: 2 pp.)
[Editorial afterword—Note by an anonymous editor: first 3 par.]

The structural pattern here looks firmer than it is, as we shall see.

The *Ariel* incident (ch. I), our narrator tells us, is offered as a preliminary adventure "by way of introduction to a longer and more momentous narrative" (p. 6).[5] A brief, separate story of disaster at sea, the episode is prologue to a world in which meaning is most nearly captured in sudden tableaux or dream pictures, marked by visual intensity and highly charged with emotion. In their purest form these images seem to flash and disappear, giving the sense of an almost instantaneous experience. Since literature is an art form which operates in time, unlike painting, this is an effect rather than a literal achievement. The sloop *Ariel* is made visible by the wand of Pym-Poe-Prospero, and it will disappear in the twinkling of an eye "amid the roaring of the tempest" (p. 14). We have entered a world ruled by magic, miracle, and fortune.

Rising from their warm Nantucket beds on a cold night in late October, young Pym and his friend Augustus Barnard are borne across a moonlit sea by the *Ariel*, crushed and "drowned" by a returning whaler, resurrected out of the deep, brought back by the whaler, and so made to appear at family breakfast without anyone being the wiser. The reader able to grant this incident his *willing suspension of disbelief* is now amply prepared for wonders to follow.

We are taken across this first threshold with considerable skill. The long first paragraph of the *Ariel* episode adopts a no-nonsense air of telling us Pym's background—name, parents, schooling, youth in Nantucket and New Bedford, friendship with Augustus and his family, fascination with far places—and then, presto, comes the night adventure. Events this night run by an absurdly careful timetable. Augustus and Pym retire in a state of intoxication following a party which breaks up at 1:00 A.M. At 1:30 A.M. Augustus startles Pym with the "mad idea" of a night sail, and "in a kind of ecstasy" (p. 7) the two boys dress, rush down to the wharf, and bail out the sloop, which is "nearly half full of water" (p. 7); at a modest reckoning it might now be 2:00 A.M. Casting off, they fly before the night wind at great speed. Augustus, standing at the tiller, his face paler in the moonlight than marble but his hand shaking with agitation, announces that their course is straight out to sea (the first tableau); for "almost half an hour" Pym stares at him in dread; then: " 'For God's sake, Augustus,' I screamed . . . , 'what ails you?—what is the matter?—what *are* you going to do?' " (p. 8); and as Augustus pitches forward into the bilge, "beastly drunk," we may estimate it is 3:00 A.M. A storm breaks, the mast goes over, but "relieved from the terror of immediate death," Pym takes the tiller after binding Augustus to a ringbolt: "when, suddenly, a loud and long scream or yell, as if from the throats of a thousand demons, seemed to pervade the whole atmosphere around and above the boat. Never while I live shall I forget the intense agony of terror I experienced at that moment" (p. 10); this dream of sound must occur at about 3:30 A.M. The rescue of Pym by the crew of the whaler which has run them down is a detailed affair which easily takes us to 4:00 A.M. His resuscitation from "a state bordering very nearly upon death" takes "three hours and a half" (p. 16), bringing us to 7:30 A.M. The whaler docks "about nine o'clock" (p. 16). Pym (with the also rescued Augustus) is thus handily back at the Barnard home for breakfast, "which, luckily, was somewhat late" (p. 16)—at, say, 9:30 A.M.?

The event in this prologue which is least susceptible to belief provides the most memorable image. When the *Penguin* strikes the *Ariel*, she comes about only after a raging argument of "nearly five minutes" (p. 12) between her captain and mate (the first appearance of the mutiny theme). The seamanship that follows is a child's improvisation: the mate launches the jolly boat in the night, in the storm, while the ship is still under way, and as she comes about he seizes the main chains and holds fast. The ship lurches far over, showing her coppered hull nearly to the keel,[6] and there, there the dream-image is:

> The body of a man was seen to be affixed in the most singular manner to the smooth and shining bottom . . . , and beating violently against it with every movement of the hull. After several ineffectual efforts, made during lurches of the ship, and at the imminent risk of swamping the boat, I was finally disengaged from my perilous situation and taken on board— for the body proved to be my own. It appeared that one of the timber-bolts having started and broken a passage through the copper, it had arrested my progress as I passed under the ship, and fastened me in so extraordinary a manner to her bottom. The head of the bolt had made its way through the collar of the green baize jacket I had on, and through the back part of my neck, forcing itself out between two sinews and just below the right ear (p. 13).

It is one of Poe's better "night scenes"—wild, impossible, violent, yet precisely detailed. The fake seamanship and Pym's unlikely endurance fall away before an apocalyptic vision of the self, spread-eagled against the hull, nailed to the copper sheathing, and drowned again and again. Five hours later Pym is eating breakfast, pleased that no one noticed his "jaded appearance" (p. 16). No one in Nantucket ever expressed "the slightest suspicion" that anything untoward had occurred to the boys, nor apparently ever questioned the loss of the *Ariel*. Dreams are private.

The *Ariel* disaster and the "miraculous deliverance" from it (p. 17) set the tone of what follows. Eighteen months later the young men (Pym is now about eighteen, Augustus twenty) again put to sea, Pym stowing away in the hold of Captain Barnard's whaler, the brig *Grampus*. This longer voyage is an exhausting one, with so many turns of the screw that even sturdy readers may be tempted to go overboard, sharks and all, before the final rescue. For the *Grampus* story is a series of violent episodes in an implacably hostile world. Pym and a grotesque half-breed named Peters will survive, but in the meantime one must run Pym's gamut of personal agonies and attend the butchering of the crew, the cannibalism of the drifting survivors, and the final hurling of Augustus' rotted body to the sharks. The successive ordeals, the random ingenuities, the catalogue of escapes, and the reiterated anguish are cloying. Our interest shifts, as it must, from whether Pym will escape to how he will escape. The only invitation the serious reader can accept must go well beyond Auden's generalized encomium that this is "one of the finest adventure stories ever written." [7] It is Poe's evocation of a subliminal kingdom that is unforgettable.

Pym is straightforward enough about the motivations that take him to sea. The usual kind of romance—hunger for exotic, lovely faraway sights and scenes—was not the lure:

> For the bright side of the painting I had a limited sympathy. My visions were of shipwreck and famine; of death or captivity among barbarian hordes; of a lifetime dragged out in sorrow and tears, upon some gray and desolate rock, in an ocean unapproachable and unknown. Such visions or desires —for they amounted to desires . . . I regarded . . . as prophetic glimpses of a destiny which I felt myself in a measure bound to fulfil (pp. 17–18).

The tempting thing, then, is annihilation, and much of the narrator's craft is expended in toying with the varieties of self-extinction. To this titillating task Pym brings an "enthusiastic temperament, and somewhat gloomy, although glowing imagination" (p. 17).

The first section of Part I (chs. II-IV) is a brilliantly sustained exploitation of this primary theme of self-destruction. For eleven days Pym is stowed away alone in the black hold of the *Grampus*. At first he is delighted with Augustus' cozy arrangements, including books, pen and paper, matches and tapers. He feels better than a "monarch" in a "new palace"; his rations of sea-biscuits and water are handsomely supplemented by "three or four immense Bologna sausages, an enormous ham, a cold leg of roast mutton, and half a dozen bottles of cordials and liqueurs" (p. 24), as befits one of Poe's young men of the world. He awakens, however, to foul air, salt food, raging thirst, seasickness, and intermittent ague. Spells of wild imaginings alternate with long, stuporous sleeps. In a final gesture of abandonment, that *perverseness* which so fascinated Poe seizes him; he downs a gill of strong peach liqueur like "a spoiled child," dashing the bottle "furiously upon the floor" (or, as sailors sometimes say, the deck). When Augustus finally calls, after endless nights, Pym is absolutely unable to reply, though not to reply is sure death. Gagging, he falls down "deadly sick." As he does so, the clatter of his knife breaks the enchantment, and with a scream—"*Augustus! oh, Augustus!*"—he is saved (pp. 44–46).

The imprisonment theme here of course goes far beyond isolation and claustrophobia: the last eight days in the hold are an entombment. This is not just a possibility, a subtle venture in latent symbols, but any reader's fact. Augustus *tells* Pym that he has been "buried" (p. 25), and Pym, attempting "to reason on the probable cause of my being thus entombed . . . gave way, unresistingly, to the most gloomy imaginings, in which the dreadful deaths of thirst, famine, suffocation, and premature interment, crowded upon me" (p. 33). In his moment of release he feels like one "suddenly redeemed from the jaws of the tomb" (p. 46). Thus the packing case in which he is confined is an undeniable coffin: "an iron-bound box . . . full six [feet] long, but very narrow," and—an exquisite bit of word-play— of the sort "used sometimes for packing fine earthenware" (p. 23). The psychiatric interpretation of Mme. Bonaparte provocatively adds that the box is also a womb within the body of the ship, wherein the unborn monarch feeds and is rocked by the sea.[8] This is an insight, rather than a fact, though it is supported by such birth imagery—not commented on by Mme. Bonaparte—as the "cord" leading to the trap door via the lumbered labyrinth of the hold (p. 24). Thus Pym alternates between prenatal harmony and posthumous agony, with life somehow lost in between. The shocking details of his awakening include a note with the word *blood* written in blood, the phosphorescent glow (decay implied) by which the note is read, and the discovery of the leg of mutton in a state of "absolute putrefaction" (p. 26).

Within the general nightmare Pym has time for actual dreams. Perhaps their literary failure helps define Poe's power:

> Among other miseries, I was smothered to death between huge pillows, by demons of the most ghastly and ferocious aspect. Immense serpents held me in their embrace, and looked earnestly in my face with their fearfully shining eyes. Then deserts, limitless, and of the most forlorn and awe-inspiring character, spread themselves out before me. . . . The

scene changed; and I stood, naked and alone, amid the burning sand-plains of Zahara. At my feet lay crouched a fierce
lion of the tropics. Suddenly his wild eyes opened and fell
upon me. With a convulsive bound he sprang to his feet . . .
(p. 28).

Struggling out of this final sequence, Pym feels "some huge
and real monster . . . pressing heavily upon my bosom,"
and wakes beneath the weight of an actual incubus. The
whole scene is much overwrought, and the clumsy half-ex-
planations by which Pym's own dog, Tiger—for such it
proves to be—is later accounted for are no more acceptable
than the failure to tell the reader what eventually happens
to Tiger. It is a measure of Poe's susceptibility to *effects* that
he could not resist spiriting Tiger aboard for the sake of a
Cerberean scene. The failure of the dreams themselves is of
course a failure in language; except perhaps for the one word
"earnestly" the passage is banal. Poe's gift was not for re-
cording dreams, as we might seem to have been suggesting,
but for dreamlike apprehensions of waking experience.
Speculating in the *Marginalia* on "fancies, or psychal impressions," Poe makes the point that "I am aware of these
'fancies' only when I am upon the very brink of sleep, with
the consciousness that I am so." He goes on to insist on "the
point of blending between wakefulness and sleep" as the
necessary "border-ground." [9] Though Poe is here speaking
of a different order of dream—delightful, spiritual—the point
stands. Pure dream is what vitiates so much of his poetry.
The oneiric power of the good fiction, however, involves
consciousness. Many events of the incarceration in the hold
have just this double vision of sleeping-waking consciousness; their power is that they keep us on the bridge where
traffic moves both ways.

Augustus' account of the mutiny (chs. IV-V), following the brilliant episode of the entombment in the hold, is a straightforward seaman's affair, a record of blunt brutality. Its importance is technical: by throwing the above-decks happenings into an after-the-fact exposition, Poe is able to keep the earlier sequence "pure." Neither Pym nor the reader knows why Augustus does not come as rescuer, why Pym cannot get out the trap door, where Tiger comes from, how long the entombment will last, and so on. In the simpler sense of plot, the role of Augustus' narrative is to "explain" the accumulated mysteries of the two preceding chapters, and it explains them well enough. But its real function is not to clean up afterward so much as it is to make the hold sequence possible in the first place. It is a matter of arranging the story in such fashion that for eight days Pym shall in fact be abandoned, immured, stifled, attacked by a beast, and deprived of food, drink, light, and fresh air. *How* all this could happen will be explained afterward; what counts, however, is not the explanations but the chance for Poe to be independent of them long enough to establish the agonizing dream of entombment.

The recapture of the ship (chs. VI-VIII) is again a series of pseudo-rational events, transitional in nature. Just as the story of the mutiny cleans up after the experience in the hold, the retaking of the ship during a rising storm is a preparation for what is to come. The political complications of the two groups of mutineers—the mate's party versus the cook's party—are mere adventures leading to the moment when the mutinous crew can be cut down far enough so that Pym's sensibility will count again. Once these maneuverings are over, we will be back with a sufficiently small remnant of the crew so that Pym's sense of things can again emerge and dominate the whole last section of Part I. When the counter-mutiny is over, only Pym, Augustus, Peters, and a spared mutineer, Parker, are left; instead of a ship, with its normal demands of navigation and communal activity, there remains only a broken hull on which nothing counts but personal survival and identity.

In the process of retaking the ship, however, one episode is more than transitional—Pym's masquerade as a corpse. Since being released, Pym has been secreted by Augustus in the empty forecastle; only Dirk Peters, the grotesque and powerful half-breed, visits them and joins in their plan to overthrow the nine drunken mutineers in the after cabin. Pym's idea, since his presence is unknown to the revelers, is that he should masquerade as the recently dead Rogers, in the hope of terrifying the mutineers into vulnerability:

> Rogers had died about eleven in the forenoon, in violent convulsions; and the corpse presented in a few minutes after death one of the most horrid and loathsome spectacles I ever remember to have seen. The stomach was swollen immensely, like that of a man who has been drowned and lain under water for many weeks. The hands were in the same condition, while the face was shrunken, shrivelled, and of a chalky whiteness, except where relieved by two or three glaring red blotches, like those occasioned by the erysipelas: one of these blotches extended diagonally across the face, completely covering up an eye as if with a band of red velvet. . . . The corpse, left to itself, was washed into the larboard scuppers, where it still lay at the time of which I speak, floundering about with the furious lurches of the brig (pp. 85–86).

Rogers may have been poisoned (p. 85); Poe doesn't really know or care, so long as he gets the kind of corpse he does. Pym's masquerade is precise. He dons Rogers' peculiarly striped shirt, stuffing it to mimic the bloated corpse, wears white mittens, chalks his face, and marks it with blood by cutting his finger. That Pym's sudden appearance, so dressed, among the mutineers causes the mate to fall "stone dead" is perhaps less interesting than Pym's reaction to his own mirror image:

> As I viewed myself in a fragment of looking-glass which hung up in the cabin, and by the dim light of a kind of battle-lantern, I was so impressed with a sense of vague awe at my appearance . . . that I was seized with a violent tremour, and could scarcely summon resolution to go on with my part (p. 88).

Now Pym has looked upon his own corpse, as it were, risen from the grave of the hold.

The real drift of the game at this point, however, is the trimming down of the crew. On June 28, the day of the mutiny, one crew member is felled with an axe as he comes up from the forecastle (p. 50), and a few minutes later the "black cook" dispatches twenty-two more with the same axe as the victims are thrust over the side. When that night four sailors are forced into an oarless boat along with Captain Barnard and set adrift (p. 54), a total of twenty-eight have gone. On July 4 a harpooner is thrown overboard during a quarrel, and the next day a drunken hand falls over the side: thirty gone. This leaves on board a total of thirteen, we are told (p. 76), including the still secreted Pym. Rogers dies on July 10 (p. 79), and just before the masquerade party begins that night, Peters throws the watch overboard, leaving eight mutineers to be taken by the three sober conspirators. In the cabin melee that follows, Peters, the Herculean primitive only four feet eight inches tall, shoots two with his pistols, beats out the brains of one with a stool, and strangles another; Augustus kills a fifth with a musket (but receives stab wounds which will prove fatal); and the forgotten Tiger reappears in the nick of time to rip the throat of number six. Pym's role is revealing: after he has literally scared the mate to death, he fells a seaman, Parker, with the blow of a pump-handle; since Parker proves to be "merely stunned," Pym emerges legally guiltless (pp. 93–94). Mme. Bonaparte suggests that "the potency-less Pym-Poe" would never dare "the glory and the guilt of the killings," as the Herculean Peters does.[10] This is perceptive, though the presumed sexual basis of Pym's actions or failures to act is an exegesis of Poe's psyche rather than of the narrative itself. So ends the bravura phase of the game of ten-little, nine-little, eight-little sailors, and we now enter the serious business of what will happen to the four survivors: Pym, Peters, the wounded Augustus, and the spared mutineer, Parker.

The gale which rose during the fight has meanwhile begun to devastate the ship, and dream again runs riot. Now that the ship's company is destroyed, the ship itself must go. Peters hacks down the mainmast, then the foremast; the bowsprit goes with them. A breaching sea sweeps away the longboat and bulwarks and shatters the windlass. A moment later "one of the most tremendous waves I had then ever known broke right on board of us, sweeping the companion-way clear off, bursting in the hatchways, and filling every inch of the vessel with water" (p. 98). This dismembering of the ship's body is recounted with the same loving care as are all other mutilations in the narrative.

The stage is now set for the second major drama of Part I (chs. IX-XIII). Hunger and thirst are announced early in the wreck sequence (p. 105) and dominate up to the very moment of deliverance (p. 145); all events of the twenty-seven-day ordeal are variations on this theme. Since "a vessel with a cargo of empty oil-casks would not sink" (p. 99), the four survivors must enact their atavistic food rituals on the stripped, unsinkable hull. Neither the joy of rescue (at the last, last moment, and after two hallucinations) nor the mercy of quick death is proffered. From the night of July 10, when the gale did its work, until daybreak of August 7, when the *Jane Guy* comes booming over the horizon, the four, then three, then two, endure.

The two central episodes, recounted with excruciating force, are the appearance of the death ship, followed two days later by the "exquisite horror" of the killing and eating of Parker (p. 129). These are preceded by elaborately unsuccessful adventures in diving into the hull in search of food. It is a long time before the "last horrible extremity" is verbalized by Parker (p. 123), but the thought has been haunting each of them separately (pp. 124, 126).

The most brilliantly conceived episode in *Pym* is the nightmare of the plague-ridden death ship, which on July 14 brings the specter of cannibalism.[11] To the four starving mariners there seems jolly promise indeed, as the Dutch brig bowls toward them, in the welcoming figure of a huge sailor hanging over the bowsprit, "nodding to us in a cheerful although rather odd way, and smiling constantly"; so things *"appeared"* (p. 111). But as the ship swings by at twenty feet and makes off, Pym and his companions are drowned in a stench of death. Twenty-five or more saffron-hued corpses in various degrees of putrefaction lie strewn across the deck. The "smiling" face is now seen for what it is: teeth bared where the flesh has been stripped away—one of Poe's most merciless *grotesques*. The swaying body of the huge sailor becomes a terrifying dream-image of man's mortality:

On his back, from which a portion of the shirt had been torn, leaving it bare, there sat a huge seagull, busily gorging itself with the horrible flesh, its bill and talons deep buried, and its white plumage spattered all over with blood. As the brig moved further round so as to bring us close in view, the bird, with much apparent difficulty, drew out its crimsoned head, and, after eyeing us for a moment as if stupefied, arose lazily from the body upon which it had been feasting, and, flying directly above our deck, hovered there a while with a portion of clotted and liver-like substance in its beak. The horrid morsel dropped at length with a sullen splash immediately at the feet of Parker (pp. 112–113).

The writing here is as brilliant as the scene is disgusting: *gorging, spattered, crimsoned, stupefied, lazily, clotted and liver-like*, and *sullen splash* are all superbly chosen; modern travelers who have seen vultures rising from animals killed on Southern highways will recognize the exactness, *not* unreality, of the images. Both Pym and Augustus refuse the awful thought that rises in them—the one careful hint of the chapter's meaning—as Pym, "with a deep shudder, threw the frightful thing into the sea"; but the symbolic tender of human flesh has been made.

For the moment they are ready to go back to diving for food, and so spend the fifteenth; by afternoon of the sixteenth the topic will not down, and Parker blurts it out. Pym is the center of opposition, voicing his own and the reader's sense of outrage, having "secretly made up my mind to suffer death in any shape or under any circumstances rather than resort to such a course"; but his "praying" and "supplicating" and naming things "sacred" does not dissuade the fated Parker (p. 124). Pym quickly enough breaks his own vow when he sees that resistance might become "sufficient excuse for refusing me fair play in the tragedy that I knew

would speedily be enacted" (p. 126). The consistently
amoral Pym is really less terrified at the prospect of eating
human flesh than of being eaten; when it comes down to
Parker or Pym, with the drawing of the final two straws, we
get an honest rendering of his "most diabolical hatred" for
his opponent (p. 128). Time stands still during the agony
of the final draw; then it is over, and Peters has his knife in
the back of Parker (chosen by the seagull). Now "the raging
thirst" of the three survivors is partly appeased "by the
blood of the victim," and after the cleaning of Parker, if
one might so describe the removal of hands, head, feet, and
entrails, the episode is closed as Pym intones: "we devoured
the rest of the body, piecemeal, during the four ever memorable days of the seventeenth, eighteenth, nineteenth, and
twentieth of the month" (p. 129). The solemn rhythm of
these phrases, and the religious quality of the terms Pym
used earlier when protesting the sacrifice, suggest a savage
communion. The gods do seem placated, in fact, for whereas more than fifteen perilous dives into the cabin had so far
produced only a single bottle of wine (p. 116), now Pym
suddenly "remembers" a lost axe; the deck over the store-
room is soon cut open. On the twenty-second the three can-
nibals feast on olives, ham, and Madeira wine, and procure
fresh water (pp. 131–134).

As the storm returns and the hull rolls further over it is
clear that more punishment is at hand. Sharks appear as
Augustus' wound begins to mortify; on August 1 (his name-
day) his putrid corpse is surrendered to them in expiation,
the clashing of their teeth being audible a mile away (p.
140). The retribution theme here illuminates strikingly the
different goals of psychiatric and literary criticism. Mme.
Bonaparte's interest in Augustus' death as an expression of
Poe's jealousy of his brother Henry is a literary irrelevance.

Her definition of the event as an Oedipus crime, however, in which "the sea mother reclaims her guilty son," is an interesting mid-point between the two types of criticism.[12] No grief is expressed by Pym or Peters, unless a casual reference the next day to "our poor companion" could be so described (p. 141). Pym is quite as incapable of love or compassion as of conscious guilt.

Thirst returns, the hull capsizes, thirst becomes agonizing; and then, the gamut being run, the *Jane Guy* appears. As Part I ends we see that it has provided us two sustained episodes which meet the promise of the Prologue: one, burial in the hold and birth into a mutinous world; the other, a cycle of primal deprivations on the wrecked hull, culminating in the feeding of man on man. The power of each lies in its literary evocation of dream forms.

Except for the haunting last chapter, Part II is far inferior to the Prologue and Part I. Cruising south (chs. XIV-XVI) is a competent but overextended seaman's log, intentionally conceived as a return to daylight after the recent night scenes: "we began to remember what had passed rather as a frightful dream from which we had been happily awakened, than as events which had taken place in sober and naked reality" (p. 150). Thus the low-key introduction before re-entering the world of dream. We become acquainted with the *Jane Guy*, her trading and sealing mission, the supplies she carries. Routine visits to Kerguelen's Island and Tristan d'Acunha are made in southern waters, with reports on flora and fauna. The tedious insistence on dates and navigational positions (some twenty-eight citations of latitude and longitude occur in three chapters) indicates Poe will shortly be up to more legerdemain.

The movement through the ice barrier (ch. XVII) keeps

the same manner, but the alert reader senses a quiver of excitement. The *Jane Guy*, at the urging of Pym, has now headed toward the polar sea and here begins to progress beyond the farthest point south yet recorded—Weddell's 1822 voyage to 74° 15′, according to Poe (p. 168). The *Jane Guy* will go to 83° 20′ S. before reaching Tsalal, and these additional nine degrees are the margin of excitement and fear this phase of the story counts on. On January 12 the passage south seems blocked by "one apparently limitless floe, backed by absolute mountains of ragged ice, one precipice of which arose frowningly above the other. We stood to the westward until the fourteenth, in the hope of finding an entrance" (p. 174). On January 14, with no change of tone in the record, the *Jane Guy* rounds the massive barrier and slides into "an open sea, without a particle of ice." Now the temperature rises, the variation per azimuth continues to diminish (verifying the movement southward), and a slow current toward the pole sets in. This "current setting southwardly" is the most interesting fictional fact so far. On the fourteenth it is only "half a mile per hour"; on the sixteenth, it is "three quarters of a mile per hour." The set of this current (by the eighteenth it is "a mile an hour") is an emotional as well as a "scientific" fact; the pull to the south is now on, and its mysterious power will reassert itself after the catastrophe at Tsalal. A huge polar bear with "blood red" eyes is captured and eaten on the seventeenth, warm air and water is noted, and a premonitory "thin vapour in the southern horizon" (p. 177) is recorded. It is a skillful chapter in which the voyagers slide quietly beyond reality and, at last, into a world where Poe can have his own latitude. The *Jane Guy* has gone behind the mirror.

Yet much of the long episode on the tropical-polar island

of Tsalal (chs. XVIII-XXIV) is unconvincing. The setting is a curious *mélange* of south-sea primitivism, pseudo-archaeological chasms (Poe has the rock-carved city of Petra in mind), and half-buried images from the American South. The recurrence of deprivations is cliché: Pym (accompanied from here on by Peters) again endures premature burial, this time in the island chasm (p. 204); again he is "marooned," now on a plateau with no descent (p. 220); and again he must hunt for food and water (pp. 214, 219, 227). The internal fantasy of the earlier scenes has given way to fancies about an eccentric and dangerous external world. The exception is the ominous and lamentable theme of black-white race hatred.

The primary event on Tsalal is the tornado of destruction let loose by the presumably friendly natives. This second major mutiny of the story again results in the wholesale slaughter of whites by blacks (it will be recalled that it was the "black cook . . . a perfect demon" who had wielded the axe on the *Grampus*). The insistent blackness of the savages—even their teeth are black (p. 241)—is matched by the total absence of white on the island and the alarm of the natives at all white objects aboard ship. Even fresh water runs purple, and the use of the word "veins" to describe its peculiar structure suggests a fantasy on negro blood (pp. 186–187). The alarm of Too-wit, the native chief, at his own mirror image betrays typical primitive fear of magic; perhaps it intimates as well a confrontation of his own blackness:

> Upon raising his eyes and seeing his reflected self in the glass, I thought the savage would go mad. . . . No persuasion could prevail upon him to take another look; but, throwing himself upon the floor, with his face buried in his hands, he

remained thus until we were obliged to drag him upon deck (p. 183).

The natives are described as grossly primitive and clearly disgust Pym; in turn, they "recoil" at the "complexion" of "the white race" (p. 182). The fear seems reciprocal. The winding rock chasms form a hieroglyph of mystical meanings which are obscurely implied to have to do with the idea of "darkness," the verb "to be white," and an Egyptian word meaning "the region of the south" (pp. 222–225; 244–245). It is Levin's provocative suggestion that the island adventure reflects Poe's buried antagonism toward Negroes, expressing "a consciousness of guilt and a fear of retribution." [13] One might risk particularizing two episodes: the gross details of the native "village" and the apprehension of the whites while visiting it (ch. XIX) might derive from some youthful experience of Poe's in visiting slave quarters in Virginia; and the wild scenes of blacks slaughtering whites might be recollections (or imaginings) of the fierce slave rebellions which, within Poe's memory, had terrorized the white South.[14] The latter images are violent: the white intruders are treacherously buried under a massive landslide prepared by the blacks (p. 203); the sailors left on board the ship are attacked and "absolutely torn to pieces in an instant" by the swarming savages (p. 213); and in counter-movement a thousand blacks are blown to fragments when the *Jane Guy* explodes. During all this Pym and Peters are on a high plateau overlooking the devastation and the swarming about of some ten thousand blacks (p. 216). Such possibly historical sources for the emotions and imagery of the Tsalal episode, while of extreme sociological interest, are no more directly a literary effect of the story than is Mme. Bonaparte's contention that the island is the body of the Mother, and that the explorations of the black chasms "represent a [child's confused] phantasy of return to the mother, expressed in anal or intestinal terms." [15] Both interpretations relate to latent dynamics more than manifest meaning; as such they need not be compatible. Each has its own use in helping to "explain" why Pym and Peters can escape destruction only by fleeing into a receiving whiteness as the story closes.

The journey into the Unknown (ch. XXV) is the climactic dream, artfully prepared for by the earlier movement through the ice barrier. The meaning of the increasing current and the far-off polar vapor becomes graphically clear when, after the diversionary and catastrophic stay at Tsalal, Pym and Peters escape in a native canoe and head to sea. The speeding current at once seizes hold and bears them toward the pole and a vast white cataract of snowlike ashes. The month-long journey of no return is recorded in journal entries that recapture the intensely personal sensibility of earlier episodes. Pym is drawn helplessly toward the Abyss, as Poe's heroes so often are, but he reports neither madness nor alarm. "I felt a *numbness* of body and mind—a dreaminess of sensation—but this was all" (p. 240). The current, then, is a superb metaphor of dream power, and Pym's passive abandonment to it is a fitting climax to his dream book. The current's fierce set, as the canoe speeds toward annihilation, is the inexorable sequel to its gentle pull when the barriers of reality were first rounded. Pym's long search for oblivion in an unknown sea is over.

Two critics help us define further the quality of the final episode. James's strictures on "the would-be portentous climax" are based on its lack of "connexions," the absence of "the indispensable history of somebody's *normal* relation to something." [16] From a novelist's view he is quite right, and the same criticism applies to the other dream projections of the story. Dreams which beget no responsibilities deny the novelist his function. With Poe we must settle for the visual and latent force of the oneiric projection, the disturbing painting nailed to the mind's wall. That James himself could not get the final scene of *Pym* from his memory is suggested by the extensive metaphor he made of it in *The Golden Bowl*, as Levin notes.[17] It was impact that Poe was after, or what he preferred to call *effect*; to deny this to Poe one would have to be able to forget how *Pym* ends.

Mme. Bonaparte sees the final episode as a consummation of the search for the mother, now envisioned as pure and undefiled.[18] This clinical analysis is still a literary irrelevance to the extent that it takes us back to Poe's childhood and away from *Pym*. But one cannot deny the female context of the last scene; it is not possible to explain away phrases such as: "heat of the water . . . of a milky consistency and hue" (March 3); "heat of the water . . . and its milky hue" (March 6); and "out the milky depths of the ocean" (March 21). The huge "shrouded human figure" that appears within "the white curtain" or "veil" and takes the long-tried voyagers into its "embraces" is surely more female than male:

> And now we rushed into the embraces of the cataract, where a chasm threw itself open to receive us. But there arose in our pathway a shrouded human figure, very far larger in its proportions than any dweller among men. And the hue of the skin of the figure was of the perfect whiteness of the snow (p. 242).

So Pym comes home at last, by-passing that corruption of the grave which he had known in the hold of the *Grampus*.

Home to mother through a warm cosmic milk bath, one has to say, savoring the apocalyptic comedy to its full. Or, if one prefers older conventions, welcomed into his dream of oblivion by the White Goddess.

Dream recital explains the peculiar, limited power of the best sections of *Pym*. The falling off of this technique during the balance of the *Jane Guy* story lets the narrative pall. Deprived of Pym's special sensibility, the polar adventure is juvenile, and the expository filler on explorations, penguins, and *bêche de mer*, a weariness; it really comes alive only in the gigantic *tableau vivant* into which Pym disappears. Poe's failure to let experience accumulate also vitiates the later narrative. In Part II Pym never broods over Augustus' death nor even recalls it. He does not wonder if Captain Barnard *was* picked up, though the possibility had been raised in Part I (p. 73). In no way does he refer to earlier events or even seem to remember them. The fact that it is Pym and Peters who come aboard the *Jane Guy*, rather than Smith and Jones, is a fact of no literary or moral consequence to the second part. We know that Poe had been driven to the idea of a long story by the exigencies of the market and his desperate need to get some prose fiction between hard covers.[19] Conflict between the demands of a longer form and his talents explains why *Pym* is not a novel, or, since Poe did not presume to that form, fails as sustained fiction.

Poe's important gift is in psychological projection from the mind of a troubled sleeper who wakes and then drops back into the self's midnight. At its best his work is witness to Emily Dickinson's dictum that "Ourself behind our self, concealed" provides "a superior spectre." The question in Poe is how much flummery one will endure in exchange for his special vision.

Notes

1. Poe's sources are summarized in Edward H. Davidson, *Poe: A Critical Study* (Cambridge, 1957), p. 280.
2. III (September, 1838), 210–211.
3. *The Letters of Edgar Allan Poe*, ed. John Ward Ostrom (Cambridge, 1948), I, 130.
4. Marie Bonaparte, *The Life and Works of Edgar Allan Poe: A Psycho-Analytic Interpretation*, Foreword by Sigmund Freud, trans. John Rodker (London, 1949), Ch. XXXII; Patrick F. Quinn, *The French Face of Edgar Poe* (Carbondale, Ill., 1957), Ch. VI; Harry Levin, *The Power of Blackness: Hawthorne, Poe, Melville* (New York, 1958), Ch. IV; and Davidson, Ch. VI.
5. All *Pym* references are to pages in the Virginia Edition: *Complete Works of Edgar Allan Poe*, ed. James A. Harrison (New York, 1902), III, 1–245.
6. That the whaler should give "an immense lurch to *windward!*" brought a horselaugh from editor Burton; so had the earlier moment when Pym, having cut away the sloop's mast, goes bowling along "under the jib!" Note 2, above.
7. Edgar Allan Poe: *Selected Prose and Poetry*, ed. W. H. Auden (New York, 1950), p. vii.
8. Bonaparte, pp. 312–313.
9. *Works*, XVI, 88–90.
10. Bonaparte, pp. 314, 344.
11. Baudelaire, in "Edgar Allan Poe, Sa Vie et Ses Ouvrages" (1852), chose only this episode for quotation. *Baudelaire on Poe: Critical Papers*, trans. and ed. Lois and Francis E. Hyslop, Jr. (State College, Pa., 1952), pp. 80–83.
12. Bonaparte, pp. 325–327.
13. Levin, p. 122.
14. E. F. Frazier, *The Negro in the United States* (New York, 1949), Ch. V. Especially relevant is the Nat Turner revolt

of 1831 in which some sixty whites and at least one hundred Negroes were killed.

15. Bonaparte, pp. 341–342.
16. Henry James, *The Art of the Novel: Critical Prefaces*, ed. Richard P. Blackmur (New York, 1946), pp. 256–257.
17. Levin, pp. 123–124.
18. Bonaparte, pp. 347–351.
19. In 1836 both Harper and Brothers and Poe's friend Paulding had made it very clear to him that the market was for long narratives, not short tales. Hervey Allen, *Israfel: The Life and Times of Edgar Allan Poe* (New York, 1934), p. 317; and Arthur Hobson Quinn, *Edgar Allan Poe: A Critical Biography* (New York, 1941), p. 251.

Niagara Revisited, by W. D. Howells

The Story of Its Publication and Suppression

BY RUDOLF AND CLARA M. KIRK

On April 3, 1880, Frederick Law Olmsted, landscape architect and conservationist, wrote to Howells, editor of the *Atlantic*, to encourage him to add his voice to the popular hue and cry against the commercialism of Niagara Falls, sending him at the same time an envelope of newspaper clippings on the subject.[1] The following year, Charles Eliot Norton, Harvard Professor of Art, urged Olmsted to renew his efforts to enlist Howells's support. "Everything is worth trying to save Niagara," he wrote. "I believe you could get Howells to write an article for Harper's, Scribner's or the Atlantic." [2] Perhaps as a result of the suggestion of Olmsted, Howells did write, at this time, a humorous little sketch, which appeared in the *Atlantic*, May, 1883.[3] It was entitled "Niagara Revisited, Twelve Years After Their Wedding Journey" and might be considered Howells's contribution to the public movement to preserve the Falls from destruction.

In this sketch, Isabel and Basil March, the now middle-aged lovers who with their children revisited the scene of their honeymoon in 1882, remarked sadly to each other that "the triviality of man in the surroundings of the Falls had increased with the lapse of time." Basil even wondered "whether the Rapids had not dwindled since his former visit" of twelve years earlier. In any case, they agreed:

> There were more booths and bazars, and more colored feather fans with whole birds spitted in the centres; and there were an offensive array of blue and green and yellow glasses on the shore, through which you were expected to look at the Falls gratis.

In spite of "the ravages of improvement about Niagara," the elder Marches abandoned themselves "to the charm of the place" and strolled "apart from the children," who were happily "examining at the news-man's booth the moccasins and the birch-bark bricabrac of the Irish aborigines, and the cups and vases of Niagara spar imported from Devonshire."

If Howells's intention in writing his little sketch was, in part, to remark upon the commercialism of Niagara, his effort was in danger for a while of bringing about exactly the reverse result, for his story was almost immediately reprinted, after its appearance in the *Atlantic*, by a Chicago advertising firm for the Fitchburg Railroad. To announce to tourists the delights of a recently completed line from Boston to the Falls,[4] *Niagara Revisited Twelve Years After Their Wedding Journey by the Hoosac Tunnel Route*, was published by D. Dalziel of Chicago, sold to the Railroad Company—and promptly suppressed. The result is that only about a dozen copies of this charming little volume, generously adorned with gaily colored lithographs, are now known to exist.[5]

An account of the publication of the story in the *Atlantic*, and the subsequent printing and suppression of the booklet, may be pieced together by an examination of the eighteen letters exchanged between the author of *Niagara Revisited* and his literary agent, James R. Osgood,[6] between July 10, 1882, and February 11, 1885.[7] This hitherto unpublished correspondence reveals the vicissitudes through which the little sketch passed, both before and after its magazine appearance. Details of the adventures of the pamphlet may be filled in by an examination of several communications from the Traffic Manager of the Fitchburg Railroad and Davison Dalziel, which are in the Howells Collection in the Houghton Library, Harvard.

That such a humorously sentimental account of a Boston family's summer excursion to the Falls could have been considered worth reprinting by the Fitchburg Railroad may surprise the modern reader unless he remembers that the hero and heroine of this mild adventure are Basil and Isabel March, the bride and bridegroom of *Their Wedding Journey*.[8] After the original publication of the serial in the *Atlantic* of 1871, it had been reprinted in a small tan and gold volume, illustrated by Augustus Hoppin (1872). A copy of *Their Wedding Journey* was tucked in the luggage of every bridal couple who made that romantic visit to the Falls during the last quarter of the nineteenth century—or so we may assume from the continued popularity of the book. News of the second trip of the well-known couple— this time accompanied by their two children—was welcome to a public as eager as the Marches "to renew fond memories." Like advertisers of all times, the Fitchburg Railroad was quick to seize upon a sentimental public mood; all that was needed were the full-page colored illustrations of the March family comfortably seated in the Fitchburg Railroad parlor car, enjoying hearty meals in the Fitchburg Railroad

Depot, and at last happily climbing about the Falls. Howells's sketch, stressing the joys of an inexpensive family excursion, was made to order—at least when enhanced by
illustrations.

Surprisingly enough, the advertiser-editors succumbed to
the temptation of changing only one sentence in the essay.
In the *Atlantic*, Basil remarked, "Come, let us get out and
breakfast at Rochester; they will give us broiled white-fish;
and we can show the children where Sam Patch jumped over
Genesee Falls, and—" [9] In the pamphlet, however, Basil
spoke a word for the new railroad station at Syracuse.
"Come," he said, "let us get our breakfast at Syracuse; they
will give us broiled white-fish; and we can show the children
the handsome new depot of the New York, West Shore
Railroad." Since the West Shore Railroad, running between
New York and Niagara and connecting with the Hoosac
Tunnel Line, advertised its route in a full page of the pamphlet, and since Sam Patch had made his fatal leap into
Genesee Falls more than fifty years before the Marches'
summer excursion, one can understand the temptation of
the editors.

We turn now to an account of the difficulties encountered
by Howells and Osgood before the sketch was finally printed
in the *Atlantic*. We will then return to the controversy with
the Fitchburg Railroad, which was not finally settled until
two years after the publication of *Niagara Revisited*.

I

Early in the summer of 1882, Howells arrived in England,
where he planned to stay at least a year to recover from a
serious illness of the previous winter induced by work and

worry. He had resigned from the *Atlantic* editorship, which had been assumed by his friend, Thomas Bailey Aldrich, and he was in communication with Henry Alden of *Harper's*, who was then trying to persuade Howells to take over "The Editor's Study." Howells was, for the time being, a freelance, anxious to sell as many articles as he could through James R. Osgood, whom he had engaged as his agent on February 2, 1881, after the dissolution of the firm of Houghton, Osgood and Company, May 1, 1880. Osgood's note of July 10, 1882, refers to a note from Howells, now lost, and probably reflects the conversations these two friends held before Howells sailed. Then they presumably agreed that Osgood should try to place the sketch—with which perhaps Howells would amuse himself further on the ship—in the *Alliance*, a Reformed Episcopal Church periodical, published in Chicago, which had recently merged with *The Western Magazine*. Osgood wrote to Howells in London: "I was glad to get your letter, and shall look with interest for the 'Niagara' article. I should think it ought to suit the 'Alliance' capitally." [10] Several weeks later Howells finished the sketch, read it to his wife, who liked it, and wrote to Osgood on August 1, 1882, in a gay and hopeful mood:

> I have finished the Niagara sketch, and I shall send it to you, after getting it put in type, on Saturday. It is not a "story," though it is largely fictitious; let me know what you do with it, and what proportion of the plunder you rend from me, or assign to me. My wife, after being ashamed of our getting $500 for it, now thinks we ought to have much more! Such is the effect of prosperity on the female mind.[11]

A few days later, when the manuscript came back from the typist, Howells reread it at his desk alone, and his mood changed. He wrote another little note to Osgood in quite a different vein, which he slipped into the envelope with the sketch.

> August 5, 1882
>
> I enclose the copy of my Niagara sketch. It doesn't seem to me very great things, as I read it over. I will send you one or two other copies for fear this should miss you.[12]

No sooner had Howells mailed off his letter to Osgood, with his manuscript enclosed, than he heard, through a mutual friend, that Osgood was on his way to England and would arrive in a few days. He, therefore, wrote hastily to Benjamin Holt Ticknor, the publisher of the *Atlantic*, since Osgood would not be in Boston to receive his letter and the enclosure. Howells had grown suspicious of the *Alliance* and was feeling out the *Atlantic*:

> So I am now sending you a sketch, which I have already sent a copy of to him, but which will not reach Boston till he has left. He was to get $500 for this thing from the publisher of the Chicago Alliance, who, however, was not to have it till he had paid for it being, as I understand, a Shepherd in Wolf's clothing.[13]

Osgood's next communication, dated October 2, 1882, reported that, "Up to now we have heard nothing from the 'Alliance' people. If they don't pony up soon I will see 'Niagara Revisited' elsewhere." [14] To this letter Howells immediately replied, on October 26, 1882, from Villeneuve in Switzerland, urging Osgood to try *Harper's*. "Why not send him [Alden] the Niagara sketch? I suppose the Alliance doesn't want it." [15] Osgood's answer on November 10, 1882—"The *Alliance* people have not yet sent the $500. I have written them three times without response," [16]—vindicated Howells's suspicions that after all "the 'Alliance' people" did not want the piece. Without much loss of time, Howells set to work on the manuscript once more, corrected it, wrote to Osgood instructing him to sell it to Aldrich for the *Atlantic*—and then, feeling apprehensive about the whole thing, mailed the letter without the manuscript!

Villeneuve, Nov. 23, 1882

My dear Osgood:

I send you a corrected copy of Niagara Revisited, which I wish you would sell to Aldrich for The Atlantic. I would really rather have it there than anywhere else—as you may tell him—for it would there find its most sympathetic audience, and it would naturally follow where The Wedding Journey was printed. But, if by the time this reaches you, you have made other arrangements for it, no matter.

Please send my share of the spoil to Mr. Sam Wells.*

A hurried footnote on the reverse of the sheet reads:

* Fix your own price on the paper, but don't *submit* it— that is, offer it on approval.

On second thoughts, I don't send the Niagara. If it had gone to the Alliance, all well and good; but I don't care, just now, to challenge criticism by an inferior thing in a prominent place. *Please don't sell it to anybody.*[17]

Osgood, meanwhile, separated from Howells by an ocean, had proceeded on Howells's earlier suggestion. He had already submitted the manuscript to Alden with no success. Several days later Osgood approached Aldrich, who seemed more favorably inclined, and wrote to Howells as follows:

Dec. 12, 1882

I note what you say about "Niagara Revisited." I had already sent the article to Alden, who had expressed a wish for it and I should think had accepted it. But after keeping it a few days he returned it saying he thought it not within the scope of the articles about which we had corresponded and agreed, that it appealed only (or rather chiefly) to the people who had read "Their Wedding Journey," and therefore "declined with thanks." Now I had already spoken to Aldrich about it, and he offered $300 for it, and I was on the point of sending it to him when your letter came. But I shall await further communication from you in the face of your present instructions. For my part, however, I don't see why you should not print it. I think it very charming. Let me know soon.[18]

Howells, always practical about disposing of his writing, was sufficiently encouraged by Osgood's words to reply on January 12, 1883, this time from Florence: "I will try to put the Niagara Revisited into better form, and send it to you for Aldrich before long." [19] Two weeks later Howells carried out his promise and mailed the corrected copy, with the stipulation that it should not be "submitted" to Aldrich for approval, but sold to him outright.

Florence, Jan. 28, 1883.

I enclose a corrected copy of Niagara Revisited, which I have concluded to let Aldrich have, if he still wants it. I don't understand that he expects it to be submitted to him, and I don't wish it to be. It will be best to have the sketch in The Atlantic, where all the matter connected with it appeared.[20]

Osgood acted on Howells's instructions promptly and effectively. However, he was forced to accept the $300 offered by Aldrich rather than the $500 which they had both earlier hoped the sketch would bring. After more than six months of haggling over the manuscript, Osgood was glad to come to terms with Aldrich. He wrote promptly to Howells:

> February 23, 1883
> Your letter of Jan. 28 came to hand a few days since and I at once sent to Aldrich to know if he still wished the "Niagara." He responded affirmatively with a check for $300, of which we have credited one-half to you and bagged the balance as arranged.[21]

Osgood's next letter, April 2, 1883, the last he wrote to Howells while he was still in England, is in reply to a letter from Howells to Osgood of March 13, in which he wrote, "I suppose we had better let Houghton & Mifflin add 'Niagara Revisited' to 'Their Wedding Journey,' " and asked Osgood so to notify them.[22] Since Osgood had quarreled with Houghton when their publishing firm was dissolved in 1881, he was somewhat irritated by the suggestion:

> Of course we shall do whatever you wish about "Niagara Revisited," but I don't quite see why you should give it to Houghton to be added to "Their Wedding Journey"—certainly not without consideration. Why not keep it to make part of a new volume bye-and-bye? Cannot this matter rest until we meet? [23]

Howells, then traveling about Italy gathering material for *Tuscan Cities*, did not receive Osgood's letter until the twentieth of April and replied to it on the same day. "There is no hurry about Niagara Revisited," he wrote; "I can decide what to do with it when I see you." [24] Howells met his publisher in London during the summer and talked the matter over, but he had his way in the end, for *Niagara Revisited* became the last chapter of all editions of *Their Wedding Journey* thereafter.

II

As we know, the agitation caused by the publication of *Niagara Revisited* was not to stop here. Osgood's suggestion that the sketch should appear in a separate volume was carried out by D. Dalziel for the Fitchburg Railroad, "by arrangement with James R. Osgood & Co." The last four letters which bear upon the history of this booklet indicate that, after its publication in the *Atlantic*, Osgood, acting for Howells, agreed with the Chicago advertising firm of Dalziel [25] to arrange for the reprinting of the essay for the Railroad, and immediately found himself engaged in a copyright controversy. The Fitchburg Railroad accepted the sketch from Dalziel—including twelve pages of colored illustrations and sixteen pages of advertisements—with the expectation of using it to promote the new route to Niagara. The only difficulty was that Dalziel failed to pay Howells the agreed-upon sum of $500.

The next letter of Howells to Osgood, written from 302 Beacon Street, and dated September 23, 1884, states the case clearly. Howells merely asked, "Has Dalziel of Chicago sent any reply to your duns?" [26] Apparently, Howells received a negative reply from Osgood, who then asked him for his advice as to how to proceed. Howells's reply, undated, is as follows:

Dear dear Osgood:
   All that I can suggest is that unless the $500 are paid we

enjoin Mr. Whitmore from publishing as soon as he notifies us of his intention. I don't know what else to say.

Yours ever

W. D. Howells [27]

Howells soon decided to take matters into his own hands and to seek legal advice. He wrote to Osgood on February 9, 1885, asking that all relevant material be sent to his lawyer:

> Will you kindly send the enclosed to our friend, Lawyer Clark, Pemberton Square, together with *all* letters of Dalziel, Whitmore, and yourself, relating to the republication of my sketch? Mr. Clark is going to write to the Fitchburg R.R. in my behalf.[28]

Osgood replied immediately, on February 11, enclosing a two-page letter from John Whitmore, the Traffic Manager of the Fitchburg Railroad, dated December 20, 1884.[29] In this letter Whitmore had reported to Osgood that Howells had called on him to state his claim, that he had assured Howells that the $500 would undoubtedly soon be forthcoming—though Whitmore would not "assume one iota of responsibility for the Fitchburg RR in the matter"—and that, to date, only a "few thousand of the books" had been printed, and that these would not be distributed until Howells was paid. After reading Whitmore's letter, Osgood wrote in his note, "you can judge as to the wisdom of taking legal proceedings."

Since the cover of the pirated pamphlet announced that it was "Published by D. Dalziel, Chicago," by arrangement with James R. Osgood & Co., Howells realized that Whitmore felt safe in refusing to assume legal responsibility for Dalziel's tardy payment of the author. He realized, too, that

Osgood himself would be implicated in any legal proceedings and hence would hesitate to press the suit against the Chicago advertising company. Howells, therefore, determined himself to make a further appeal to Whitmore before taking the necessary legal action. On February 20, 1885, he drafted a hurried scrawl to "Mr. W." which begins abruptly, without superscripture:

> It is now 2 mos. since you were kind enuf to answer me that Mr. D. wd pay me within a very short time for the use of my paper in your pamphlet.

> Mr. D. has not pd me & I have no belief that he will voluntarily do so. I venture to recur to you and beg to know whether you can give me any information in regard to him.
>
> Y.t.
>
> W. D. H.

Whitmore replied on February 21, the day on which he received Howells's note, saying that he had written to Dalziel for an explanation and would forward his reply when he received it. Howells sent the note on to Osgood, with the following remark written in the corner, "I saw him 6 wks or so ago & he told me he sh'd remit you the $500 in a few days." Apparently, in the interview between Howells and the traffic manager, Whitmore had, in fact, promised to stand behind Dalziel's debt, even though he did not believe that the Fitchburg Railroad could be legally held accountable. However, the $500 was not remitted to Howells's agent by either Whitmore or Dalziel.

After a lapse of a month, Whitmore wrote again to Howells, enclosing a copy of a letter and a telegram which he had just received from Dalziel. "Surely," wrote Whitmore in his brief note of March 23, 1885, "the matter is approaching consummation at last. Permit me to enquire if you have received your $500—" Since we know that Howells had not received the promised $500, we are prepared to share Howells's feeling when he perused the two-page copy of Dalziel's letter to Whitmore, March 21, 1885, and a copy of his telegram added to the second page. The entire letter is an elaborate apology and explanation of why Dalziel was not able at an earlier date to ship on to Boston a second batch of *Niagara Revisited* pamphlets. Dalziel himself appears to be in financial difficulties and expects, he writes, "to sustain some loss in this matter"; however, he intends to send on the second shipment of the book by April 1. Dalziel did not refer in the letter to any debt owed the author of the essay.

Howells lost no time in threatening suit, through his lawyer, against the Fitchburg Railroad. Without the support of Osgood, his publishing agent, Howells coped with the delaying tactics of an advertising agent and the ambiguous replies of a railroad company, and succeeded in suppressing the issue of *Niagara Revisited*. One can readily imagine how a few copies of this charming little pamphlet were secreted in the pockets of those who were supposed to destroy them.[30]

Niagara Revisited, Howells's contribution to the Save-Niagara campaign, with some difficulty found its way into print in the May, 1883, issue of the *Atlantic*; when it reappeared the following year as a separate illustrated advertising pamphlet, it was speedily consigned to oblivion by its author.[31] However, when *Their Wedding Journey* was reissued in 1887, *Niagara Revisited* was included as a final chapter of this immortal account of honeymooners at Niagara.[32] The pamphlet itself is seldom seen in a bookdealer's catalogue, for Howells's unaided fight for his rights as an author was all too successful.

NOTES

1. Unpublished letter, Houghton Library, Harvard. In 1879, a Save-Niagara campaign was launched by Olmsted and Charles Eliot Norton in an effort to restore the Falls area scenically and to make it an international reservation. Senators, scientists, artists, writers, lawyers, were enlisted both in this country and in England to preserve Niagara. Olmsted was asked in 1880, by the New York State Legislature, to help prepare a Report on the Condition and Prospect of Niagara, which resulted, in 1885, in establishing the International Park for the protection of the natural beauties of the Falls. For a full account of the state of Niagara Falls at that time and for the part played by Olmsted in rescuing the area, see an unsigned article in *The Nation*, 33 (Sept., 1881), 171–172. For the part played by Norton in the Save-Niagara campaign, see Kermit Vanderbilt, *Charles Eliot Norton, Apostle of Culture in a Democracy* (1959), 188–192.

2. Unpublished letter, Houghton Library, Harvard. June 2, 1881. For further comment on Niagara and the public effort to preserve its beauties, see the two articles by Henry James, Jr., in *The Nation*, 13 (Oct. 12, 1871), 238–239; *idem*. (Oct. 19, 1871), 254–255. See also: "The Editor's Easy Chair," *Harper's*, LXIV (Dec., 1881), 151–152; *idem.*, (Dec., 1882), 146–147; "The Story of the Hoosac Tunnel," N. H. Egleston, *Atlantic Monthly*, XLIX (March, 1882), 291–301.

3. *Atlantic Monthly*, LI (May, 1883), 598–610.

4. The Hoosac Tunnel, through which the trains on the Fitchburg line passed on their run from Boston to Niagara, had become a popular tourist attraction since its opening on July 1, 1878.

5. Copies of *Niagara Revisited* which have been examined by the writers of this article are to be found in the following

libraries: Huntington, Houghton, Clark, Newberry, Yale, and Columbia. Mr. C. Waller Barrett of New York also owns a copy. See "Niagara Revisited," by Clara M. Kirk, *Columbia Library Columns*, VII (Feb., 1958), 5–12.

6. James Ripley Osgood, head of the firm of James R. Osgood and Co., was Howells's agent from 1881 to 1885.

7. We quote from the seventeen unpublished letters with the permission of Professor W. W. Howells. No one may make further use of these letters without his written consent. We are also indebted to Mr. William A. Jackson and the Houghton Library for allowing us to study the letters and for furnishing us with photostats. The Library of Congress and the Library of the University of Southern California have aided us in our search for manuscript letters. The eighteenth letter in this correspondence is reproduced in *The Life in Letters of William Dean Howells* (1928), edited by Mildred Howells. Permission to reproduce a portion of this letter has been granted by Professor W. W. Howells under the same conditions already cited.

8. *Atlantic Monthly*, XXVIII (July–Dec., 1871). For a full account of the March family, which played a part in ten of Howells's stories and novels, see "Reality and Actuality in the March Family Narratives," Clara M. Kirk, *PMLA*, LXXIV (March, 1959), 137–152.

9. *Op. cit.*, p. 601.

10. Osgood to Howells. Boston, July 10, 1882. Manuscript letter in the Houghton Library, Harvard. In October, 1881, the *Alliance* ceased to appear. It then merged with *The Western Magazine*, which soon merged with *The Weekly Magazine*.

11. *Life in Letters*, I, 316.

12. Howells to Osgood, August 5, 1882. Manuscript letter in the Houghton Library, Harvard.

13. Unpublished letter of Howells to Ticknor. (Undated) Library of Congress.

14. Osgood to Howells, October 2, 1882. Manuscript letter in the Houghton Library, Harvard.

15. Howells to Osgood, Villeneuve, October 26, 1882. Manuscript letter in the Houghton Library, Harvard.

16. Osgood to Howells, Boston, November 10, 1882. Manuscript letter in the Houghton Library, Harvard.

17. Manuscript letter in the Library of the University of Southern California, Los Angeles. Samuel Wells was of the law firm of Bangs and Wells, Boston.

18. Osgood to Howells. December 12, 1882. Manuscript letter in the Houghton Library, Harvard.

19. Howells to Osgood, January 12, 1883. Manuscript letter in the Houghton Library, Harvard.

20. Howells to Osgood, Florence, January 28, 1883. Manuscript letter in the Houghton Library, Harvard.

21. Osgood to Howells, February 23, 1883. Manuscript letter in the Houghton Library, Harvard.

22. Howells to Osgood, March 13, 1883. Manuscript letter in possession of C. Waller Barrett, New York.

23. Osgood to Howells, April 2, 1883. Manuscript letter in the Houghton Library, Harvard.

24. Howells to Osgood, April 20, 1884. Manuscript letter, Columbia University.

25. Davison Dalziel, President of the Dalziel National Printing Co. Dalziel was born in London, 1853; he started a journal called *The Echo* in Sidney, Australia, in 1876; he went to San Francisco in 1878, where he launched the *San Francisco Daily Mail*; in 1880 Dalziel arrived in Chicago and began the *Newsletter*. He also founded the Dalziel Advertising Company for advertising railroad lines. A. T. Andreas, *History of Chicago* (1884–1886), III, 672.

26. Howells to Osgood, September 23, 1884. Manuscript letter in the Houghton Library, Harvard.

27. Undated manuscript letter in the Houghton Library, Har-

vard. Mr. Whitmore was Traffic Manager of the Fitchburg Railroad.

28. Howells to Osgood, February 9, 1885. Manuscript letter in the Houghton Library, Harvard. Thomas William Clarke is listed in the *Harvard Alumni Directory* as of the class of 1855. He died in 1895. His name also occurs in the *Boston City Directory*, 1883, p. 223:

"Clarke, Thomas W. (Clarke & Raymond) lawyer and solicitor of patents, 29 Pemberton Sq." On p. 1507 is the advertisement:

Thomas William Clarke & F. F. Raymond, 2d.
Counsellors at Law.
Specialties of Practice:
  Patent, Copyright and Trade Mark
  Causes, and soliciting of Patents.
Offices, 29 Pembroke Square (Rooms 4, 5 and 6),
  Boston, Mass.

29. Dr. George Arms, of the University of New Mexico, drew our attention to these two letters, the draft of a letter from Howells, and the communications from John Whitmore and D. Dalziel which follow. They are all in the Howells Collection, Houghton Library, Harvard.

30. A letter written on the stationery of the Fitchburg Railroad is pasted on the inside cover of the Huntington Library copy of *Niagara Revisited*. The letter, which is signed "C. E. Foster," reads: "Dr. Sir—Yours of the 31st ultimo re. the book 'Niagara Revisited, etc.' This publication was never circulated on account of litigation arising and the supply was destroyed." The writer was perhaps Charles Elwood Foster, patent attorney (1841–193–?). The copy of *Niagara Revisited* in the Newberry Library is inscribed "Joshua Merill Boston Mass 1885."

31. Our account of this controversy is briefly authenticated by Howells himself, who personally sanctioned the following

statement, which is to be found in *The Book Buyer*, March, 1897. It was written by Albert Lee, editor of "Harper's Round Table," who attempted at that time to make a bibliography of the writings of Howells. "The whole has been revised personally by Mr. Howells," Lee wrote, and he then gave the following account of *Niagara Revisited*:

> This book was made by a Chicago firm for the Fitchburg Railroad Company, and the Chicago people were to pay Mr. Howells a certain sum for the privilege of using his sketch, which had already appeared in the *Atlantic Monthly*. But they failed to meet their obligations toward the author, and consequently Mr. Howells served a notice upon the railroad company, through his attorneys, which prevented the publication of the book. A very few copies got into circulation, but not more than ten or a dozen, and these are now carefully preserved as curiosities by the fortunate owners.

In 1912, a book dealer, Henry E. Lower, wrote to Howells, "Do you know where a copy of *Niagara Revisited* may be seen for description?" Howells replied, "Never published; printed by the Boston and Fitchburg R.R. but held back because of my proposing to sue for violation of copyright. Published in Atlantic Monthly." A photostat of this question sheet, sent to Howells by Lower, who was preparing a Howells bibliography, is in the writers' possession.

One reference to *Niagara Revisited* is to be found in *The Life in Letters of William Dean Howells*, I, 315. The editor tells us that the story

> was published in the May *Atlantic*, 1883. It was reprinted, without Howells's consent, as an advertisement for the Hoosac Tunnel Route of the Fitchburg railroad, but the author made the railroad suppress the whole edition. He afterwards added *Niagara Revisited* as a final chapter to *Their Wedding Journey*.

32. *Niagara Revisited* has been included in every American edition of *Their Wedding Journey* since 1887. It is to be noted that the reference to the new depot at Syracuse does not appear in these editions. Drawings of the March family by C. Carleton accompany the essay in the 1895 edition of *Their Wedding Journey* and show the Marches in the clothes of the 1890's.

A Reading of Tess of the D'Urbervilles

BY HORACE E. HAMILTON

In the sequence of Hardy's novels, from 1871 to 1895, the last two [1] prove to have engaged him more deeply than any of his previous writings. The author of *Tess*, of *Jude*, and the projector of *The Dynasts*, seems to have reached a stage in his art when he needed a wider, a more universal, metaphor. His device of personifying nature—already familiar to us in such scenes as Egdon Heath—is extended in *Tess of the D'Urbervilles* to a symbolizing of action and character. These elements of a resultant allegory, because not seen in their connected pattern, have frequently been cited as mere distortions of realism.

Although Hardy designates seven "phases" in his story, the general structure might have been the five acts of a tragic morality play. The title would be: England's Paradise Lost. The first act would offer the initial propositions from which the fateful demonstration would follow: Tess's meeting with Clare; her father's assumption of a defunct title; the hastening of his economic ruin which indirectly results from a whim that his daughter marry into the wealthy D'Urber-villes; and, finally, the poor instruction the girl has had at home. The second act would be Tess's seduction and her subsequent efforts to regain her integrity. Depending upon which face of Hardy's compound metaphor we see at a given moment, we read here either Eve's forfeit of Paradise, or England's loss of her rural domain. In the third act Tess seeks regeneration in the bosom of Nature (Talbothays). Rising from this is the intended union between Tess-Eve-Nature and Angel-Adam-Mind. The fourth act brings about the marriage-and-no-marriage of the two, the attempted harmony between an Apollonian principle and that of Cybele or earth-mother (with the fateful defection of the Apollonian). The fifth, bringing us full circle, is the harvest of Angel's rejection of Tess and her gradual conquest by the wrong forces (the various guises of Alec D'Urberville). As the first act sees the seeds scattered, the last reaps the tares: the folk world of agrarian England has had to sell out to economic exploitation, while high ideals and the new Science stand impotently by.

Tess Durbeyfield and Angel Clare have their first glimpse of each other during the Maytime rites held near the girl's home in the Vale of Blackmoor. In this "Cerelia," as Hardy calls it, each girl carries a peeled willow wand and bunch of white flowers and is dressed in white. But Tess, in whom "you could sometimes see her twelfth year in her cheeks," is not the one whom the youngest of the Clare brothers leads off in the dance.

Pedigree, ancestral skeletons, monumental record, the D'Urberville lineaments, did not help Tess in her life's battle as yet, even to the extent of attracting to her a dancing partner over the heads of the commonest peasantry.[2]

When he leaves to overtake his brothers, Angel looks back and "could see the white figures of the girls in the green enclosure whirling about as they had when he was among them. They seemed to have quite forgotten him already" (p. 16). All but one—the one with whom he had not danced. This white shape "stood apart by the hedge alone."

Thus Tess has already been identified with a seasonal phase of nature. Clare's is a seemingly casual encounter with Tess in her springtime; but actually it is a foreshadowing of the blindness accompanying his intellectuality. The light of mind (which his very name suggests) will be insufficient in the crisis to preserve the girl from her fall. Two years later, resisting Clare's courtship at the great dairy, she asks: " 'Why didn't you stay and love me when I—was sixteen; living with my little sisters and brothers, and you danced on the green?' " (p. 250). Like Milton's angel Raphael, Clare might have brought to her some of his divine wisdom as armor against the advances of the Tempter. On the night of the seduction in The Chase, mist hung and timeless, it is a sleeping Eve who half hears Satan whispering into her dreams:

> He knelt and bent lower, till her breath warmed his face. . . . Darkness and silence ruled everywhere around. Above them rose the primeval yews and oaks of The Chase, in which were poised gentle roosting birds in their last nap, and about them stole the hopping rabbits and hares. Where, might some say, was Tess's guardian angel? Where was providence in her simple need? (p. 90).

The triad of Tess, Alec, and Clare have now emerged to play the elemental morality of nature, worldly corruption, and pure intellect. As usual with Hardy, the point of view is woman's, in this case Tess's, through whom we see the personal events unfold that will be emblematic of a kind of national tragedy.

The fall of Tess does not so much lead to a theological denouement as a struggle between the daughter of nature and the tyranny of society. In the economic reverses of the Durbeyfields—an authentic but deteriorated branch of the once proud D'Urbervilles—Tess becomes the sport or mutation of a nobler but dying species. Although seduced by a son of the new-rich borrower of the D'Urberville name, she scorns assists from her despoiler. Her deeper instincts transcend the strictures of conventional morality. With healthy independence she prefers the hard labor of a harvester, loyally keeping her infant by her side. Working in the sun-bathed fields in a ritual older than her race, she takes on the protective coloration designed by Nature. "A fieldman," says Hardy, "is a personality afield; a field-woman is a portion of the field" (p. 111). In this environment, her own people accept her unquestioningly. She is not a woman in disgrace, but an embodiment of fertility, her inherent grace suggesting a sort of pagan deity. The sun itself imparts benevolence, explaining "the old-time heliolatries in a moment. . . . One could feel that a saner religion had never prevailed under the sky" (p. 109). And we think ahead to the final scene in the book in which Tess stretches out on the sacrificial sun altar of Stonehenge.

In her simplicity she baptizes her baby on the eve of its death. She assumes then—as repeatedly in her moments of self-reliance—almost superhuman proportions, appearing to the awakened younger sisters and brothers "singularly tall and imposing . . . a being large, towering and awful—a divine personage with whom they had nothing in common . . ." (pp. 119–120). But for the degrading eyes of society, Hardy implies, she would remain nature's noblewoman. "She had been made to break an accepted social law, but no law known to the environment in which she fancied herself such an anomaly" (p. 108). Or again, "Alone in a desert island would she have been wretched at what had happened to her? Not greatly" (p. 115).

To stifle her parents' naïve hopes of marrying her into the family of bogus D'Urbervilles and to check any source of embarrassment, she leaves home to find such work as she can do. "On one point she was resolved: there should be no more d'Urberville air-castles in the dreams and deeds of her new life" (p. 126). Here, as when Angel Clare dismisses illustrious ancestry as a spurious asset, and near the book's close when Tess and her family are forced to bed down by the ancestral chapel at Kingsbere, Hardy's intent is to show that the ethos of the country was worthy of preservation for its own sake. Preserve it, he means, from exploitation by the commercial D'Urbervilles on the one hand; on the other, withstand such fatuous ambitions as John and Joan Durbeyfield's of reviving a lost identity with forebears who were themselves predatory in the feudal past.

But even as Angel Clare, guided by a divine light of reason,[3] points out some such truth to his bride on their wedding night, he fails her—the very *desiderium* of his superior understanding.

II

While the theme of lost virtue in a degraded society dominates the section discussed, Hardy has not abandoned his Biblical analogy: there is a temporary Eden in which Tess and Clare must come together. The great dairy of Talbothays in the Frome Valley of Dorset is the setting of Tess's new life; and it is here, in scenes unforgettable in their images of natural fecundity, that she comes again under the awakening eye of Angel Clare. "All the while," says Hardy, "they were converging, under an irresistible law as surely as two streams in one vale" (p. 165).

Tess becomes part of surroundings rich in the natural detail of Hardy's finest description. Here diminish opposing views of the world: the one that shrugged with her mother's "Well, we must make the best of it I suppose. 'Tis nater, afterall, and what do please God!" and the other expressing its harsh evangelism in fiery red paint on roadside walls: "THY,DAMNATION,SLUMBERETH,NOT" and "THOU,SHALT,NOT, COMMIT" (pp. 101; 102). The beginning of Chapter XIX, all of XX, and much of XXII and XXIII build up the most palpable Eden, its vividness hard to equal anywhere in Hardy's writing. In the dawns of this summertime, Tess was early awake, having the job of rousing the others:

> The first two persons to get up at the dairy-house, they [Tess and Clare] seemed to themselves the first persons up of all the world. . . . The spectral, half-compounded, aqueous light which pervaded the open mead impressed them with a feeling of isolation, as if they were Adam and Eve. At this dim inceptive stage of the day Tess seemed to Clare to exhibit a dignified largeness both of disposition and physique, an almost regnant power. . . .
> She was no longer the milkmaid, but a visionary essence of woman—a whole sex condensed into one typical form. He called her Artemis, Demeter, and other fanciful names half teasingly, which she did not like because she did not understand them (p. 167).

Here in her true setting, as in the harvest field, or in the dark of night baptizing her dying child, she is transformed. Here her pedigree scarcely requires the fussy validations of a particular generation.

But any outlines of a Biblical allegory invariably merge with other associations: at this point with contrasts of Christian and pagan culture. Back in his father's vicarage at Emminster, Clare has ample opportunity for revisions of perspective. Here he may enjoy the erudite company of his rather priggish brothers, not to mention earnest talk with the unquestionably chaste Mercy Chant. But the earth of Talbothays still draws more powerfully than the Bible classes of Miss Chant. "Clare's mind flew to the impassioned, summer-steeped heathens in the Var Vale, their rosy faces court-patched with cow droppings; and to one the most impassioned of them all" (p. 201). Yet his preference for the pagan is to be far from consistent. He is enamored of the idea, the theory, while it permits him the illusion of living by reason. Even as he has the skeptic's capacity to decline the Church as a calling (for its fancied narrowness), he has less capacity to set aside purely intellectual concepts when they blind him as a man. He had told his father "in a moment of irritation, that it might have resulted better for mankind if Greece had been the source of the religion of modern civilization, and not Palestine" (p. 203).

But even when flirting with the attractions of paganism, Clare's logic is less sound than Tess's instinct with its simple code forgotten or unrecognized by the changing world. Even as honesty constrains her to speak out, she senses the risk of laying before the uncompromising mind of her suitor the question of her past. Already, to her revelation that she is a D'Urberville by blood, Clare displays strong prejudices: " 'I should have been glad to know you to be descended exclusively from the long-suffering dumb, unrecorded rank and file of the English nation, and not from the self-seeking few

who made themselves powerful at the expense of the rest' "
(p. 242). Not until Tess sleeps on the sacrificial altar at
Stonehenge does it dawn on him that the girl, over whose
nominal heredity he quibbles, is very much one of the "long-
suffering dumb, unrecorded rank and file of the English
nation."

III

Whatever the inhibiters at work on each, Angel needs his
milkmaid, and the milkmaid needs her Angel. Clare, whose
apprenticeship at Talbothays is to bring practical experience
to an agricultural career, needs not only a healthy farm girl
for a mate, but in a wider sense needs the complement of
Tess's instinctive nature to his lofty ideals. Tess, whose
physical attractions cannot survive the defilements of a
cynical world, needs not only a responsible mate to salvage
her fallen estate, but in a wider sense needs the guidance of
a superior intellect to complete her as a symbol of the
domestic integrity of rural Britain. If the dual themes may
be joined at this point, that integrity would resemble a kind
of Eden before false values invaded it, and a sort of fission
of body and soul had resulted.

The end of the old year, the eve of the new, is chosen for
their wedding date. It is a precarious moment when Tess
asks herself, "Could it ever be? Their two selves together,
nothing to divide them . . . ?" (p. 261). As usual, her
doubts are instinctively right. Fate will quickly conspire with
the weaknesses of each to disunite such a logical union. The
letter with her explanation goes untimely astray. After the
private wedding, Clare's platonic kisses pressed as consolation on Retty, Izz, and Marian, seem only to stir their half-
reconciled feminine feelings. Tess notices, and is sad for

them. But—"of all this, Clare was unconscious" (p. 274). Nor do any but Mr. Crick the dairyman note the unaccustomed crowing of a cock in the afternoon as Clare takes Tess through the wicker gate. The second time the cock crew "straight at Clare" (p. 274). After the third crow, Mr. Crick drives it off impatiently. "It only means a change in the weather," says Mrs. Crick, "not what you think: 'tis impossible!" (p. 275)

Back to the Biblical—the New Testament now—Hardy's symbolism here is obvious and deliberate. Perhaps for this reason the effect seems more forced, less effective than elsewhere. Despite the scriptural source of the cockcrow, the context again unites the Biblical with the broader cultural allegory. For all his benevolence, Angel Clare is to betray the very life force the country most needs. Later at Wellbridge House silently gazing at his bride, Clare thinks in terms of a one-way obligation: "What I am in worldly estate, she is. What I become, she must become. What I cannot be, she cannot be" (p. 278). Meanwhile outside their room in the old abbey, "the restful leaves of the preceding autumn were stirred to irritated resurrection, and whirled about unwillingly. . . . It soon began to rain. 'That cock knew the weather was going to change,' said Clare" (p. 278). The leaves seem to stir as with the deeply repressed instincts of Clare himself. By the fire, shortly after, while "imagination might have beheld a Last Day luridness in this red-coaled glow," which gives to Tess's heirloom necklace of diamonds "a sinister wink like a toad's" (p. 287), his bride is permitted at last to tell the story of her fall.

The betrayal is, of course, Angel's rejection of womanhood's innocence even in her fallen estate. In Genesis, Adam ate also of the fruit: according to Milton, in order to share Eve's disgrace. Angel, instead, wants to "work it out in his mind" (p. 297). As he falls back on cold reason, we feel Tess's dismay that life itself—complex and ineffable—is to be determined by this ethical dogmatism. It is preposterous —whatever the best interests considered—that Clare should pronounce a sort of death by inanition. The ancient Cistercian abbey, like the D'Urberville estate to which it belongs, is in ruins. But "the mill still worked on, food being a perennial necessity; the abbey had perished, creeds being transient" (p. 299). Clare is obsessed now with the resemblance of Tess to a sinister-looking D'Urberville gazing down from one of the portraits. His own face, on the other hand, wears "that terrible sterile expression which had spread thereon since her disclosure" (p. 300). At which point the name of Angel Clare, itself, assumes ironic incongruity. "With more animalism," says Hardy, "he would have been a nobleman" (p. 312). And Tess is "appalled by the determination revealed in the depths of this gentle being she had married—the will to subdue the grosser to the subtler emotion, the substance to the conception, the flesh to the spirit" (p. 313).

The sleepwalking scene, vexing as it has usually been to reconcile aesthetically, actually opens another—a subliminal —dimension to the complex relationship of Angel and Tess. As in few—if any—other instances, Hardy here adds a cloudy ingredient to the clear prescription of Angel's behavior. It is Adam with a buried self; Adam finding a heritage of affinities unidentified by his mentor Raphael. We may suppose that only in sleep—as when he carries Tess in his arms to the coffin in the ruined abbey church—does Angel's inhibited self do what his waking consciousness forbids.[4] She suffers him, grateful if only for his sleeping touch, sensing his un-conscious self as a part of him that cannot reject her. It does not occur to her that his act may also express an un-conscious desire to bury the flesh, the corruption of which he cannot endure. In any event, she is reluctant to startle him from his sleep, trying gently instead to persuade him back in from the chill night. " 'Let us walk on, darling.' . . . To her relief, he unresistingly acquiesced; her words had apparently thrown him back into his dream, which thence-forward seemed to enter on a new phase, wherein he fancied she had risen as a spirit, and was leading him to Heaven" (p. 319). Tess senses that she has been rejected by a part of him only. Later, at breakfast, she is on the verge of men-tioning the sleepwalking, but hesitates. For him to know that

> he had instinctively manifested a fondness for her which his common sense did not approve; that his inclination had com-promised his dignity when reason slept, again deterred her. It was too much like laughing at a man when sober for his er-ratic deeds during intoxication (p. 320).

Since she had acknowledged her mistake at the hands of Alec D'Urberville, Tess's natural instincts would probably have carried her over the mere social disaster, the original sin, to accept a healthy continuance of life. The moral de-termination of the enlightening Angel, on the other hand, shakes her faith in life as the effect of the sin originally could not do. "Don't make it more than I can bear!" she cries when her mate announces his plan to go ahead with his farming venture in Brazil. Ironically, the woman whom even his mother comes to see as an ideal helpmeet in his ambi-tion is to be rejected on abstract principle. And in that primitive land, of all places, principle alone would seem to be of doubtful use. At the parsonage the kindly vicar and his wife are not told the secret of the new bride—"sincere and simple souls whom he loved so well; who knew neither the world, the flesh, nor the devil in their own hearts; only as something vague and external to themselves" (p. 336). The son assumes that the father's moral limitations are the same as those smothering the simple humanity in himself.

IV

Clare goes to Brazil alone. Through spring and summer, with characteristic self-reliance, Tess works in a dairy—though not at Talbothays, with its memory of her husband. It is a vegetative existence now, without the stimulus of an Angel Clare. "Mentally she remained in utter stagnation, a condition which the mechanical occupation rather fostered than checked" (p. 337). She is shorn of the stature and impressiveness that was hers in the days before her expulsion from Eden. And meanwhile to farmer Clare's ambitions the promise of the new world proves hollow. He has abandoned old England, which well might have used his passion for scientific farming, and soon lies ill of fever in the alien "clay lands near Curitaba." Tess, "fearing towns, large houses, people of means and social sophistication, and manners other than rural" (p. 350), makes but limited use of the funds left her by Clare, preferring as always her own resources. "Society might be better than she supposed from her slight experience of it. But she had no proof of this, and her instinct in the circumstances was to avoid its purlieus" (p. 350).

With the winter and lack of work, she seeks an out-of-the-way farm at Flintcomb-Ash, as dreary and sterile as Talbothays had been congenial and productive. On her way she thinks it necessary to clip her eyebrows, shorten her hair, and wrap up her face to avoid molestation along the road. Out of her element—her Eden—fending off a world that had no Clare, she finds comeliness an embarrassment. She must hide it. Diminished now in her wintertime, she can yet remind us of the simple adjustment of which she was capable just after her motherhood, "a figure which is part of the landscape; a field-woman pure and simple, in winter guise; a gray serge cape, a red woolen cravat, a stuff shirt covered by a whitey-brown rough wrapper, and buff-leather gloves" (p. 357).

At night, retiring among some trees on an estate, she is shocked by the sight of some mutilated pheasants which had been shot at by hunters and left to die. In pity she wrings their necks, reflecting meanwhile how she has exaggerated her own plight in the face of a heedless world—"so unmannerly and so unchivalrous towards their weaker fellows in Nature's teeming family" (p. 355). Taking the side of nature, she despises society, cruel to the victims of its sport. But to ignore its opinion—"that she could not do so long as it was held by Clare" (p. 356).

Consistently the bleak landscape of the Dorset hills (near the Egdon Heath of Eustacia Vie) is contrasted with the fertile pastures of the great dairies. Tess is the forlorn stepchild of this land, as she was the nubile essence of the other. Its oppressiveness increases as she approaches her destination:

> Towards the second evening she reached the irregular chalk tableland . . . bosomed with semi-globular tumuli—as if Cybele the many-breasted were supinely extended there—which

stretched between the valley of her birth and the valley of her love [that is, between Marlott in the north and Talbothays in the south] (p. 358).

Flintcomb-Ash is "a starve-acre place," one of a type of village "uncared for either by itself or by its lord" (p. 363); in fact, a sample of the absentee ownership which is crowding out the little farmer. In contrast to the budding associations of the earlier country, this place has "a complexion without features, as if a face, from chin to brow, should be only an expanse of skin" (p. 363). Here Mrs. Angel Clare is set to work with Marian and Izz, two of her husband's earlier admirers, grubbing out the half-mutilated turnips for cattle fodder. They were silhouetted on a field "rising above stony lanchets or lynchets—the outcrop of siliceous veins in the chalk formation, composed of myriads of loose white flints in bulbous, cusped, and phallic shapes" (p. 363). The rougher sensibilities of Marian make her "shriek with laughter" as she uproots the "queer-shaped flints aforesaid," while Tess remains "severely obtuse" (p. 366). In this chilled, arid place Hardy's associations are with male hardness—later, negation—against the soft fruitfulness of woman, as frustrated here as the wracked imprisoned form of "Cybele the many-breasted . . . supinely extended there." It is in this gross and alienated place—so close, yet so far from her Eden of promise—that Satan turns up again.

The two themes are once more intermingled: the persecution of Eve and the socio-cultural problem of England. However different the strands, Hardy sees them as complementary: the archetypal myth and its protean variations ramifying into a form of national tragedy. The ratio between the theological symbol, the story, and the wider social analogy is something like that of the musical signature, the melody, and the counterpoint.

With the return of Alec D'Urberville—blacksuited now as an evangelical preacher—the assault on Mrs. Clare's hard-pressed integrity is renewed. Now, if ever, she needs a strong defender, and in the logic of things, whom if not Angel himself? But acting on other logic, he has left her more imperiled than ever. In her over-tried love and shaken ideal of him, she faces the last great temptation alone, the final corruption. Now, as the devil can quote Scripture, Alec can rationalize his interest in Tess as his new-found Christian charity. But the "conversion" which makes him so cocky is quickly sloughed off like his black colthes. As soon as Tess crosses his path, he is secularized once more; she is, as he asserts, *his* corrupter now. Sensing her own disruptive influence, Tess feels the "wretched sentiment which had often come to her before, that in inhabiting the fleshly tabernacle with which Nature had endowed her she was somehow doing wrong" (p. 395).

Even as the rats are hunted down when the hayrick is leveled, Tess knows that Alec is only waiting till her work is done to begin his gameful stalking. It is nip and tuck with time now; for as Angel acquires perspective far away in his own adversity, the assault on his true wife progresses inexorably.

After the hayrick incident Tess returns in desperation to Marlott—to the family which has received over half of the money left by Clare. Here she merely encounters afresh the improvidence of her father, "Sir John." Amiably irresponsible all along, into his mouth is now put a wry commentary on the assiduous antiquarians who "spend lots o' money in keeping up old ruins, and finding the bones o' things, and

such like," when "living remains must be more interesting
to 'em still, if they only knowed of me" (p. 441).

V

Having tracked her down at Marlott,[5] Alec discovers Tess at
dusk with some neighbors burning dead weeds in their
garden plots. Unnoticed, he takes his place on the other side
of the fire and falls to with a pitchfork. " 'A jester might say
this is just like Paradise,' " he says, startling her out of a
momentary peace. " 'You are Eve and I am the old Other
One come to tempt you in the disguise of an inferior animal' " (p. 444). She tries to get rid of him, having already
spurned his offer of financial help; yet later, when her father
has died and the family must give up its lifelong freehold,
she is again confronted, and again must refuse. Because of
her family's need, she knows how costly is this independence.

Twice she has written to Clare, the last time a brief
despairing note; but he does not receive this word until he
arrives some time later at Emminster. Meanwhile the Durbeyfields must move; and with no clear object in mind they
set out for the ancestral village of Kingsbere. Ancestral indeed! they find it holds nothing for them, with the one little
inn already filled. The carter unloads their heaped possessions in the lea of the ruined chapel which holds the tombs
of the long dead D'Urbervilles. What follows is a temporary
shift from the Eve-Satan analogy to the Faustian. As Tess
wanders disconsolately among them, Alec is revealed
stretched across "an altar-tomb, the oldest of them all." It is
his macabre joke, which he follows up with a final Mephis-
tophelian offer of "The Slopes," a house on his estate. "He

stamped," it says, "with his heel heavily on the floor; where-upon there arose a hollow echo from below."

> "That shook them a bit, I'll warrant! . . . The old order changeth. The little finger of the sham D'Urberville can do more for you than the whole dynasty of the real underneath. . . . Now command me. What shall I do?"
> "Go away!" she murmured (p. 464).

Hardy seems to anticipate the scene at Stonehenge, though reversing it here. Where Alec, of the sham D'Urber-villes, mocks the spirit of her ancestors, Tess, on the altar stone of that vastly more ancient landmark, unconsciously invokes another spirit, the Sun itself—"older than the cen-turies; older than the D'Urbervilles" (p. 501). "One of my mother's people was a shepherd hereabouts," she observes to Clare. "And you used to say at Talbothays that I was a heathen. So now I am at home" (p. 502). In the dark she chooses the altar stone because it still retains the warmth of the sun.[6] This, then, is where she finally belongs, as she belonged the day he first saw her dancing in the village rites of spring. Neither her father's claim to D'Urberville blood, nor Alec's claim of her body, nor Clare's for her moral purity did justice to the woman who awaits her arrest for murder. But there she lies, feeling the last warmth of the sun in the stone—an unmistakable figure for sacrifice. The offering is of a creature of Nature, a woman of the farms, fertility itself, worshiped once by the earliest Britons. In-stead of returning, as it were, to the Eden motif (the signa-ture already established for the music), the author has now shifted his basic key completely to the natural heritage of England. Tess is no longer Eve; she is the embodiment of an agrarian spirit out of England's past, sacrificed to the no-god principle of a sterile England.

Whatever its aesthetic merits, the sun-stone scene is given extra poignancy when we note the preparation for it in Tess's earlier surrender to Alec in the synthetic, mushrooming resort of Sandbourne (Bournemouth). Hardy draws the paradox of a rootless city sprung up in the almost primeval setting of the surrounding country:

> Within the space of a mile from its outskirts every irregularity of the soil was prehistoric, every channel an undisturbed British trackway; not a sod having been turned there since the days of the Caesars. Yet the exotic had grown here suddenly as the prophet's gourd; and had drawn hither Tess (p. 480).

The incongruity of "a cottage girl, his young wife, amidst all this wealth and fashion" (p. 481) is the more appalling to Angel as he realizes that his own neglect has driven her to it. In a sense, Alec is Sandbourne; Tess is the "irregularity of the soil" rapidly yielding to the new and careless trade in pleasure, and Clare is the diverted knowledge of the modern world standing impotently by. Tess has sold herself—to the false D'Urberville for the survival of the shabby Durbeyfields. Tragic justice requires a drastic stroke. The fatal stabbing of Alec is that stroke—desperate, antisocial, fatal for herself, yet a stroke nevertheless for freedom.

Together they fly from the villas and hotels into the concealing depths of New Forest. Society will be paid, as Tess knows—even when Angel talks of flight from the country. Their plight is desperate, but that fact fades before the brief interlude of an ineffable union. Body and soul, they are at last one. Half lost in the shadows of New Forest, they come upon an empty mansion for rent. There is nothing else near it, no one around it; and though it is not theirs, they occupy it. Its singular, unexpected appearance in this place leads up to the altar scene which completes the socio-cultural anal-

ogy: the Kingdom is about to be let; the owners are elsewhere. For three days—their long-deferred honeymoon—
they live in a kind of twilight bliss, peaceful even in the
knowledge that their time is short. England has little to hold
out for these long alienated halves of herself; but Hardy may
be suggesting that even temporary fulfillment must be taken
for the brief taste of impossible Eden that it may afford.

It can be seen throughout *Tess of the D'Urbervilles* that
a complex of symbolic images ramify from two compli-
mentary metaphors: the Biblical-Miltonic Eden and coun-
try-England's lost heritage. The allegory begins with the
ritual of Tess's seduction by the new man of fortune, and
ends with an atavistic sacrifice on the pagan altar of Stonehenge. In between, with the theological and pagan principles interacting, are the half-resolutions, conflicts, and
wrong turns of inevitable tragedy: the regeneration of Tess
the earth-figure; her abortive union with the idealistic, progressive, but impotent Clare; the exploitation and ultimate
corruption of the abandoned earth-figure; and the anar-
chistic resolution of evil by violence in the death of Alec and
the illegal appropriation of the empty house. How explicit
Hardy may have wished this pattern to be, it is hard to say.
But implicit it certainly is. And such a pattern (apart from
the richness it imparts to the whole) seems indispensable as
a justification of otherwise random emphasis on incidents
and behavior unharmonious to strictly naturalistic narrative.

Notes

1. That is, beginning with *Desperate Remedies* and ending
   with *Jude. The Well-Beloved*, 1897, is actually the last.

2. *Tess of the D'Urbervilles*, Harper's Modern Classics (New York, 1950), p. 16. Subsequent references to *Tess* will be parenthesized within the text.

3. "Divine light of reason" is just about what the name Angel Clare means; so does D'Urberville suggest "city-country," by compound Latin derivation; while Tess (Teresa) calls to mind the Spanish Carmelite saint of perfect purity and devotion (cf. the novel's subtitle—"A Pure Woman"). Hardy had originally chosen the name Sue (later used in *Jude*), then changed it to Rose Mary. Not until the thirty-fifth chapter did she finally become Tess.

4. This is like a ghostly repetition of the incident at Talbothays when Angel carried Tess and her two friends across a rain pool on their way to church. That was before he knew Tess's story. The interpretation might be that the new knowledge would inhibit such an intimacy—save in his sleep.

5. As with various other names in the book, Marlott (the home of the Durbeyfields) suggests ill fortune—the *marred lot* of Tess's family. Others invite speculation: "The Slopes," for Alec's home—a place of moral retrograde? the *barren* suggestion in the name, Flintcomb-Ash; Kingsbere, for Bere Regis; Sandbourne, for Bournemouth—a place of impermanence or instability, etc.

6. Later, with the sunrise, Angel observes that this particular stone lies in an axis with the flame-shaped sun stone. It is an archaeological fact, of course, that this axis points exactly to the rising of the sun on Midsummer Day.

The Death of Gissing: A Fourth Report

BY ARTHUR C. YOUNG

George Gissing sailed from England for France on May 6, 1899, leaving behind him his termagant second wife, Edith Underwood Gissing, and two sons; he knew that there was little chance of his ever taking up his life again on English soil. Since 1897 he had been separated from his wife, whose irascible temper and sublime vulgarity had driven him away. In France Gissing hoped to find some region where he could nurse his various illnesses which could not be cured in the English climate. But health was not his first consideration; he was on his way to meet Mlle. Gabrielle Fleury, a twenty-nine-year-old Frenchwoman, with whom he planned to set up a new home. He had met Gabrielle when she had come to England to ask for permission to translate New Grub Street. She was intelligent, attractive, and sympathetic, and to her Gissing explained why it was impossible for him ever to live with his wife again. Within a year Gabrielle and Gissing had decided that they would have to live in France if they wanted to share their lives. So on

May 7, 1899, at Rouen, the couple went through an illegal marriage ceremony.[1] From that date on, Gabrielle was known in both England and France as "Mrs. Gissing." [2] Among the reading public and Gissing's friends, this deception was childishly simple. Edith had never been seen by her husband's friends nor was she known at all outside the immediate family.

After their marriage, Gabrielle and Gissing, in company with her invalid mother, moved their household frequently in search of a healthful climate which might ease his emphysema and rheumatism. They finally settled in a rented villa at St. Jean Pied de Port, near the Spanish border, where Gissing hoped the mountain air from the Pyrenees might restore him. Throughout the summer of 1903, Gissing suffered constantly from his rheumatism and lung disorder, and then in early winter he contracted a cold which led to his death in December.

Three English friends of Gissing, Theodore Cooper, Morley Roberts, and H. G. Wells, who were present either shortly before or immediately after his death on December 28, 1903, published accounts of his last days and hours. The Reverend Mr. Theodore Cooper, an Anglican clergyman stationed at St. Jean de Luz, had one of his friends write an account for the *London Church Times*, announcing Gissing's eleventh-hour conversion to Anglicanism.[3] The report drew an immediate denial from Morley Roberts, who had arrived at Gissing's villa shortly after the death; Cooper, according to Roberts, was a kind of ecclesiastical vulture or body snatcher. When Cooper refused to be drawn into battle, the furor faded away, although neither Roberts nor Wells forgot the incident. Cooper's own words were printed many years later when a letter he wrote Gissing's sisters was published in an edition of the novelist's letters; [4] but the editors selected only excerpts which gave the history of the friendship and some details of events preceding Gissing's death.

When Morley Roberts published his masked biography of Gissing, *The Private Life of Henry Maitland* (1912), he discussed Gissing's last hours thoroughly and explained that Cooper, through some twist in his professional mind, had mistaken Gissing's hallucination about the supernatural world for a rational pronunciamento of religious conviction. Although Roberts had not been an eyewitness in the sickroom, he had spoken with Gabrielle Gissing and had interviewed the practical nurse so that his account is detailed and agrees with Cooper's except for the alleged conversion.

The third friend, H. G. Wells, who had raced to Gissing's side on receipt of an urgent telegram from Gabrielle, did not publish his version until much later. Wells reached Gissing on Christmas Day 1903 and stayed with him until the afternoon of December 27. During this three-day period, Wells helped to nurse Gissing and watched the gradual dissolution of his mind. Wells corroborated Roberts's belief that the hymns Gissing shouted and the mystical beings he described circling the room sprang from a fevered, disorganized brain. However, Wells did not publish the complete account of what he had seen until 1934; it appears in a section of his autobiography.[5] Thirty-one years had elapsed since Gissing's death, and it is likely that Wells refreshed his memory by leafing through Roberts's earlier publication. At any rate, there are few discrepancies in the two accounts as far as the factual information is concerned, but there is a wide difference in attitude on one count. Wells and Roberts express divergent impressions of the behavior and personality of Gabrielle Gissing and of Cooper; Wells lets the Reverend Mr. Cooper escape with a token lashing, but Gabrielle bears the full blow of the whip. According to Wells, Gabrielle was not "the nursing type of woman." "Her sense of proportion was inadequate and her need for sympathy untimely." [6] While the practical nurse rested, Wells had to assume the sickroom duties, since Gabrielle did nothing but pose and posture as the stricken wife unable to do as much as smooth a rumpled coverlet. But where Wells is stringent and derogatory in speaking of Gabrielle, Roberts praises her and says that she was genuinely "broken down by the anxiety and distress which had come upon her so suddenly." [7] It is Cooper who infuriates Roberts, and the defenseless clergyman receives the loud blast of his attack.

Gabrielle might have made a public statement in an effort to explain what actually did happen in the death chamber, but she was reluctant, because of her questionable situation as Gissing's mistress, to do anything that might attract vulgar publicity. However, in a series of letters, hitherto unpublished, she wrote her story to a friend of her husband.

This chronicle exists in five letters written by Gabrielle to Eduard Bertz, a German critic and novelist, who had known Gissing in London and had kept up a monthly correspondence with him for eighteen years.[8] While her husband was alive, Gabrielle had occasionally sent notes to Bertz commenting on his work and giving a kind of health report on Gissing so that a pattern of exchange had already been established. The most interesting letters are those sent to Bertz in the year following Gissing's death. These letters, now in the Rare Book Room of the Yale University Library, clear up some minor factual points, but they excite some speculation in other ways. Since Gabrielle was, naturally, the person most deeply affected by her husband's death, her letters have a certain validity which the printed records lack; and they also have the freshness and urgency that accompany a personal revelation. The five letters sent to Bertz in

1904 are dated January 17, April 2, May (the day is not given), September 29, and November 29; the first two were written at St. Jean de Luz, the third in London, the fourth at Lourmarin (Vaucluse), and the fifth at St. Jean de Luz. The two most important missives are those of January 17 and November 29, in which Gabrielle tried to give Bertz the full history of the death.

The January 17 letter says that Gissing became ill on Tuesday, December 8, and went to bed more out of precaution than necessity. The local doctor at St. Jean Pied de Port examined him and declared that there was nothing morbidly wrong. But on the following Saturday, Gissing suddenly became alarmingly feverish, and when his fever had not lessened by Monday, Gabrielle, apprehensive about the attending doctor's skill, telegraphed for a physician to come from Bayonne.[9] Although he examined Gissing on his arrival that same day, the doctor from Bayonne was not able to diagnose the illness as bronchopneumonia until Thursday, December 17. Assuring Gabrielle that the prognosis was hopeful, the doctor thought that the disease was progressing classically; the patient's heart was sound and his vitality high. Then wrote Gabrielle:

> Le Lundi matin, son état empire subitement, il se plaint de malaises étranges. Je télégraphie à Bayonne; le docteur accourt, ausculte et me dit qu'il est perdu, que les poumons sont guéris, c'est vrai, mais que le cœur a fléchi, qu'une *miocardite* s'est déclarée dont on ne guérit pour ainsi dire jamais. Le médecin s'attend(ait) même à ce qu'il passât dans la nuit tandis qu'il a résisté 8 jours encore; 8 jours *d'atroces souffrances*, de véritables tortures, de délire, de cris nerveux devenant presque, vers la fin, convulsions, et tout à fait aux dernières heures un peu de fièvre cérébrale. Je devrais dire plutôt la dernière nuit car, après une injection de morphine

le Lundi vers 7ʰ du matin, la connaissance lui est revenue, il m'a reconnue et a manifesté une vive émotion et ses yeux ne m'ont plus quittée jusqu'au dernier soupir, et il (a) fait les adieux muets les plus émouvants, les plus navrants; je dis *muet* car, en effet, avec le connaisance revenue, il a perdu la faculté de parler. . . .

Apparently Gissing lay paralyzed until his death at 1:15 in the afternoon.

In a later paragraph, Gabrielle mourns that she was unable to "collect" her husband's last words:

J'aurais tant voulu recueillir ses dernières paroles, dernières pensées, et pas même cette suprême consolation ne m'a été accordée! L'horrible délire, coupé d'instants de demi-lucidité où il était trop faible pour être bien en possession de sa pensée, était le plus souvent occupé des réminiscences de son travail, des lectures qui s'y étaient rapportées. Ainsi, dans sa dernière nuit, il récitait le Te Deum puis s'écriait qu'il voyait l'autre monde, l'enfer et les diables.

The hallucinations which the Reverend Mr. Cooper transmogrified into flights of angels and a prevision of heaven seem more likely to have been based in Gissing's reading and thinking about the early days of Christianity in Rome, the subject of his unfinished novel *Veranilda*, which was published posthumously in 1904. Although Gissing was either in delirium or speechless in his last hours, Gabrielle did recollect that earlier in his illness he had called her to the bedside, lamenting his unfinished novel and the brevity of his happiness with her; but then he abruptly ceased his complaint and said:

No, no, I must not give way to these feelings; it is unmanly and moreover unphilosophical. If I am to die, after all, it is by law of nature and I must not rebel against it. And I have to remember that my life has not been altogether unhappy. I have had an immense power of enjoyment, so that in spite of all my poverty and miseries, I have enjoyed life more than many happy people. I have done a work which, I think, will not be entirely forgotten tomorrow.[10]

Roberts, says Gabrielle, had heard indirectly about Gissing's illness and had set out for France, arriving just in time to follow the body to its tomb at St. Jean de Luz, which was selected for the burial because there was an English colony in the town.[11]

In spite of the importance Wells assigned to himself in outlining his visit, Gabrielle avoids any word at all about him, although she speaks of Cooper and Roberts; the letter closes with a request to tell her what disposition to make of the collection of letters which had passed between Gissing and Bertz.

The next three letters contain little information about Gissing, but here and there a few remarks are worth noting. The second letter, dated April 2, was written when Gabrielle had recognized and tried to accept the disaster. She mentions that she has thought of suicide but that she must live in order to care for her ailing mother. By this time, the article inspired by Cooper had come to her attention, but Gabrielle disposes of the announcement as worthless and wonders at the tactlessness of the parson. The May letter, sent from London, simply recounts her twelve-day visit to Wakefield, where she stayed with Gissing's mother and sisters and where she observed almost enviously the religious certainty of his family; they knew without qualms that Gissing was in bliss awaiting the reassembly of his friends. She also says that she has heard that Wells has been asked to write a preface for *Veranilda,* which was to appear in the autumn.

J'ai appris que Mr. Wells avait fait paraître sa Préface à "Veranilda"—ou plutôt ce qu'il destinait comme Préface—en article dans le "Monthly Magazine." [12] Plusieurs personnes m'ont écrit des lettres indiguées s'étonnant que "anyone could have written such [an] unsympathetic, misleading, objectionable article." Et ce n'est pas tout. La "Sphere," ayant sans doute exprimé un avis semblable, Mr. Wells s'est empressé d'y écrire que "Mr. Morley Roberts had fully endorsed his literary criticism on Gissing." Or, Mr. Roberts m'a écrit que cela l'avait fort contrarié car ce n'était pas exact, qu'il l'avait dit a Mr. Wells, mais que, d'autre part, le voyant dans cette fâcheuse posture il lui avait promis de ne pas contredire publiquement son assertion erronée. Là-dessus je lui ai répondu qu'à mon sens il devrait au contraire rétablir la vérité, car enfin sa vieille amitié avec G. lui imposait un devoir envers lui qu'il n'avait pas envers Mr. Wells. Que d'ailleurs si celui-ci s'attirait quelque ennui, il n'avait que ce qu'il méritait par son inconvenance, son extraordinaire manque de tact en saisissant l'occasion d'une préface au dernier ouvrage de son ami pour s'exprimer défavorablement et fort injustement sur tous ses autres ouvrages. Que s'il avait une opinion pareille, ce n'était ni le lieu ni le temps de l'émettre, surtout quand il se présentait comme un ami personnel de l'auteur, qualité qui oblige à plus de réserve encore. (Je suis fort heureuse de voir que vos réflexions sur cette manière d'agir sont identiques aux miennes, mon cher ami.) Enfin j'ajoutai que je trouvais aussi dépourvu de tact, et de plus absurde, que Mr. Wells ait mêlé à ses dires Mr. Roberts lui-même et prétendu étayer ses opinions littéraires des siennes. D'abord il lui en a gratuitement prêtées, et ensuite, quand bien même leurs deux appréciations eussent concordé, aurait-il *prouvé* par là leur justesse?

Est-ce qu'une appréciation d'œuvres d'art n'est pas toute personnelle, et comment ferait-on la démonstration de la justesse de son goût?—Pour finir, je priais Mr. Roberts de se souvenir que le public n'était que trop enclin aux malicieuses interprétations, et que bien des gens s'étonneraient sans doute du singulier et choquant empressement des amis de George à tâcher de jeter la défaveur sur ses œuvres,—ce qui me peinerait beaucoup, appliquées si faussement à lui (Mr. Roberts). Je n'en ai pas reçu de réponse, je ne sais si ma franchise l'a froissé; j'espère que non. Le grand thème, c'est que G. n'a écrit de romans que parce qu'il y a été contraint par la nécessité de gagner sa vie, que, livré à ses seules tendances, il se fut adonné entièrement à l'érudition pure, l'étude de l'antiquité, la visite des pays classiques etc. et Mr. Wells part de là pour déclarer qu'en conséquence ses romans *forcés* ne valent pour ainsi dire rien, qu'il y traite de sujets qui lui étaient antipathiques, ou qu'il ne connaissait pas ou ne comprenait pas, qu'il avait pour visée d'imiter Balzac tout simplement, qu'enfin il ne devenait original qu'avec *Veranilda*. Tout le reste peut-être rayé—ou à peu de chose près—de la littérature anglaise. Voilà en résumé l'article.

Gabrielle's virulence toward Wells, swollen by the appearance of the "Impression," flowed over the barriers decreed by taste, and in her final letter for 1904, she made plain and serious charges against him.

In this last epistle, dated November 29, Gabrielle summed up her grievances. On Gissing's request, she had sent a wire to Wells, asking him to come to France. He had complied, and on December 25, he arrived at St. Jean Pied de Port. At this time, Gissing had been in bed for nearly three weeks, and although he was weak, he still had enough energy to battle the myocarditis which had succeeded the pneumonia. According to the letter:

Il reprenait même appétit et réclamait à grands cris de la nourriture. Mais, comme toujours en pareil cas, le docteur avait prescrit de l'alimenter très fréquemment, mais très légèrement, surtout à très petites doses à la fois, afin de ne pas donner plus à faire au cœur malade. Or, dans la nuit du Samedi au Dimanche (26 au 27), Mr. Wells me dit qu'il va rester près de George jusqu'à minuit et insiste vivement pour que j'aille prendre un peu de repos pendant ce temps (nous n'avions pas de garde-malade!) en assurant qu'il fera parfaitement tout ce qu'il faut pour le malade. Quoique à contre cœur, je cède à ses instances, je vais m'étendre sur mon lit, mais, tourmentée, inquiète, je n'y reste qu'à peine une heure et je retourne dans la chambre. Et qu'y trouve-je? Mr. Wells m'annonçant triomphalement qu'il a profité de mon heure d'absence pour ingurgiter au pauvre malade, coup sur coup: un demi-litre de *beef-tea*, extrêmement fort, deux ou trois verres de champagne, une tasse de café, du thé, du lait,—enfin tout ce qu'il avait eu sous la main! Il déclarait avec satisfaction que George avant pris tout cela sans faire de difficulté, c'était la preuve que les médecins se tromperaient dans leur diagnostic et que G. tout simplement mourait de faim et avait besoin d'être *suralimenté*!! Le résultat en fut tout naturellement que le médecin qui, ce soir, avait laissé G. presque sans fièvre, et fort calme, le retrouva le lendemain matin dans une agitation violente, avec une fièvre ardente, le délire, etc., et qu'il me dit: "Je n'y comprends rien. Qu'est-il donc arrivé?" Et lorsque je lui eus raconté la chose, il leva les bras au ciel, en disant: "Il l'a tué!"

Wells's recollections agree with Gabrielle's statements on two points: the beef tea made by the Coopers was given to Gissing; and Gabrielle did leave the room, having been sent out to rest by Wells, who found her a nuisance instead of an aid in nursing the patient.[18] But Gabrielle's curious charge collapses when her own words are examined. In the January

17 letter, she reports unequivocally that the second doctor had told her eight days before Gissing's death that the myocarditis would be fatal. If Wells had so stuffed Gissing that his heart buckled under the strain, then such a tragedy could not have been passed over without a single reference for nearly a year.

The only explanation for Gabrielle's bitter words seems to be in the spate of charges and countercharges over Gissing's supposed deathbed conversion and the crushing evaluation of his work by Wells. These two incidents obviously irritated her sensibilities, and she turned her indignation and venom on Wells. That she did not appreciate Wells even before his article appeared is quite clear. Since Wells had originally arranged her first meeting with Gissing, Gabrielle may have nursed a spark of resentment toward him for his thorough knowledge of their history.

Each of the three reports written by Gissing's friends must be read judiciously: Cooper interpreted what he saw and heard from an ecclesiastical position; Roberts's whole biography of Gissing is a compound of imagination, self-interest, and inaccurate detail; Wells had to dig up old notes and rely on his memory many years after the event. This fourth report, contained in Gabrielle's letters, seems the most accurate in detail, and, except for the possibly malicious accusation about Wells, her account, not intended for publication, is as close to the truth as any of the other three.

NOTES

1. A. C. Young, "A Note on George Gissing," *The Journal of the Rutgers University Library*, XXII (December 1958), pp. 23–4.

2. Edith Underwood Gissing was committed to an asylum in 1902, remaining there until her death in 1917.

3. Morley Roberts, *The Private Life of Henry Maitland*, ed. Morchand Bishop (London, 1958), p. 223.

4. *The Letters of George Gissing to Members of His Family*, ed. Algernon and Ellen Gissing (London, 1927), pp. 397–9.

5. *Experiment in Autobiography* (New York, 1934), pp. 481–93.

6. *Ibid.*, p. 493.

7. Roberts, p. 215.

8. See A. C. Young, "George Gissing's Friendship with Eduard Bertz," *Nineteenth-Century Fiction*, XII (December, 1958), pp. 227–37.

9. Cooper says that he, on Gissing's request, telegraphed for his physician, a Dr. Malpas, to come from Biarritz (A. and E. Gissing, p. 397). The doctor's name has an uncomfortable denotation, but it is not significant in any way.

10. This quotation is in English in the letter.

11. Wells writes that Gabrielle had sent for him and Roberts, begging them both to come over (Wells, p. 491); Roberts, agreeing with Gabrielle, states that he had heard nothing until Wells sent him a telegram (Roberts, pp. 212–13).

12. "George Gissing, An Impression," *Monthly Review*, August, 1904, pp. 160–72.

13. Wells, p. 493.

Ambrose Bierce and the Art of War

BY DAVID R. WEIMER

As American commentators on Ambrose Bierce have universally remembered and then forgotten, there is something to be gained from sitting down with his stories and reading them—as stories. History in the twentieth century has, to be sure, furnished causes for our having spent less time with what Bierce wrote than with what he stood for. At the same time that two world wars have stimulated an interest in his fiction, particularly in the war stories, they have made still more intriguing to postwar sensibilities the remote, lonely figure Bierce was. The faintly sensational nature of his public life has served, also, to divert attention from his writings.

This biographical questing seems to me regrettable, but not entirely so. A momentary loss in literary appreciation may, after all, be a gain elsewhere; and so it has proved with Bierce. In undervaluing him as a writer, we have elevated him as a symbol—with results suggestive of fundamental ideas shared by American intellectuals and perhaps the public generally. It tells us something valuable about ourselves,

I believe, to learn that in the 1920's Americans conceived of Bierce as a Rebel, an Alienated Artist, an Iconoclast—all fundamentally social ideas implying the possibility of the individual's reconciliation with society—whereas our own postwar era has seen him as a Nihilist or Stoic, that is, in terms of isolated moral positions, as either denying all values or preserving one's own. It is worth a small literary sacrifice to know that.

But the same argument does not apply to the long run. Like Juvenal, his spiritual brother-in-arms, Ambrose Bierce will eventually be known only by his few scribblings. It is time that we become better acquainted with some of them.

Because the most thoughtful and eloquent appraisals of Bierce's work have appeared in the wake of World Wars I and II, it is worthwhile to discover what he was about in his battle fiction, a literary type of predictable appeal to post-war generations. Bierce wrote twenty such short pieces, all told, fifteen of them brought together (with eleven tales of unmilitary terror) in 1891 as *Tales of Soldiers and Civilians*. The best known of these Civil War episodes is "An Occurrence at Owl Creek Bridge," but equally typical of the subject matter and approach of the whole collection are "A Horseman in the Sky," "Chickamauga," "A Son of the Gods," "One of the Missing," "The Coup de Grâce" and "One Officer, One Man." Since these seven are, I think, also the best of his war stories, we may appropriately look at them more closely than at the others.

What are their characteristic features? They usually have one main character and are simply plotted. As a rule, they begin *in medias res*, follow a B-A-B structure (with a chronological reversion or flash back in the middle section), and end ironically. Frequently they depend on extreme devices to shock the reader, as when (in "The Coup de Grâce") a soldier discovers that swine have ripped open the abdomen of a wounded friend of his, still alive on the ground, and have been feeding on his entrails. (How cautious we should be in dismissing such incidents in the tales as *mere* contrivances is nicely illustrated by the fact that in the Cheat Mountains of western Virginia in 1861 Bierce had actually seen corpses whose faces had been eaten away by wild swine.) Furthermore, like Poe, to whom he owed a great literary debt, Bierce was strongly concerned with creating an effect. He also had a flair for building and sustaining mood, for developing motivation realistically and selecting the most cogent detail.

Now these observations are all pretty fragmentary, and I offer them here partly as evidence of the sort of criticism Bierce's war stories have commonly received to date. From H. L. Mencken, who argued in 1929 that Bierce's tales "are probably read today, not as literature, but as shockers," to Harry T. Levin twenty years after, who perceived in the war tales chiefly the thematic contrast "between the civilian's preconceptions of military glory and the soldier's experience of ugliness and brutality," critics of the war stories have viewed them from one angle or another, but never in the round. Even Carey McWilliams, who offered the fullest and in many respects the most sensible literary account of the short stories in his biography of some thirty years ago, played them down as coherent artistic achievements.

While I am as susceptible as anyone to quarreling with readers who see a short story only as bits and pieces, I find a certain justice in the piecemeal comments on Bierce's work. Too many of his stories lean heavily on crafty mechanics, on a kind of literary gadgeteering. Small wonder that critics have given tit for tat.

But despite all this, each of Bierce's best war tales does

have an artistic center. Many have sensed it, if no one has yet squarely confronted and described it. "A Horseman in the Sky" is the clearest example. Almost the entire action of this twelve-page story occurs near the top of a steep cliff in the mountains of Virginia. A Union soldier, Carter Druse, awakes as if intuitively from a forbidden sleep at his sentinel post:

> He quietly raised his forehead from his arm and looked between the masking stems of the laurels, instinctively closing his right hand about the stock of his rifle.
>
> His first feeling was a keen artistic delight. On a colossal pedestal, the cliff,—motionless at the extreme edge of the capping rock and sharply outlined against the sky,—was an equestrian statue of impressive dignity. The figure of the man sat the figure of the horse, straight and soldierly, but with the repose of a Grecian god carved in the marble. . . . The gray costume harmonized with its aerial background; the metal of accoutrement and caparison was softened and subdued by the shadow; the animal's skin had no points of high light. A carbine strikingly foreshortened lay across the pommel of the saddle, kept in place by the right hand grasping it at the "grip"; the left hand, holding the bridle rein, was invisible. In silhouette against the sky the profile of the horse was cut with the sharpness of a cameo; it looked across the heights of air to the confronting cliffs beyond. The face of the rider, turned slightly away, showed only an outline of temple and beard; he was looking downward to the bottom of the valley. Magnified by its lift against the sky and by the soldier's testifying sense of the formidableness of a near enemy the group appeared of heroic, almost colossal, size.

Private Druse raises his rifle, pauses, recognizes the rider, then fires at the horse. Abruptly the point of view shifts to that of an officer in the Union army. Climbing from below the mountain on which Druse reposes, the officer hesitates:

> Lifting his eyes to the dizzy altitude of its summit the officer saw an astonishing sight—a man on horseback riding down into the valley through the air!
>
> Straight upright sat the rider, in military fashion, with a firm seat in the saddle, a strong clutch upon the rein to hold his charger from too impetuous a plunge. From his bare head his long hair streamed upward, waving like a plume. His hands were concealed in the cloud of the horse's lifted mane. The animal's body was as level as if every hoof-stroke encountered the resistant earth. Its motions were those of a wild gallop, but even as the officer looked they ceased, with all the legs thrown sharply forward as in the act of alighting from a leap. But this was a flight!

As we suspected, the man whom the dying horse carries to his death is Private Druse's father. That is the trick of the thing. But one is likely to remember from the story, I believe, not so much the trick as the sharply sketched images of the motionless rider astride the horse. These images give us the most intense, most expressive part of the narrative, even as they interrupt it momentarily. They provide the emotional center of the story, the point which should—and I think for the most part in Bierce's battle tales does—coincide with the center of the author's implicit values.

Bierce's values will be clearer if we examine another passage from the tales. In "Chickamauga," a six-year-old boy, a deaf-mute, wanders from home, plays soldier in the woods and becomes lost. Suddenly he sees strange creatures moving with a terrific slowness on the ground among the trees. They are men, hundreds of them, wounded in battle, now crawling away from it. To the child, observing this dreadful scene,

> it was a merry spectacle. He had seen his father's negroes creep upon their hands and knees for his amusement—had ridden them so, "making believe" they were his horses. He now approached one of these crawling figures from behind and with an agile movement mounted it astride. The man sank upon his breast, recovered, flung the small boy fiercely to the ground as an unbroken colt might have done, then turned upon him a face that lacked a lower jaw—from the upper teeth to the throat was a great red gap fringed with hanging shreds of flesh and splinters of bone. The unnatural prominence of nose, the absence of chin, the fierce eyes, gave this man the appearance of a great bird of prey crimsoned in throat and breast by the blood of its quarry. The man rose to his knees, the child to his feet. The man shook his fist at the child; the child, terrified at last, ran to a tree near by, got upon the farther side of it and took a more serious view of the situation. And so the clumsy multitude dragged itself slowly and painfully along in hideous pantomime—moved forward down the slope like a swarm of great black beetles, with never a sound of going—in silence profound, absolute.

Here, as in "A Horseman in the Sky," the image is set amidst utter silence, but against an implied background of shattering sound—of the rifle shot or the battle just past, the crash of the horse and rider or the shrieks of the wounded about to come.

Both images are of motion, too, yet of no motion at all. In the first story the man and horse are initially "motionless," form "an equestrian statue"; plunging from the cliff, the man still does not change position, while the horse only seems to gallop on the earth. Similarly, in "Chickamauga" the great black beetles move so slowly as to make their motion appear as illusory as the rest of their "hideous pantomime." Equestrian statuary, cameos, pantomimes, beetles —Bierce's metaphors are drawn from different spheres of art and nature, but they all imply the ideas of arrested motion, of suspended sound.

We would seem to be in the presence of a writer whose treatment of his materials, indeed whose conception of external reality, is highly pictorial; and so we are. If Bierce is a slighter artist than Henry James or Faulkner, as he unquestionably is, the way he visualizes experience nonetheless has a great deal in common with that of the creator of the famous scene in *The Ambassadors* in which Lambert Strether, coming unexpectedly upon Mme. de Vionnet and Chad Newsome together in a boat, is forced to take a new view of the pair ("It was suddenly as if these figures, or something like them, had been wanted in the picture . . . and had now drifted into sight, with the slow current, on purpose to fill up the measure"); or with the creator of that natural world where the moment of a ten-year-old boy's first confronting an enormous bear takes on mythic proportions ("It did not emerge, appear: it was just there, immobile, fixed in the green and windless noon's hot dappling, not as big as he had dreamed it but as big as he had expected, bigger, dimensionless against the dappled obscurity, looking at him").

Still other features of the war stories become artistically significant when we place them in the light of Bierce's graphic intentions. As in his handling of sound and motion, Bierce interrupts, restrains, telescopes time. His most signal use of this device is in "An Occurrence at Owl Creek Bridge," a tour de force in which elaborate memories and fantasies flood through a hanged man's mind in the few seconds between his drop from the gallows (the bridge) and his losing consciousness. But Bierce manipulates time frequently in the stories, nearly always in constructing the type of scene already described.

He likewise exhibits a marked interest in light, shadow, and color and in exact, sparing description. He favors dramatic presentation over narrative, a restricted point of view (with only occasional shifts to the omniscient author), and the use of his main character in the role of spectator—all elements that work directly toward the creation of a single, vivid, static scene. This pictorial focus has been felt, rather than articulated, by American critics. They have shown an awareness of it chiefly in their metaphors, as when Bertha Clark Pope observed, in the course of introducing an edition of the *Letters* (1922), that "above all writers Bierce can present—brilliantly present—startling fragments of life, carved out from attendant circumstance . . . sharply bitten etchings of individual men under momentary stresses and in bizarre situations." In his *Portrait of the Artist as American* (1930), Matthew Josephson came closest of all the critics to touching the mainspring of the war stories, commenting on the equestrian scene in "A Horseman in the Sky" as "almost sculptural" in quality, on "the picture of the lost child" in "Chickamauga" and also on Bierce's "love for the purely kaleidoscopic, through his perception of form and mysterious beauty in each accidental effect of light."

Though Pope and Josephson stopped this side of developing their insights, both sensed that the painter's eye was not peripheral to the method of the war stories but somehow right in the middle of it. Roaming around a bit more among the better stories, they might have noted the central, organizing image in each. In "A Son of the Gods," a young officer braves enemy fire to reconnoiter the opposing troop positions and (after a few suspenseful minutes of astonishing bravery) is killed. In "One of the Missing," a courageous private scouts Confederate gun emplacements only to be trapped by a freak accident in a wooden shed where (after a brief, disciplined attempt to free himself from the wreckage) he dies of terror. In "The Coup de Grâce," an officer (glancing in a second from a herd of swine to his wounded friend upon the ground) realizes that he must kill the man to spare him further agony. In "One Officer, One Man," a well-intentioned army captain (during the first, shocking barrage of enemy gunfire) abruptly commits suicide.

While the arrested moment in these stories sometimes brings self-discovery to one of the characters, that is not really Bierce's main point. What the characters undergo—and what matters to Bierce—is an instant, always brightly attractive in its brief duration, of intensely felt or intensely perceived experience.

It is not in every case a moment of heroism, though often it is. Acute and pleasurable intensity—that is the distinguishing characteristic. And there is another: transience. The horse and rider will surely, swiftly fall, the groans of the dying soldiers resound, the courage go for naught. This is almost certainly what Josephson meant in referring to the war stories as creating "moments of instability—as in a dance—of ingenious, dire paradox on the part of the universe." The grotesquely unstable, fragile, precarious nature of the individual's rare and therefore valuable experience is precisely Bierce's theme.

A recognition of this theme makes it possible to understand both the incompleteness and the force of Carey McWilliams's statement that the war fiction conveys "the sense of an indescribable malevolence . . . mixed up in a strangely inseparable manner with the good and beautiful." And it makes possible, too, the proper evaluation of other critical judgments, such as Mencken's assertion (in his *Prejudices*, 1927) that Bierce's "war stories, even when they deal with the heroic, do not depict soldiers as heroes; they depict them as bewildered fools, doing things without sense, submitting to torture and outrage without resistance, dying at last like hogs in Chicago. . . ." Mencken had a surer grasp of Bierce's over-all place in American letters (minor but important) than of the literary subtleties.

We can judge, furthermore, what is sound and what is not in Ludwig Lewisohn's condemnation of all Bierce's tales as "morally and therefore in the last analysis creatively sterile, because Bierce showed himself conscious of no implication and disengaged no idea. The naked horror sufficed him." The remark is, within limits, perspicacious. Bierce was assuredly not conscious *enough* of the implications of his imagined world, not conscious enough to be thought of as a first-rate literary mind. But the naked horror did not suffice him. If less deeply, less complexly than his literary superiors of a later day, Bierce saw very far into the ambiguities of the war experience.

The "Traditional" Presidential Inaugural Address

BY ALBERT A. AUSTEN

On March 4, 1889, President Benjamin Harrison began his inaugural address by noting: "There is no constitutional or legal requirement that the President shall take the oath of office in the presence of the people, but there is so manifest an appropriateness in the public induction to office of the chief executive officer of the nation that from the beginning of the Government the people, . . . have been called to witness the solemn ceremonial." [1] Mr. Harrison was not only President, he was right. In fact, practically all of our inaugural procedures have come about through custom or, what might be termed, historical accident, rather than through constitutional requirement.[2] For example, though the oath of office may be given by any public official, it has traditionally been administered by the Chief Justice of the Supreme Court. On the other hand, the first open-air inauguration—that of President Monroe in 1817—resulted from the refusal of Henry Clay, as Speaker of the House of

Representatives, to allow the inaugural committee to replace the "plain, democratic" chairs of the House, where the ceremony was to take place, with the ornate red chairs of the Senate. Clay's friends argued that he was really concerned lest the floor of the House chamber prove to be too weak to hold the large number of people that was to be admitted. His critics, however, attributed his action to the fact that Clay was angry with Monroe because the latter had failed to appoint him Secretary of State. Whatever the truth of the matter, President Monroe addressed a crowd of eight thousand people outside the Capitol instead of a much smaller group inside it, and the most notable absentee was Henry Clay. Since that time all but two of our regular, public presidential inaugurations have been held outdoors.

The inaugural address, second in significance to the taking of the oath itself, is the result of custom rather than of political accident. It was established by Washington with his first inauguration in New York in 1789. Four years later, in Philadelphia, Washington almost discontinued the practice by delivering the shortest initial address on record—a speech of just four sentences or 135 words—in which he postponed his inaugural speech until the occasion of his fifth annual message to Congress. In 1797, however, John Adams followed the form of the first inauguration with an address which saluted at length the people, the Revolution, the Constitution, and his illustrious predecessor who had "merited the gratitude of his fellow-citizens, commanded the highest praises of foreign nations, and secured immortal glory with posterity." [3]

The speeches of Washington and Adams established a precedent, but it fell to Thomas Jefferson to set the pattern. Fully four fifths of these speeches follow the very simple pattern of organization used by Jefferson in his first inaugural address of 1801. Indeed, there is a substantial body of internal evidence to support the probability that our Presidents-elect have read the addresses of their predecessors and that they have found security in what might be called the traditional structure of the inaugural address. In President Monroe's first inaugural address of 1817, for example, he said that he was following the practice of the "distinguished men who have gone before me . . ." [4] Grover Cleveland, in his inaugural address of 1893, drew an analogy between the nation and a strong man who, though otherwise healthy, "may still have lurking near his vitals the unheeded disease that dooms him to sudden collapse." [5] Three and a half decades later Herbert Hoover used the same figure of speech in his inaugural speech of 1929 when he warned, "The strong man must at all times be alert to the attack of insidious disease." [6] The metaphor is a common one, but the fact that it occurs at very nearly the same place in both speeches is further indication that its use by Hoover was more than merely coincidental.

The striking similarity of most of our presidential inaugural addresses is evident not only in their predominant three-part organization, which consists of an introduction, a body, and a conclusion, but in the time given to each of these parts and in the nature of the observations made in each phase of the speech.

The conventional introduction consists of a brief but humble confession of the speaker's awareness of the great responsibilities involved in the office of President and an expression of gratitude for the confidence which the people have placed in him. The two sentiments are ordinarily briefly and simply phrased. Though Pierce, Grant, and William Henry Harrison stated or implied in their addresses that they did not seek the office but were called to it, the common tone of the introduction of the inaugural address is one of humility and thankfulness. Quite representative of this spirit are these early lines from President Zachary Taylor's inaugural address of 1849:

> The confidence and respect shown by my countrymen in calling me to be the Chief Magistrate of a Republic holding a high rank among the nations of the earth have inspired me with feelings of the most profound gratitude; but when I reflect that the acceptance of the office which their partiality has bestowed imposes the discharge of the most arduous duties and involves the weightiest obligations, I am conscious that the position which I have been called to fill, though sufficient to satisfy the loftiest ambition, is surrounded by fearful responsibilities.[7]

The body of the typical inaugural address is, as it is usually declared to be, a review of the principles of administration which will guide the President in office. This section of the speech most commonly takes the form of a quickly moving series of opinions or statements on specific issues of foreign and domestic policy. Here our Presidents have taken the opportunity to discuss the leading questions of the day, as they have seen them. To this discussion they have invariably devoted from seventy-five to ninety-five per cent of their speeches. In the variety of topics treated and in the emphasis given to them may be traced the origin, the persistence, and the resolution of most of the important questions that have shaped our history. Neutrality, for instance, stressed by almost every President from Washington to McKinley, yields at the beginning of the twentieth century to the concept of internationalism and to the determined search for world peace upon which we are now engaged. The question of slavery, gingerly and briefly touched

upon by Monroe in 1817 as a question of harmony of opinion in the Union, is not openly identified in the inaugural
speeches until Van Buren's address of 1837, and it is really
not discussed as such at any length until the addresses of
Lincoln's predecessors, Pierce and Buchanan. Economy in
government finance, of course, has been a perennial topic, as
have been matters relating to national defense, tariffs, and
taxes. At various times, war, a sound currency, the powers
of the executive, the use of public lands, civil service reform,
patronage, immigration, labor legislation, the enforcement
of the Eighteenth Amendment, and, of late, the rising tide
of Communism have all been given attention in these
speeches. The full list would be impressive and would, in
itself, represent a fairly complete summary of American
history. The common effect of these discussions, however, is
that they are a preliminary report on the state of the nation,
a summary or review of goals achieved or to be achieved in
domestic and foreign affairs. They are, of course, accompanied by the time-honored appeals to patriotism, to a sense
of national unity, to pride in the growth and prosperity of
our nation, and to a faith in our ability to solve our problems within the letter and the spirit of the Constitution.

The conclusion of the representative inaugural address
is most frequently an appeal to the President's colleagues
in government and to the people for aid and counsel. This
appeal is almost invariably heightened by a final brief prayer
to God for guidance. Occasionally a President has opened
and closed his speech with a prayer, as President Eisen-
hower did in his first inaugural address in 1953. Here, by
way of illustration of a traditional conclusion, are the closing lines from President Garfield's inaugural address of
1881:

And now, fellow-citizens, I am about to assume the great trust which you have committed to my hands. I appeal to you for that earnest and thoughtful support which makes this Government in fact, as it is in law, a government of the people.

I shall greatly rely upon the wisdom and patriotism of Congress and of those who may share with me the responsibilities and duties of administration, and, above all, upon our efforts to promote the welfare of this great people and their Government I reverently invoke the support and blessings of Almighty God.[8]

The form and content of the typical inaugural address are not unusual in any respect. The former represents the basic structure of practically every type of speech; the latter consists of matters one would expect a President to discuss on such an occasion. The surprising fact is, however, that so many of our Presidents have followed the tradition as faithfully as they have. Perhaps the force of the tradition itself, strengthened by the formal, ceremonial nature of the occasion, has been the chief cause of the development of a standard pattern in these speeches. The topical, time-bound, expendable nature of the speech, coupled with the desirability of cautious, nonargumentative statement inherent in the situation, may also have operated to bring about a practical conformity in the structure and substance of these addresses. The inaugural address is, after all, only a preface; it is ordinarily received in an attitude of expectancy rather than in one of acceptance, for the nation waits to see whether or not the President's actions will speak more loudly than his words.

The only aspect of these speeches in which there is appreciable variety is their length. Because Washington's speech at his second inauguration was only a token address, the distinction of having delivered the shortest, true inaugural address belongs to Franklin Delano Roosevelt. His fourth inaugural address, which he delivered from the portico of the White House in 1945, consisted of twenty-six sentences, or a total of about five hundred and sixty words. Sentences, it may be noted, are of little value in judging the length of inaugural addresses. More than one third of John Adams's address of 1797 consists of a single, monumental period of well over seven hundred words. The lengthiest inaugural speech is that of William Henry Harrison, our ninth President. Some 60,000 more or less patient spectators braved a bitter northeast wind for nearly two hours while the President discussed general questions in vague terms and in language heavily laden with the classical allusions which were fashionable in his day.[9]

Between Franklin Roosevelt's brief fourth inaugural address and William Henry Harrison's presidential dissertation lie the other forty-one public Presidential inaugural addresses. Only a third of these speeches, however, are substantially greater in length than their approximate average of twenty-two hundred words. Thus, in the critical moment between promise and performance, most of our Presidents have wisely decided to be brief rather than verbose.

Few, if any, of the inaugural addresses which conform to the pattern described would be judged to be great inaugural addresses. Treating, as they commonly do, a variety of topics, the attention of the speaker has been too widely dispersed to produce a speech of durable significance. The great inaugural address, on the other hand, is the product of concentrated effort upon a single theme and of what Professor Toynbee has called "the interplay between 'forces' and 'personalities' "[10] The early inaugural addresses (those of the two Adamses, Jefferson, and Madison) are notable examples of classical inaugural exposition; but the initial addresses of Lincoln tower above those of the Presidents of his own and the previous century because they were the products of a concern with a tremendous pressure placed upon one point in our Constitution—the permanency of the Union—and of the interplay between a unique personality and forces more violent than any that have been felt in our entire history.[11]

Lincoln, however, is not alone; the mold of the inaugural tradition has been broken on several occasions in our own century. In both form and content Theodore Roosevelt's inaugural address of 1905 contrasts sharply with those of his predecessors. It is exceptionally brief; no specific measures of foreign or domestic policy are discussed; and the usual opening and closing sentiments are omitted. In tone and purpose his speech is philosophical and inspirational rather than ceremonial and reportorial.

The impress of tradition is plainly visible in Woodrow Wilson's inaugural speeches of 1913 and 1917. However, in vigor of language, in level of statement, motive, and concept, in the vitality and intensity of their concern for the nation's future they are closer in kind to Theodore Roosevelt's speech. Like his and Lincoln's they give us not merely a measure of the moment but of the man.

The most sustained and consistent break with common inaugural practice may be found in the four inaugural addresses of Franklin Delano Roosevelt, which are reminiscent of Lincoln's inaugural addresses in the strength and originality of their statement. Each, too, is dedicated to a single, specific theme, namely: recovery, social justice, the rediscovery of the spirit of America, and the search for peace after victory. In each the form is made subordinate to substance. At no point in these speeches is Roosevelt's language that of a man who has to say something; throughout it is that of one who has something to say.

Chief Executives of the United States have addressed their countrymen on Inauguration Day forty-three times since Washington stood before the burghers of New York in 1789. The world has often noted, but seldom remembered, their words. The student of the history of ideas can find in these speeches an index to the problems—and to the lack of problems—facing the American people throughout our national history. All can find in these speeches evidence that memorable oratory stems not from glibness, but from competence and courage; not from an important occasion, but from a significant challenge. When competence, courage, and challenge meet, our heritage is enriched by the words of another Demosthenes, Lincoln, Churchill, or Roosevelt.

NOTES

1. *Inaugural Addresses of the Presidents of the United States from George Washington 1789 to Harry S. Truman 1949* (82d Congress, 2d Session, House Document No. 540 [U.S. Government Printing Office, Washington, D.C., 1952]), p. 143; hereinafter cited as *Addresses*.
2. The oath of office was stated in the original Constitution. The day of the inauguration, first left to Congress to determine, was changed from March 4 to January 20 by the Twentieth Amendment in 1933. Except for these two details, the Constitution is silent on other matters of inauguration procedure.
3. *Addresses*, p. 7.

4. *Addresses*, p. 27.
5. *Addresses*, p. 153.
6. *Addresses*, p. 215.
7. *Addresses*, p. 91.
8. *Addresses*, p. 137.
9. Robert G. Gunderson, *The Log-Cabin Campaign* (Lexington, Ky., 1955), pp. 265–268. Apparently the style was even more ornate before Webster took a hand in revising the speech. The story is told that upon returning to his lodgings, after having finished his task, the mistress of the house told Webster that he looked tired and asked him if anything had happened. "You would think something had happened," said Webster, "if you knew what I have done. I have killed seventeen Roman proconsuls." See John Bach McMaster, A *History of the People of the United States* (New York, 1906), Vol. 5, p. 600.
10. Arnold J. Toynbee, "Seventeen 'Great Men'—Or Great Forces?" New York *Times Magazine*, November 8, 1959, Sec. 6, p. 16.
11. Two excellent studies of Lincoln's First Inaugural are those by Marie Hochmuth and Richard M. Weaver. The former is in the volume by Wayland M. Parrish and Marie Hochmuth, *American Speeches* (New York, 1954), pp. 21–71; the latter is in the volume by Richard M. Weaver, *The Ethics of Rhetoric* (Chicago, 1953), pp. 85–114.

The Fictional Values of 1984

BY JOSEPH SLATER

When 1984 was published in the summer of 1949, it seemed primarily a work of political importance. It was a prophecy and a *reductio ad terrorem*. It administered a kind of shock therapy to readers who had long before freed their minds from the verities of Marxism-Leninism but whose emotional reflexes still responded in the old way to, say, the record album called *Six Songs for Democracy*. It was a decisive and liberating book, and it will always have a place, along with *Witness* and *The God That Failed*, in a strange chapter of Anglo-American intellectual history.

The past decade has certainly not lessened the accuracy of Orwell's ugly vision. The years of brainwashing—and how easily *that* word would have found its place in the Newspeak dictionary!—the years of McCarthy and Hiss, of the "controlled schizophrenia" of Klaus Fuchs, of the downgrading of Stalin, of the blue-overalled communes of the People's Republic of China, these could hardly be said to show that Orwell is a prophet discredited by history. Nevertheless, rereading 1984 in 1960 is to some extent like rereading *Uncle Tom's Cabin* in 1875; the war is over, on this front at least; American Communists are as few and feeble as advocates of secession; and O'Brien has acquired some of the remoteness of Simon Legree.

What remains? What will remain? Has 1984 already become a paragraph in intellectual history, or does it live as a work of art, having outlived, as art sometimes does, the circumstances which brought it to birth? This tenth anniversary of an influential novel seems an appropriate time to examine certain fictional matters which were at first obscured by matters of fact.

1984, like most books and places which have had a shattering initial impact, cannot be revisited without misgivings. Is Room 101 schoolboyish, as the *TLS* reviewer thought? Are the rats funny? They didn't seem very funny ten years ago. Can the third part really be—as it seemed to Alfred Kazin—"as brilliant as the 'Grand Inquisitor' scene"? What sort of prose is to be expected from the man who announced, "The modern writer who has influenced me most is Somerset Maugham"?

And indeed a slight smell of stale adjectives does hang over 1984, a Maugham-like facility and predictability. There is a certain cheapness, too, in wisecracks like "the Junior Anti-Sex League," of the sort which made Huxley's *Ape and Essence* such a disaster. Nevertheless, from the first few pages it is apparent that Orwell has a comfortable mastery of his medium. His writing is clear and clean in diction and syntax, unpretentious, unaffected, and on the whole unhackneyed. Nor are its virtues merely negative; it is verbally concrete and evocative, varied and effective in sentence pattern and rhythm:

Under the window somebody was singing. Winston peeped out, secure in the protection of the muslin curtain. The June sun was still high in the sky, and in the sun-filled court below a monstrous woman, solid as a Norman pillar, with brawny red forearms and a sacking apron strapped about her middle, was stumping to and fro between a washtub and a clothesline, pegging out a series of square white things which Winston recognized as babies' diapers. Whenever her mouth was not corked with clothes pegs she was singing in a powerful contralto.

It ranges from parody, in the question-and-answer bluntness of Big Brother's oratory and the subtle pedanticism of Goldstein's *Theory and Practice of Oligarchical Collectivism,* to pastoral, as in this description of the dreamland which Winston calls the Golden Country:

It was an old, rabbit-bitten pasture, with a foot track wandering across it and a molehill here and there. In the ragged hedge on the opposite side of the field the boughs of the elm trees were swaying very faintly in the breeze, their leaves just stirring in dense masses like women's hair. Somewhere near at hand, though out of sight, there was a clear, slow-moving stream where dace were swimming in the pools under the willow trees.

It is a twentieth-century style, to be sure, but one which often echoes with the prose of other times:

To know and not to know, to be conscious of complete truthfulness while telling carefully constructed lies, to hold simultaneously two opinions which canceled out, knowing them to be contradictory and believing in both of them, to use logic against logic, to repudiate morality while laying claim to it, to believe that democracy was impossible and that the Party was the guardian of democracy, to forget whatever it was necessary to forget, then to draw it back into memory again at the moment when it was needed, and then promptly to forget it again, and above all, to apply the same process to the process itself—that was the ultimate subtlety: consciously to induce unconsciousness, and then, once again, to become unconscious of the act of hypnosis you had just performed. Even to understand the word "doublethink" involved the use of doublethink.

It would be easy to argue that not only in his politics and his satirical temper but also in his style Orwell was a man of the eighteenth century. There is rhetorical as well as political significance in the fact that the next-to-the-last paragraph of 1984 is concerned with a Newspeak translation of the Declaration of Independence.

In other technical respects too, Orwell, though he is no innovator or virtuoso, works with unobtrusive sureness. His dialogue is convincing and varied. It catches accurately, at least for an American ear, the rhythms of Cockney speech:

" 'Ark at 'im! Calls 'isself a barman and don't know what a pint is! Why a pint's the 'alf of a quart, and there's four quarts to the gallon. 'Ave to teach you the A,B,C next."

"Never heard of 'em," said the barman shortly. "Liter and half liter—that's all we serve. There's the glasses on the shelf in front of you."

And it distinguishes between these sounds and the "less debased accent" of Charrington:

"That's coral, that is," said the old man. "It must have come from the Indian Ocean. They used to kind of embed it in the glass. That wasn't made less than a hundred years ago. More, by the look of it."

His characters, major and minor, are clearly individualized by their speech: Julia ("Yes, my love, I'm listening. Go on. It's marvelous."); Ampleforth ("To tell you the truth— There is only one offense, is there not?"); Parsons ("*You* know what kind of a chap I was. Not a bad chap in my way. Not brainy, of course, but keen."). And at a higher level, it is in dialogue that some of the most effective scenes are done and some of the subtlest relationships realized:

> "You are a slow learner, Winston," said O'Brien gently.
> "How can I help it?" he blubbered. "How can I help seeing what is in front of my eyes? Two and two are four."
> "Sometimes, Winston. Sometimes they are five. Sometimes they are three. Sometimes they are all of them at once. You must try harder. It is not easy to become sane."

But dialogue is a less important technique in 1984 than interior monologue. The greater part of the action takes place in the mind of Winston Smith, as he does calisthenics before his two-way telescreen or drinks Victory Gin at the Chestnut Tree Café. The flow of his thought is set down inconspicuously in the third person and the past tense, but it is always Winston's thought and never Orwell's statement. Or rather, only once or twice, as when Julia subversively paints her face and Orwell comments, "It was not very skillfully done, but Winston's standards in such matters were not high," does the reader know anything about life in Airstrip One which does not come to him through the mind of Winston Smith. The political history of the 'fifties and 'sixties, the sexual practices of the Outer Party, the life of the proles: these are the subjects of Winston's meditations as he tries to touch his toes or writes in his suicidal diary. Even Goldstein's book enters the novel through Winston's eyes or through his voice as he reads to Julia. In 1984 the restricted point of view is not merely a convention or a tour de force; it is the means by which prophecy, parody, satire, and political theory are fused into fictional reality.

Asked in 1940 about his work in progress, Orwell described it not as prophetic fantasy nor as political satire, but as "a novel in three parts." After a rereading of 1984 one feels that Orwell's answer came less from reticence than from preoccupation with form. The three parts are almost three acts of a well-made play, each boldly punctuated with an opening line and a curtain line. Indeed, this novel is "well-made" in the old-fashioned theatrical sense—as if it followed the practice of Scribe or the theory of Freytag. Part I is entirely Exposition: it even ends with a kind of expository refrain, "Like a leaden knell the words came back at him: WAR IS PEACE   FREEDOM IS SLAVERY   IGNORANCE IS STRENGTH." Part II is Rising Action: it begins with Julia's note, reaches its Climax in the reading of Goldstein's book, and turns downward almost immediately thereafter when the metallic voice speaks from the telescreen. Part III is Falling Action: interrupted only once, in what Freytag would have called the Moment of Final Suspense, by Winston's discovery of his immortal hatred for the Party, it moves gradually and inexorably toward a Catastrophe which is not complete until the final curtain line, "He loved Big Brother." In structure, as in style and doctrine, 1984 might be called—for want of a better word—classical.

Each chapter has a clear function as dramatic scene and as unit of exposition. Chapters 1 and 2 of Part I introduce the diary, the main characters, and the three sacred principles of Ingsoc: Newspeak, Doublethink, and the Mutability of the Past. Chapter 3 shows Winston dreaming, waking, exercising—and thinking about Doublethink. Chapter 4 shows him at work in the Ministry of Truth—demonstrating the Mutability of the Past. Chapter 5 shows him at lunch—talking about Newspeak. In Chapter 6 he is writing in his diary—about sex under Ingsoc. Chapter 7 is another diary scene, with entries and meditations about the proles and the past. Chapter 8 records Winston's search for the past among the proles of London, fruitless except for the symbolic paperweight he finds in the junk shop where he bought his diary.

Part II is less intricately organized than Part I; a mere listing of synoptic chapter titles, of the sort Orwell might have written if he had lived in a century more congenial to him, will trace the clear steps by which the action rises: 1. A Message and a Meeting; 2. Love in the Country; 3. Love in the Belfry; 4. A Room of Their Own; 5. Julia; 6. O'Brien; 7. They Can't Get Inside You; 8. O'Brien's Apartment; 9. The Book; 10. The Arrest.

The six chapters of Part III, except for the first scene in the windowless porcelain reception cell of the Ministry of Love, are organized around what O'Brien calls the three stages of reintegration: learning, understanding, and acceptance. Chapter 2 is concerned with learning through torture that two and two make five. Chapter 3 is concerned with understanding, through lecture and torture, the motivation of the Party. Chapter 4 recounts Winston's efforts, unassisted, to accept Ingsoc and to love Big Brother and his discovery of the core of hatred and defiance in his heart. Chapter 5 shows how that core is removed in Room 101. Chapter 6 shows the triumph of love and acceptance of a table in the Chestnut Tree Cafe.

But the structural tightness of 1984 is not solely the result of such careful engineering. Within the larger structure of the novel are recurrent settings, actions, motifs, and symbols, which rivet the parts and chapters into coherence. The Chestnut Tree Cafe, for example, appears in I,5 as the ill-omened haunt of Winston's too-intelligent friend Syme. It appears again in I,7 as the place where Winston had seen Jones, Aaronson, and Rutherford, shortly before their re-arrest, blankly drinking clove-flavored Victory Gin while the telescreen jeered. And there is Charrington's junk shop, where Winston buys the keepsake album before the novel begins, where he returns in I,8 to buy the paperweight and encounters Julia, and where in II,4 he rents the telescreenless room upstairs. There are parallel actions: the first meeting with O'Brien occurs at the same place in the corridor where Julia had slipped the note into Winston's hand; the skull-faced man betrays the chinless man in almost the same words which Winston later uses to betray Julia. The refrain "We are the dead" is used by Winston in the belfry scene, by O'Brien in the apartment scene, and by Winston again just before the iron voice comes from the picture of St. Clement's. Other refrains echo through the book: "Oranges and lemons, say the bells of St. Clement's," a symbol of the past, an ironical tie between O'Brien and Winston, and a structural tie between Part I and Part II; "it was only an 'opeless fancy," recurrent symbol of proletarian strength and weakness; and "Under the spreading chestnut tree/ I sold you and you sold me," symbol of the Party's omnis-cience and malevolence, which is heard by Jones, Aaronson, and Rutherford in I,7 and by Winston Smith in the last chapter of Part III. Dreams recur like refrains. They fuse with reality, as Winston's mother becomes the refugee woman of the newsreel in a symbolic fusion of guilt and sympathy. They come true, almost, in the close-bitten pasture and the contemptuous, annihilating gesture with which Julia flings aside her party overalls. They come true finally, in the place where there is no darkness, to reveal that the events of 1984 and the six years preceding have been a consistent, coherent pattern of omnipotence and evil.

The plot which moves within this structure is simple and swift, taut with surprise and suspense, sharpened by irony, and, within the limits of fantasy, credible. Its *dramatis personae* are few and functional, and all of the minor characters are neatly tucked into the main plot before the falling action really begins. The main plot is, in fact, the only plot: in 1984 love and subversion are identical. Just as the first five paragraphs swiftly display the chief backdrops of the novel —the dreary austerity, the dirt, the smell of boiled cabbage, "the blue overalls which were the uniform of the Party," the ubiquitous posters with the caption "Big Brother Is Watching You," the Thought Police, the two-way telescreen—so the first chapter introduces the major elements of the plot. During the Two Minutes Hate, to which Winston's mind flashes back as he begins his diary, appear not only O'Brien and Julia, Goldstein, the Brotherhood, *the book*, and the Junior Anti-Sex League, but, more important, the affinity which Winston feels for O'Brien, the lust-hatred he feels for Julia, and his certainty that through the *thoughtcrime* of which he has long been guilty he is already doomed.

The first chapter ends with an ominous knocking on the door; when Winston, his heart thumping, opens, he sees, instead of the Thought Police, his neighbor Mrs. Parsons, who needs help with a blocked-up sink. Throughout the novel such devices of suspense and surprise keep the plot from decelerating and help it to carry its heavy, though by no means dead, weight of exposition. Winston must wait five minutes before he can read the message which the dark-haired girl, perhaps an agent of the Thought Police, perhaps a member of the Brotherhood, has slipped into his hand; when he does, it says, "I Love you." During the frantic five days that follow the Oceanic-Eurasian Pact, Winston carries a copy of *the book* in his unopened briefcase. When, reading it to Julia, he discovers that she has fallen asleep, he breaks off, sleepy and confident, in the middle of a sentence: "This motive really consists . . ." Charrington turns out to be a member of the Thought Police. Parsons, of all people, turns up at the Ministry of Love. O'Brien says, mildly and ironically, "They got me a long time ago." O'Brien rejects as stupid the answer that the Party holds power for the good of the majority. O'Brien says drily, after the electrical rack has flooded Winston with ultraviolet pain, "You know what is in Room 101, Winston. Everybody knows what is in Room 101."

Listed out of context, these turns of plot perhaps resemble the facile thrills of Hitchcock and Reed. In the context of Orwell's terrible prophecy, however, they are rather the fears and shocks and betrayals of life. They grow out of character and earlier situation; they are motivated; they are significant. Even the contrived and familiar knocking at the door is made thematically meaningful by the paragraph that follows:

> As he put his hand to the doorknob Winston saw that he had left the diary open on the table. DOWN WITH BIG BROTHER was written all over it, in letters almost big enough to be legible across the room. It was an inconceivably stupid thing to have done. But, he realized, even in his panic, he had not wanted to smudge the creamy paper by shutting the book while the ink was wet.

And the betrayal by O'Brien is not merely shocking; it is traumatic and integral: from it, as much as from Winston's final victory over himself, come the darkest meanings of the novel.

Further, the simplicities of suspense and surprise are balanced by ironies of action and situation. Winston, the enemy of the party, the lover of the past, works happily and well at the rectification of history. The lovers plan their tryst in the safety of a crowd which is watching a convoy of Eurasian prisoners:

> With hands locked together, invisible among the press of bodies, they stared steadily in front of them, and instead of the eyes of the girl, the eyes of the aged prisoner gazed mournfully at Winston out of nests of hair.

The thrush rhapsodizes in the thicket where Winston and Julia, wary of microphones even in the country, have hardly dared to whisper. Is there, Winston thinks, a beetlelike man at the other end of a wire listening intently to *that*? The telescreen is hidden behind the picture of St. Clement's, directly over the rat hole in the wainscotting. Julia, the skeptic and nihilist, cannot remember that four years ago Oceania was at war with Eastasia. The world of 1984 is complex enough to be credible.

Also, the shocks and surprises of the plot are believable because, unconsciously, the reader has been prepared for them. The rats of Room 101 are no beasts from the machine; they are truly for Winston the worst thing in the world, and the reader knows how O'Brien knows. And so O'Brien wrote *the book*! But of course: Winston had felt as he read that "it was the product of a mind similar to his own, but enormously more powerful." Even the minutiae of satirical action are meticulously prepared for. At noon on the first day Winston hears from his telescreen that the chocolate ration has been reduced from 30 grams to 20; next morning at work one of his assignments reads: "times 14.2.84 miniplenty malquoted chocolate rectify"; at lunch he learns that the workers have thanked Big Brother in spontaneous demonstrations for raising the chocolate ration to 20 grams a week. And the same care appears in the design of emotional and thematic developments. At the end of Part I, many chapters distant from his conversion in Room 101, Winston meditates on the tyranny which the pain-filled body exercises over the mind; in the reception cell he shrinks from the thought of the pain which even the Brotherhood's merciful razor blade would bring; after the first truncheon blow has crushed his elbow, he knows that "nothing in the world [is] so bad as physical pain." In an early entry in his diary he writes the axiom, "Freedom is the freedom to say that two plus two make four"; the same sum appears with symbolic force in Goldstein's book; and just before the arrest it flashes through Winston's mind as the secret doctrine which must be passed on to the future. In a novel of the real world such prefiguration produces coherence and singleness of effect; in a fantasy it serves also to make the incredible credible.

But how incredible, after all, is Airstrip One? Orwell's political vision created a stagnant society, a stunted technology, a London little different physically, except for telescreens and helicopters, from the London of 1949. The canteen, the Parsonses' flat, the clearing, the room above the junk shop, the reception cell at the Ministry of Love: these have a familiar reality which deepens the terror of the major action. Similarly, the educational techniques of the Ministry of Love are not merely extensions of those of the Gestapo and the GPU; they have older and more significant antecedents in the history of religion: there have been other times when hatred of a god was the deadliest sin, when kindly pedants used torture to teach that faith was higher than reason, when sinners wept with happiness on discovering that they had divested themselves of the love of created beings and now loved their god alone. Orwell's future is a projection of the present and the past, his nightmare a distortion of every man's day.

The characters of 1984 have received little critical attention and almost no praise. Thin and flat they have been called; and in comparison with Lambert Strether or Cyril Fielding they are flat indeed. But that is to judge them by improper standards; place them with Bernard Marx, Julian West, or Raphael Hythlodaye, and they seem the most complex, convincing, poignant characters who ever inhabited a utopia.

The minor figures are sharply carved and memorable: Katherine, who despite her "duty to the Party" is about as funny as the rats; the Parsonses, grotesque, pathetic creatures of stale sweat and mindless orthodoxy; Syme, who loves the bright-blue tongues at the hangings but whose intelligence has made him a security risk; Ampleforth; Charrington; the chinless man; the skull-faced man; the proles, in whose strength and humanity there seems, until the washtub is flung across the yard, to be some hope; Julia. It would be easy to set Julia down as a failure, too uncomplicated in mind and emotion to be interesting, too sophisticated in political affairs, considering her intellectual equipment, to be believable. But if she is thought of as a minor character, important only in her relationship to Winston, she becomes a satisfactory embodiment of the sexuality, the tenderness, the luxury, the domesticity which Ingsoc puritanism has destroyed.

O'Brien, unlike Julia, exists dramatically, in speech and action. It is by his calculated reference to the *unperson* Syme that he reveals his disloyalty and his subtlety. He speaks the melodrama of conspiracy with the faint irony which intelligence requires. He makes his collective paranoia ("I could float off this floor like a soap bubble if I wished to. I do not wish to, because the Party does not wish it.") seem as sane as Euclidean geometry. He carries out his holy office of inquisition and instruction with a hideous gentleness, an intertwining of genuine priestly love with a transcendent sadism. Of all the horrors of the novel, the character of O'Brien is deepest and darkest. Consistent, familiar, understated, timeless—no more a figure of 1984 than of 1484—he is terrifyingly believable. The evil father, the perverted priest, the cruel physician, he is nevertheless physician, priest, and father; and the ultimate pessimism of the novel lies less in Winston's submission than in his love for his inquisitor.

When Winston Smith pauses at the door and realizes why he has not closed his diary, it is apparent that he is a man—and not Everyman, the Little Man, or the Common Man. And yet he is those abstractions too. He is thirty-nine years old, sickly and undersized. He has varicose veins and five false teeth. He is a physical coward. Intelligent and creative enough for his job at the Ministry of Truth, he is yet, as O'Brien says, no metaphysician. He is gnawed by guilty memories of childhood. He has been corrupted, not merely by Victory Gin, but by the moral poison of the world he lives in. And yet he has other qualities not little or common in 1984, or in any year: a capacity for love and a tough, sullen, instinctive hatred of orthodoxy. His relationship with Julia develops from nihilistic carnality to love to something much like marriage. His heresy and his hope of revolution disintegrate under torture and the irresistible power of O'Brien's personality, but until almost the last he preserves a nucleus of hatred. He will conceal it from them and from himself until the few seconds before they shoot him; then it will "fill him like an enormous roaring flame. . . . To die hating them, that was freedom." This love and hatred, strangely identical, are strong enough so that when they are burned out in Room 101 we feel that something heroic has been destroyed. And when, at the Chestnut Tree Café, Winston finally wins the victory over himself, we are moved by more than political despair.

1984 is of course a political novel and a satire, a sharp and effective weapon for the wars of its time. But it is more important as an anatomy of power, as a document of despair, as a lament for the fragility of love, courage, and reason, as a book of praise for those qualities and for the immutable past, the double bed, the private room, the piece of coral, and the silky texture that sugar gives to coffee. Its highest literary accomplishments are perhaps those extended satirical sequences which become a kind of intellectual drama: Winston at work in the Ministry of Truth, Syme's exposition of Newspeak, *the book*'s analysis of the economic and political function of war. But the value which chiefly distinguishes 1984 from other works in its genre is human reality. *Looking Backward, News from Nowhere, Brave New World, The Aerodrome, Ape and Essence*—from none of them do scenes and characters and emotions survive. 1984 is better written than they, and better designed; it is intellectually richer and subtler; most important, it has a fictional intensity and vitality which will keep it alive when the forces that called it forth are as dead as Torquemada. To compare it with *The Brothers Karamazov* is to do it more than justice: it is not that kind of book. Of its kind, however, it is very good indeed, and to call it the best of English utopian novels is not extravagance and is only in part an act of gratitude.

Books and Articles by J. Milton French

I. BOOKS

A. ALONE

1. Editor, George Wither's *History of the Pestilence*, Harvard, 1932.
2. Editor, *Charles Lamb: Essays and Letters*, Odyssey, 1937.
3. *Milton in Chancery*, Modern Language Association (Monograph Series, number 10), 1939.
4. *The Life Records of John Milton*, 5 volumes, Rutgers (Rutgers Studies in English, number 7), 1949–1958.

B. IN COLLABORATION

1. Volumes 13 and 18 of the *Works of John Milton*, Columbia, 1937–1938. With Thomas O. Mabbott. *Letters of State* and *Uncollected Writings*.
2. A *Bibliography of the Theophrastan Character in English*, Harvard, 1947. Compiled by Chester Noyes Greenough and prepared for publication by J.M.F.
3. *Complete Prose Works of John Milton*, 7 volumes, Yale, 1953—. Member of supervising editorial board.

II. ARTICLES AND REVIEWS

1. "A Defence of Troilus," PMLA, XLIV (1929), 1246–1251.
2. "Poor Little America," Atlantic Monthly, CXLIV (1929), 785–788.
3. "George Wither in Prison," PMLA, XLV (1930), 959–966.
4. "Four Scarce Poems of George Wither," Huntington Library Bulletin, II (1931), 91–121.
5. "Lamb and Spenser," Studies in Philology, XXX (1933), 205–207.
6. "Lamb and Milton," Studies in Philology, XXXI (1934), 92–103.
7. "Othello among the Anthropophagi," PMLA, XLIX (1934), 807–809.
8. "A New Letter by John Milton," PMLA, XLIX (1934), 1069–1070.
9. "Milton and an Epitaph on Mazarin," Notes and Queries, CLXXI (1935), 445.
10. "Milton as a Historian," PMLA, L (1935), 469–479.
11. "An Action against Milton," London Times Literary Supplement, December 21, 1935, and March 14, 1936.
12. "Milton as Satirist," PMLA, LI (1936), 414–429.
13. "Milton's Blindness," Philological Quarterly, XV (1936), 93–94.
14. "Milton and the Politicians," Philological Quarterly, XV (1936), 94–95.
15. "Milton, Needham, and Mercurius Politicus," Studies in Philology, XXXIII (1936), 236–252.
16. "Bowman and Donne," London Times Literary Supplement, December 12, 1936.
17. "The Autographs of John Milton," ELH, IV (1937), 301–330.
18. "'A Satyr against J.M.,' 1655," Notes and Queries, CLXXIII (1937), 45. (In collaboration with Thomas O. Mabbott.)
19. "Milton's 'Proposalls of Certain Expedients,' 1659," Notes

and Queries, CLXXIII (1937), 66. (In collaboration with Thomas O. Mabbott.)

20. "The Milton-Powell Bond," *Harvard Studies in Philology,* XX (1938), 61–73.
21. "Milton's Copy of Gildas," *Harvard Studies in Philology,* XX (1938), 75–80.
22. "Milton's Family Bible," *PMLA,* LIII (1938), 363–366.
23. "Notes on . . . Marvell and Wither," *Notes and Queries,* CLXXIV (1938), 273–274.
24. "Raleigh, Frobisher, and the Great Carack of Spain," *Notes and Queries,* CLXXIV (1938), 327–330.
25. "Freshman Appreciation of Literature," *Akron Journal of Education,* XIV (1939), number 7, 10–12; reprinted in *English Journal,* XXIX (1940), 311–315.
26. "First Supplement to the Columbia Milton," *Notes and Queries,* CLXXVII (1939), 329–330. (In collaboration with Thomas O. Mabbott.)
27. "That Late Villain Milton," *PMLA,* LV (1940), 102–115.
28. "A Chip from Elia's Workshop," *Studies in Philology,* XXXVII (1940), 88–99.
29. "Mute Inglorious Miltons," *Modern Language Quarterly,* I (1940), 367–381.
30. "Second Supplement to the Columbia Milton," *Notes and Queries,* CLXXIX (1940), 20–21. (In collaboration with Thomas O. Mabbott.)
31. "The Burning of Milton's *Defensio* in France," *Modern Language Notes,* LVI (1941), 275–277.
32. "Recent Acquisitions in English," *Journal of the Rutgers University Library,* IV (1940), number 1, p. 22.
33. Review of *English Institute Annual* for 1940, *Rutgers Alumni Monthly,* XX (December, 1940), 15.
34. "John Milton, Scrivener, the Temples of Stowe, and Sir John Lenthall," *Huntington Library Quarterly,* IV (1941), 303–308.
35. "The Columbia Milton: Third Supplement," *Notes and*

Queries, CLXXXI (1941), 16. (In collaboration with Thomas O. Mabbott.)

36. "The Introductory Course in Literature," *College English,* III (1941), 53–63.

37. "Milton—An Apocryphal Story," *Notes and Queries,* CLXXXI (1941), 204. (In collaboration with Thomas O. Mabbott.)

38. "Milton's Supplicats," *Huntington Library Quarterly,* V (1942), 349–359.

39. *The Seventeenth-Century News-Letter.* Edited with James M. Osborn and James G. McManaway. Several issues per year, 1942–1944.

40. "Chips from Milton's Workshop," *E L H,* X (1943), 230–242.

41. "'The Grand Case of Conscience,' wrongly attributed to Milton," *Notes and Queries,* CLXXXV (1943), 302–303. (In collaboration with Thomas O. Mabbott.)

42. "Seventeenth-Century English Newsbooks," *Journal of the Rutgers University Library,* VII (1943), i, 1–8.

43. Review of Harris Fletcher's facsimile edition of Milton's *Complete Poetical Works,* vol. I, *Journal of English and Germanic Philology,* XLIII (1944), 473–478.

44. "Magic Casements" (a Phi Beta Kappa Address at Rutgers), Rutgers University, 1944. (Separate booklet.)

45. "A Parliamentary Satire of 1675," *Journal of the Rutgers University Library,* VIII (1945), 65–69.

46. "Some Notes on Milton," *Notes and Queries,* CLXXXVIII (1945), 52–55.

47. Review of Douglas Bush's *Paradise Lost in Our Time,* in *Journal of English and Germanic Philology,* XLV (1946), 110–114.

48. "The New Curriculums of Harvard, Yale, and Princeton," *College English,* VIII (1946), 73–82.

49. Review of Harris Fletcher's facsimile edition of Milton's *Complete Poetical Works,* vol. II, *Journal of English and Germanic Philology,* XLV (1946), 458–464.

50. Review of Irene Samuel's *Plato and Milton,* in *Modern Language Notes,* LXIII (1948), 280–282.
51. "The Baptism of Milton's Daughter Mary," *Modern Language Notes,* LXIII (1948), 264–265.
52. Review of Benjamin Boyce's *The Theophrastan Character in England to 1642,* in *Journal of English and Germanic Philology,* XLVII (1948), 198–202.
53. "George Wither's Verses to Dr. John Raven," *PMLA,* LXIII (1948), 749–751.
54. "Elia," *Journal of the Rutgers University Library,* XI (1948), 92–94.
55. "The Date of Milton's First *Defense,*" *Library,* 5th Series, III (1948), 56–58.
56. Review of Rudolf Kirk's edition of Joseph Hall's *Heaven upon Earth and Characters of Vertues and Vices,* in *Rutgers Alumni Monthly,* XXVIII (1949), vii, 21.
57. "Milton's Homes and Investments," *Philological Quarterly,* XXVIII ("Studies in Milton: Essays in Memory of Elbert N. S. Thompson, 1949), 77–97.
58. Review of Harris Fletcher's facsimile edition of Milton's *Complete Poetical Works,* vols. III and IV, in *Journal of English and Germanic Philology,* XLVIII (1949), 413–420.
59. "Milton, Ramus, and Edward Phillips," *Modern Philology,* XLVII (1949), 82–87.
60. Review of D. C. Allen's *A Strange Metamorphosis of Man,* in *Modern Language Notes,* LXV (1950), 566–567.
61. "The Columbia Milton: Fourth Supplement," *Notes and Queries,* CXCV (1950), 244–246. (With Thomas O. Mabbott and Maurice Kelley.)
62. "Blind Milton Ridiculed in *Poor Robin,*" *Notes and Queries,* CXCVI (1951), 470–471.
63. "The Columbia Milton: Fifth Supplement," *Notes and Queries,* CXCVII (1952), 376–379. (With Thomas O. Mabbott and Maurice Kelley.)
64. "Milton's Two-Handed Engine," *Modern Language Notes,* LXVIII (1953), 229–231.

65. "The Digressions in Milton's 'Lycidas,' " *Studies in Philology*, L (1953), 485–490.

66. "That Immortal Garland" [*Areopagitica*], *Journal of the Rutgers University Library*, XXXIII (1954), 10–11.

67. "Two Notes on Milton and Wither," *Notes and Queries*, N.S. I (1954), 472–473.

68. Review of E. L. Marilla's *The Central Problem of Paradise Lost*, in *Studia Neophilologica*, XXVI (1953–54), 201–202.

69. "A Comment on 'A Book Was Written,' " *Modern Language Notes*, LXX (1955), 404–405.

70. "An Unrecorded Edition of Milton's *Defensio Secunda*, 1654," *Papers of the Bibliographical Society of America*, XLIX (1955), 262–268.

71. "Mr. Secretary Milton at Work," *South Atlantic Quarterly*, LV (1956), 313–321.

72. "The Survey of English Literature," Scott Foresman Company, 1956. (An address to the College Conference on English in the Central Atlantic States, published as a separate pamphlet with Robert Warnock's "The Survey of World Literature," delivered on the same occasion.)

73. "John Milton's 'Songs of Experience,' " *Seventeenth-Century News*, XV, i (1957), 6–7. (An address to the Milton Society of America.)

74. "An Unpublished Reply (1659) to Milton's *Defensio*," *Modern Philology*, LV (1958), 164–169.

75. "Seventeenth-Century English Authors and Chancery," *Notes and Queries*, N.S. V (1958), 219–220.

76. "Light and Work in 'L'Allegro' and 'Il Penseroso,' " *South Atlantic Quarterly*, LVIII (1958–59), 123–127.

77. "The Reliability of Anthony Wood and Milton's Oxford M.A.," PMLA, LXXV (1960), 22–30.